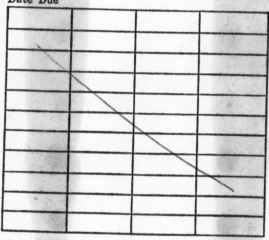

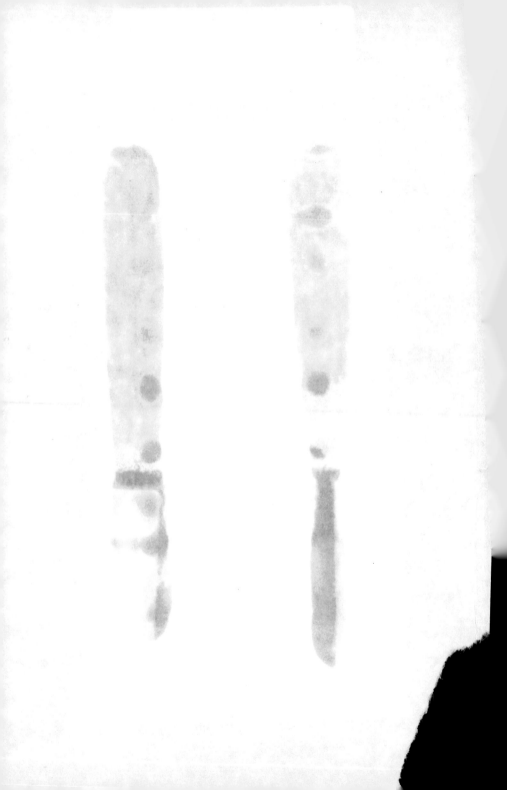

HEGEL'S *PHENOMENOLOGY, PART I:*

ANALYSIS AND COMMENTARY

HEGEL'S *PHENOMENOLOGY, PART I:*
ANALYSIS AND COMMENTARY

Howard P. Kainz

Studies in the Humanities No. 12
Philosophy

THE UNIVERSITY OF ALABAMA PRESS
University, Alabama

Contents

Introduction

Immanuel Kant, in his *Prolegomena to Any Future Metaphysics,* describes what he means by the process of "a priori synthetic judgment": It is, he says, to begin with certain a priori concepts of the understanding; and then to proceed in a manner analogous to the way that the eye and the other senses proceed by empirical intuition to expand the initial perception of an object by means of predicates added to it by way of synthesis.[1] Thus in mathematics, a priori synthetic judgment consists in expanding initial quantitative intuitions into concepts constructed actively and directly from these intuitions.[2] Then Kant asks the question—the main question of the *Prolegomena*—whether it is valid to proceed this way in metaphysics. And he concludes in the negative.

Hegel's philosophic methodology, however, seems to show a contempt for the problem as to whether such a thing "can be done." Anyone reading his *Phenomenology of Mind* easily gets the impression that this, if anything, must be what Kant means by "a priori synthetic reasoning" in philosophy. The question of whether we can apply this Kantian terminology to the context of Hegel will be discussed in detail in the conclusion to this study. But for the present, where we are concerned with giving a preliminary indication of what Hegel "does" in the *Phenomenology,* we could say that he seems to present us with a prototype of "a priori synthetic metaphysical reasoning." Beginning from the ideas of the mind and from the forms of knowledge as if from developments taking place before our eyes, he proceeds from his own determinate vantage point to focus on one such development, set it up (vaguely, at first) against a context of other mental developments appearing on the horizon, and then pass on to these others in succession. As he does this, every successive point of view "proves itself" to be imperfect, limited, one-sided; and gives way naturally to a higher point of view, such that we approximate ever closer and closer to the *truth*—which would consist in some final all-embracing point of view, retaining the gist or positive content of all "former" vantage points, while eschewing everything that smacks of one-sidedness.

Thus Hegel's *Phenomenology* is "the science of knowledge in the various appearances it makes,"[3] and Hegel describes its composition as his "voyage of discovery" in the realm of thought. In a way, his methodology reminds one of Jung's chapter on "The Type Problem in Philosophy" in his book, *Psychological Types*. For just as Jung tries in that chapter to explain the differences in philosophical systems by delving into basic psychic dispositions and irreducible presuppositions, so also Hegel in his *Phenomenology* tries to capture or recapture basic "attitudes" or "stages" in the development of human consciousness, to show their mutual dialectic relationship, and thus gradually to gain the best possible vantage point for understanding certain necessary relationships of knowledge to the world of knowledge.

Hegel did not plan to stop with this voyage around the world of thought. It was but a preliminary, exploratory voyage, and the "maps"–the *Logic*, the *Philosophy of Right*, etc.,–would come later to elucidate in more accurate, scientific, "speculative"[4] fashion the concepts that he encounters in their immediacy[5] in this initial expedition.

But at any rate one who wishes to make even this initial voyage with Hegel as pilot is in for some rough sailing. Apropos this voyage, one nineteenth century wit remarked that Hegel was "the man who sailed around the world of the spirit and intrepidly advanced to the north pole of thought where one's brain freezes in the abstract ice."[6] One more sympathetic to Hegel's undertaking might merely express the wish that Hegel had been equipped with a more readable and lucid style as his "vessel" for making the trip. Hegel himself gives a foreboding intimation of the difficulties the reader may expect when he says in the Preface,

> We note here the basis for that special charge which is often made against philosophical writings–that "most of them have to be read many times before they can be understood" .... What happens is that opinion discovers that the philosophical content is meant differently from what it had expected, and this correction of opinion obliges knowledge to return to the propositional content again, and construe it differently.[7]

This indeed is an accurate description of the experience of this reader of Hegel, and apparently of many others. For one thing, one is continually encountering terms in the *Phenomenology*–such as "universal," "form," "intuition," "consciousness," "category," etc. which are used in ways very different from the ways philosophers used them in the past. For another thing, the context is so important that no part of the *Phenomenology* has much intelligible meaning by itself. One very often finds himself in the predicament of the person who is reading a Russian novel and must continually refer back to early chapters to recall names and events that have significance later on as the plot thickens. Thus it happens that the reader expends so much energy in simply understanding the *Phenomenology,* that he has little left over for critical evaluation of the points made in the book. As Kaufmann puts it,

> "What is the man talking about? *Whom* does he have in mind?" ... The obscurity and whole manner of the text are such that these questions are almost bound to replace the question of whether what Hegel says is right.[8]

The student of Kant, or Aristotle, or Leibniz, or Descartes can without too much trouble grasp the pivotal doctrines of the philosopher in question–e.g. the categorical imperative, the prime mover, the immanence of the monads, the methodological doubt–and then fruitfully compare these doctrines with the opinions of other philosophers or defend or critically evaluate them. But with Hegel, there is even much doubt as to what are his "pivotal doctrines." Does he say that reality becomes explicit in triads of thesis, antithesis, synthesis? Does he opt for ideas as the only true reality, and disparage the value of the material world? Does he try to deduce nature from abstract concepts? These and other "pivotal doctrines" have long been associated with Hegel. But there is considerable doubt whether Hegel could be effectively charged with fathering them, if a paternity suit were brought against him. And thus much of modern Hegelian scholarship has concerned itself with disassociating many traditional "Hegelian" ideas from Hegel.[9]

In view of these problems, the main purpose of this book is to give a coherent and not too unreadable account of "what Hegel is talking about" in the *Phenomenology*. The instruments used for achieving this purpose are the following:

1) *A detailed consideration of certain problems relating to the "Phenomenology" as a whole.* The specific questions considered are: I. What is the literary form of the *Phenomenology*? II. What is the "plot" of the *Phenomenology*? III. Is the *Phenomenology* an introduction to Hegel's System, a part of it, or both? IV. What is the subject-matter of the *Phenomenology*? V. Is it possible to choose a vantage point which is neither "subjective" nor "objective"? VI. What is the meaning of the "dialectical necessity" joining the various "moments" in the *Phenomenology*? VII. What is the meaning of "experience" in the context of the *Phenomenology*? VIII. How can consciousness be both measurer and measured? IX. What is the relation of the point of view being studied to the point of view of the "phenomenologist"? and X. What is a "phenomenology" in the Hegelian sense?

2) *A running analysis of Part I (Sections I-V) of the "Phenomenology."* This running analysis aspires neither merely to capture the form of the *Phenomenology* in summary fashion, nor to recapture the content in such elaborate detail that one might as well read Hegel himself. Its objective is to present a union of form and content in such a way as to supply a bridge to an understanding of Part I and of the *Phenomenology* as a whole. A "Hegel Made Simple" is, of course, out of the question, as those who have read Hegel will corroborate. And so the "bridge" is not a mere stepping-stone or even a footbridge. But hopefully, its ponderousness and complexity falls short of that of the *Phenomenology* itself.

3) *A commentary supplementing the running analysis.* The commentary will: a) note apparent differences in Hegel's usage of terms from traditional usage; b) elucidate a few statements or transitions in the analysis, in cases where a straightforward analysis must needs reproduce the obscurities of the original; c) supply cross-references and indices pertaining to the *Phenomenology* itself; d) refer to historical philosophical positions which are intimated by the text; and e) comment on the parallels to the *Phenomenology* that one finds in the writings of

some philosophers after Hegel. By disengaging the analysis from the commentary, it is hoped that clarity and reader convenience will be enhanced. It should be noted, however, that the commentary proper stops short of considering the question, "Is Hegel right?"

4) *A Glossary of some common terms used in the "Phenomenology."* The purpose of this glossary is to give brief definitions for a core of terms which are strictly Hegelian in connotation, and whose understanding is necessary for an understanding of the *Phenomenology*.

5) *A table of correlation between the indices of our analysis and of the Baillie translation of Part I.* Most of the sections of the *Phenomenology* appearing in the running analysis of Part I have been retitled with a view to clarity (i.e., to denote more accurately the content of the sections). A table of correlation hence appears in the back matter, in order to indicate what retitling has been done.

In the Conclusion, we address ourselves to the following three "afterthoughts": (I) How is Part II of the *Phenomenology* related to Part I? (II) Does Hegel's *Phenomenology* give us any new insight into the problem raised by Kant: "Are synthetic a-priori judgements possible in philosophy?" and (III) How is the transition made from the *Phenomenology* to the *Encyclopedia?*

TEN QUESTIONS

I. WHAT IS THE LITERARY FORM OF THE "PHENOMENOLOGY"?

Although form is largely an extrinsic feature in a literary work, some understanding of the form of a particular work is almost a necessity if a reader is to approach the work intelligently and derive as much value and significance as possible from it. Ordinarily, when one picks up a writing for the first time and begins to peruse it, he will catch a glimpse of a certain structure, he will be able to "categorize" that work in terms of certain conventional literary structures with which he is familiar; and this is the first, as it were, primordial step to the appreciation of that writing. For example, one would be hindered from the outset if he began to read a chapter from a novel on the assumption that it was a short story, or a newspaper article on the assumption that it was an editorial, or a biography on the assumption that it was a novel. In reading philosophic writings, one also goes on the presupposition that there are a certain number of basic, conventional forms, all of them allowing an infinity of variations according to individual purposes and temperament, according to the specific content, etc. And in reading such a work, it is again *very important* that one knows whether it is a dialogue on the Platonic pattern, a confrontation with distinct questions after the manner of the *Quaestiones disputatae* of Thomas Aquinas, an examination and explication of certain pivotal concepts after the manner of Berkeley's *The Principles of Human Knowledge,* a critique of currently-held views in the vein of Kant's Critiques, and so forth. We may temporarily be deceived by the title, but some perusal of the content will ordinarily undeceive us as to the structure of the entitled work. For example, from the title of Spinoza's *Ethics* we would get the impression offhand that we were approaching a systematic presentation of the principles and problems pertaining to a certain limited field of philosophy. But a certain amount of reading in the *Ethics* would show us that it was really a metaphysical system built after the model of a textbook in geometry. And our reading of the *Ethics* would prove much more fruitful, after we had come to that realization.

Unfortunately, the reader of Hegel's *Phenomenology* will be hard put to find any intelligible conventional structure in the work, even after having exerted much effort on reading it. He bypasses the title, which gives him no indication of the structure of the content, and begins to study the Preface, or the Introduction, or the first chapter; or browses through the middle parts, or looks to the end to garner an intimation of its teleology. All to no avail. And as a result, he will characteristically find himself in the grips of an extremely embarrassing and seemingly absurd question: *What is he reading?* To be sure, he is reading the *Phenomenology of Spirit.* But a little reading will suffice to show that the book is not concerned with simply expanding on, or analyzing the notion of "spirit"; that it does not seem to be a description (taking "phenomenology" to mean morphological description) of any determinate subject-matter that you could put your finger on; that, in short, it is a moot question just exactly what is the problem considered, or the subject treated of, or the objection rebutted; or? If we look to the history of philosophy for enlightenment, we find that the *Phenomenology* is without precedent, a *sui generis* production. If we turn to contemporary "phenomenologies"—treatises on the phenomenology of sleep, the phenomenology of perception, the phenomenology of the body, the phenomenology of time-consciousness, etc.—we do not receive any great increment in enlightenment. For although in certain cases there may be a proximity in subject-matter, nevertheless in procedure of development and general structure these contemporary phenomenologies seem to be different from whatever conception Hegel had of what a phenomenology ought to be. So we conclude tentatively that our inability to comprehend Hegel's style in the *Phenomenology* is a result of the fact that this work is *completely* unique in the annals of philosophy.

But this realization does not help us to read the work. Uniqueness must be reduced to some common denominator if it is ever to become public property (or even the property of a coterie). To this end, the following five considerations may conduce:

a) Beyond literary form in the more conventional sense—prose fiction, essays, treatises, Renaissance Style, Naturalism, Symbolism, etc.—there is a form of individuality which the author gives to his work. Rehder, in his article, "Of Structure and Symbol: the Significance of Hegel's Phenomenology for Literary Criticism," describes this form or vehicle of individuality in the following terms:

> There is an . . . aspect of form which owes little allegiance to the style of
> a historical period or taste. . . . I should like to distinguish it by the term
> *inward form.* . . . Constituent components of this formative principle—
> rhythm, sound, pitch, configuration, structure . . . have been bent to serve
> the purpose of a singular, designing intellect.[1]

In other words, in spite of a particular book's apparent lack of conformity to any recognized structural patterns, we might still penetrate to its "inward form" and find there clues of the extraordinarily individual purposes in the mind of the author—clues which will give us much-needed aid in coming to a comprehension of his book as a whole. This inner form will be present to a greater or lesser degree in any work of import; but when we are on a very unfamiliar type of terrain, it behooves us to pay especially close attention to "natural markings."

b) Hegel, as heir to the rationalist persuasion in philosophy, shared two of the main objectives of rationalism:

1) the objective of coming to a comprehension of the All *(das Ganze)*, the totality of being, or, as they frequently called it, the "Absolute";

2) the objective of describing the world precisely as an organized system of Reason.

c) Fichte, a little more than a decade before Hegel wrote the *Phenomenology*, had attempted, in his rationalistic way, to demonstrate the "deduction" of absolute self-knowledge from ordinary sensory awareness—an attempt that takes on a certain superficial resemblance to the task Hegel was going to undertake in the *Phenomenology*. As Hyppolite says,

> In Fichte, in that part of his *Doctrine of Science* in which he proposed to give a "pragmatic account of the human spirit," and which he named the "Deduction of Representation,"—we find the first model for the type of task that would later be accomplished in Hegel's *Phenomenology of Spirit*. In this "Deduction," Fichte proposes, in effect, to lead ordinary consciousness from immediate sensible knowledge to philosophical self-knowledge.[2]

d) Schelling, Hegel's friend and immediate predecessor in philosophy, suggested in one place[3] that one might effectively approach an understanding of actual individuals in the actual world by taking the present as the starting point, and then trying to recapture the historical progressions that brought these actualities about.

e) Finally, Hegel was much influenced by sources which were not explicitly philosophical—in particular by the romantics in literature. And from the romantics one could find certain hints as to how Schelling's above-mentioned "idea" might best flourish. For example, Rousseau in his *Emile* attempts to show how the development of the *individual* from sensation to reflection parallels a similar development in the *human race* as a whole. Rousseau also has it in mind in this novel to chart out the journey of the *natural consciousness* from a prosaic view of the world to a poetic vision; and this is largely the same objective that Goethe has in his *Wilhelm Meisters Lehrajahre* and Novalis has in his *Heinrich von Ofterdingen*. Curiously, in the Classical Walpurgis Night (Part II of Goethe's *Faust*), we have an indication that the influence may have been reciprocal.[4] As Rehder says,

> If it were nothing else, this Walpurgis Night might be considered a phenomenology of emerging language, embracing the whole scale of expression from primitive sounds to the most intricate forms of speech and chant.[5]

The idea is that Goethe does here with speech what Hegel had accomplished with ideas—leading from the most primitive "abstract" ideas to the most intricate and concrete.

Rehder also points out that the Walpurgis Night is comparable to the *Phenom-*

enology on another count—namely, that it has to do with uncovering the presence of spirit to the world:

> The Classical Walpurgis Night deals with the problem of the materialization of energy: it is a *Phänomenologie des Geistes* in poetic form.[6]

Whatever may have been the particular works of literature that influenced Hegel most, it seems obvious that there was a sufficiency of models in the Romantic literature of Hegel's time, which Hegel might conform to in order to implement the speculative vision of Schelling.

In conclusion, as to the precise structure of the *Phenomenology,* we might say that

a) Hegel conceived the philosophical objective of presenting the All of "Spirit" according to a rationally coherent system.

b) He failed to find any recognized literary structure of the specifically philosophical type for implementing this aim. Fichte's "Deduction of Representation" could not supply a suitable model for the venture—since it ended up in a typical Rationalist *circulus vitiosus:* the "deduction" of something which had already been a presupposition. For in this work of Fichte,

> the philosophical self-consciousness is presupposed from the start, and this history or account of the development of consciousness—in spite of its intentions (which are quite similar to those of the *Phenomenology*)—is rather arbitrarily concocted, for this very reason.[7]

c) Nevertheless, he was impressed by the suggestion of Schelling about giving an empirical or phenomenal presentation of Absolute Spirit. And he was inspired by the descriptive style of the romanticists to achieve this objective *sans* rationalism: by drawing a word-portrait showing the parallel between the development of the individual and the development of his race, and methodically describing the ascent of the human spirit from natural consciousness to the highest possible philosophical vision of reality.

d) Insofar as he subscribed to Schelling's idea of describing the *present* of man and his world by going into the historical antecedents, he was also led to utilize something like what we call the "flashback" technique—beginning with a certain *fait accompli,* and then, by a series of reminiscences, weaving the thread of incidents, facts, motivations, or ideas that lead up to it. But note that a novelist who uses the flashback technique 1) sometimes gives little or no detail as to the *fait accompli* he is beginning with, but plunges forthwith at the outset into the series of reminiscences; and 2) often recites these reminiscences in an order other than the temporal order in which they took place. And so likewise Hegel 1) does not make explicit the *fait accompli* he is beginning with in the *Phenomenology* —namely, the particular philosophical view of the world that he personally had arrived at in the milieu of German idealism; and 2) does not proceed in any specifically temporal order in his reminiscences (the processes of *Erinnerung*).

e) But not even the realization of the above factors will make the *Phenomenology* into a familiar type of terrain. One continually, on every page, gets intimations of the massive effort that was needed to incarnate a philosophical work into a literary structure never meant for (or at least never successfully used for) philosophy.

f) In view of this latter consideration, it is of the utmost importance to pay close attention to what we have called the "inward form," i.e. the form or vehicle of individuality. That is, it is necessary to pay close attention to the context in which every word or paragraph is set—to garner the host of unique and unusual meanings given to them. Otherwise, if one accepts them according to their outward structure and their more conventional meanings—he will find himself (or Hegel) in a labyrinth of contradictions not amenable to synthesis.

II. WHAT IS THE "PLOT" OF THE "PHENOMENOLOGY"?

As was mentioned in the preceding section, Hegel seems to start from a *fait accompli*—his own particular philosophical view of the world—and then describes the currents leading up to this viewpoint after the manner of a literary flashback. In order to understand the "plot" of the Phenomenology, it would help if we examined first of all this philosophical viewpoint, and then go into the considerations and motivations that might have led him to adopt certain specific types of "flashback." In this way, we may come to see the "plot" unfold in its conceptual genesis.

One of the most essential characteristics of Hegel's philosophical viewpoint is that it involved the realization that our objective world is permeated with the alterations made by subjectivity; and that subjectivity itself is essentially oriented to, and conditioned and determined by, some type of objectivity. Obviously, the reality which we encounter is the result of the interaction between these two poles. And—theoretically—we could best understand any facet of reality only if it was veridically deduced from the context of this interaction (an interaction which might be termed "spirit," insofar as it brings man and men to spiritual awareness, and conversely also brings the material world to spiritual significance).

How can we best approach the portrayal of this interaction? If one wanted fully to describe a physical reaction like combustion, he would have to separate the reaction into components, dissect and analyze them, and in this way elucidate the way in which they "come together."

In describing the spiritual interaction between thought and being, it is important first of all that the one describing it have the vantage point where he sees it precisely as an *interaction*. Aristotle did not have this vantage point, but was immersed in objectivity; and thus he describes reality in terms of objectively different categories of external being. Kant did not have this standpoint, but was immersed in the insight that thought determines being; and in accord with this standpoint, he analyzes reality in terms of the different modes of thought possible in the apprehension of being—i.e., the categories of the understanding and the forms of sensibility.

But if one escapes the "provincialism" of the Aristotelian or Kantian view-points, the problem still remains: how can he approach a description of this most complex of all subject-matters? Could he approach it historically, showing how subject and object have *de facto* met and interpenetrated, and do meet and interpenetrate? If by "historically" we mean "temporally," this would not seem to be feasible. For being does not progress to consciousness on the basis of any time schedule; and time itself seems to be attributable in large part to subjectivi-ty (so that we would be continually begging the question as to the value of any temporally progressing analysis *of* subjectivity). Then again, subjectively speak-ing, thought itself, which observes and becomes related to time as to just *one* of its objects, and transcends temporality in its abstract thought processes—would not seem to be readily amenable to description purely in terms of temporal progression. If one were to approach the description of the temporal progression of the *objective pole* to *subjectivity*, his description would be perhaps something like Teilhard de Chardin's *Phenomenon of Man* or Bergson's *Creative Evolution.* If one were to approach the description of the temporal progression of the *subjectivity* to mature *existence,* his description would possibly be something on the order of a philosophy of developmental psychology. But Hegel's stand-point, as we have seen, was neither objectivity nor subjectivity, but the reciproci-ty between the two poles; and furthermore, he wished to describe this reciproci-ty in a complete, systematic, and relatively presupposition-less way—which would seem to preclude immersion in any sort of historical progression. How go about this?

We are taking for granted here that philosophy represents a final reflection of knowledge upon itself, a gathering together of the whole scheme of things into an all-encompassing view. This, at least, seemed to be Hegel's understanding of "philosophy." The "total view" envisaged here will, of course, differ in accord with the state of knowledge and the state of the world. But since we are presup-posing a state of knowledge which realizes that it is conditioned by objects, and a state of the world which is known to be a product of subjectivity—we are faced with a clear-cut choice: either unreflectively accept some philosophical presup-positions, and give a partial one-sided reflection upon reality, on the basis of these presuppositions; or give a truly new philosophical total view of this subjec-tive-objective dynamism, precisely *as* subjective-objective.

This seems to be the task Hegel faced in the *Phenomenology.* And if he wanted to describe the interaction in terms of its progression, he would have to describe it in terms of a non-temporal progression—something analogous perhaps to the progression of thought (one idea "leading to" another) or the progression of the parts of an organism (one organ or function leading into another).

In the face of this problem, it was natural that Hegel should adopt a procedure something like that of the novelist who wants fully to elucidate the relationship of two characters—e.g. a lover and his beloved—to each other. For just as the novelist goes into each of the characters, showing their formation, and the incidents that led up to their mutual realtionship—so also Hegel goes into both objectivity and subjectivity, gives their facets and antecedents, and leads up to their "marriage." Time enters into the picture, but is subservient to the description, just as it is in the novel which utilizes flashbacks of varying temporal spans, takes up the thread of the narrative here and there, etc.

But the "romance" that Hegel is describing is the most complex imaginable. In describing the relationship of the individual consciousness to the object, he must take into account that the "object" is culturally conditioned by the historical antecedents of one's race or nation; in describing the religious self-consciousness of men-in-general, he must take into account that this is conditioned by the progression of the individual to self-consciousness; and so forth.

The "tale" that Hegel eventually weaves is one that is designed to take into account all possible essential factors, viz.: a) the relationship of the individual subjectivity to its object; b) the relationship of the individual spirit to the universal spirit; c) the relationship of the cognitive and volitive "object" to the cultural objective world created by spirit; and d) the relationship of the cognitive and volitive "object" to the subjective attitude of the individual consciousness. All of this involves a concentration on now one aspect, now another, without losing the thread of the narrative—which to a large extent is an artistic problem as well as a philosophical one.

Whether or not Hegel's artistry is on par with his philosophy, these would be the major outlines of the "plot" developed in the *Phenomenology*. And in the final chapter of the *Phenomenology*—as a sort of climax (or perhaps the denoument)—he tries to bring all the various threads together, so that the reader can get a final glimpse of the essential dynamisms of spirit in the part and in the whole.

III. IS THE "PHENOMENOLOGY" AN INTRODUCTION TO HEGEL'S SYSTEM' A PART OF IT, OR BOTH?

Hegel in his Jena period began to announce, in the summer of 1805, the publication of his "System," which would comprise a) *philosophiam speculativam (logicam et metaphysicam), naturae et mentis, ex libro per aestatem prodituro, et* b) *jus naturae, ex eodem.* There was no mention at this time of any "introduction" to his system.

But as Hyppolite says,[1] when Hegel began to write part (a) of his System, he started with an introduction which, in the winter of 1806-1807, received the name of a *Phenomenology of Spirit*; and gradually went beyond the initial triad of consciousness/self-consciousness/reason (cf. Part I[2] of the *Phenomenology*) to comprise the "phenomena" of spirit, religion, and absolute knowledge (in Part II of the *Phenomenology*)—and to contain, for all practical purposes, his whole envisaged system in "phenomenological" form.

But then—and this is where the confusion enters—when he finally wrote the

System (the *Encyclopedia,* comprising a) the *Logic,* b) the *Philosophy of nature,* and c) the *Philosophy of Spirit*), he includes "phenomenology" in the *Philosophy of Spirit,* under the heading of "Subjective Spirit," and more precisely as the moment of "antithesis" in the dialectic unfolding of subjective spirit.

And finally—to bring this initial confusion to full bloom—he restricts the term "phenomenology" in the *Encyclopedia* exclusively to the subject-matter of *Part I* of the *Phenomenology of Spirit* (consciousness/self-consciousness/reason). And lest we think this was an abridgment to save time, it should also be noted that in his *Propedeutics*—a summary of his system for the use of high school students—the restriction of the term "phenomenology" to the triad of consciousness/self-consciousness/reason receives additional corroboration.

The resultant confusion as to the relation of the *Phenomenology of Spirit* to the System can accordingly be expressed in terms of two distinct questions:

a) How can the *Phenomenology* be both an introduction to the System, and included in that System? and

b) Why is only Part I of the *Phenomenology* included in the *Encyclopedia* and in the *Propedeutics* under the heading, "phenomenology?"

Before answering these questions, it would be well to recall Hegel's apparent incentive or motivation in writing the *Phenomenology.* Hegel's personal vantage point was the insight to which Schelling had led him without partaking of it himself—namely, the insight into Absolute Spirit as a transcendent unity pervading all subject-object relationships, and having the status not just of an abstraction apprehensible only to "intellectual intuition" but of a concrete reality comprehensible to "reason" (in Hegel's sense of the word). How could Hegel best introduce others to this same insight? As we have seen, he chose to use a method roughly comparable to a flashback technique, to introduce the novice in philosophy to all the currents and cross-currents and counter-currents of Absolute Spirit in its interactions. He gradually[3] conceived the plan of bringing the novice to a vivid "immediate" insight (at the end of the *Phenomenology,* the Chapter on "Absolute Knowledge") into Spirit as the prime actuality pervading the actual world and all individual "spirits" in this world. Then, having brought his readers to this realization, he would be in a position to consider this Absolute in-itself, organizing all its aspects and attributes into an organized system of science. (After one has demonstrated the existence of God, he is then in a position to develop a theodicy.)

Hence Hegel purposed to bring his readers first to an extensive "empirical" apprehension of the workings of Spirit on all levels, and then to construct an Absolute Science, demonstrating in a dialectically necessary way what are the "internal characteristics," so to speak, of this Spirit, in a comprehensive sytem.

With this in mind, we can consider now the two questions mentioned above:

a) It is not absolutely contradictory that x should be an introduction to a scientific system, and also part of that system.

For example, if one became sufficiently versed in all extant sciences to know their primary and secondary laws, their elements and subdivisions—we could not say that his knowledge of all these sciences would not be a "science" (i.e., scientific knowledge). Granted, his knowledge of any individual science would probably not be as extensive as the knowledge of a person specializing in that science. But still, there is something to be said for having a fairly extensive knowledge of *all* sciences. For want of a better word, let us call this state of knowledge of *all* sciences "scientific-knowledge-in-general." If a person arrived at this state of "scientific-knowledge-in-general," he would then be able, other factors being equal, to conduct a scientific meta-study of these sciences, arrange them in a systematic way according to their elements, principles, common and distinctive features, etc. This latter arrangement, if it amounted to an extensive organized system, would then be worthy to be called a "science of sciences," or a "meta-science." If this meta-science were complete, it is not improbable that in its catalogue of scientific disciplines, both "scientific-knowledge-in-general" and "meta-science" would appear as distinct and autonomous sciences. So if we may assume that "scientific-knowledge-in-general" is an *introduction* to meta-science, we here have a case where x is an introduction to a scientific system, and also a part of that system.

To take one further example which is closer to the case of phenomenology in its relationship to the science of Spirit: One could no doubt be introduced (Aristotle certainly was) to traditional logic by an inductive method, becoming acquainted experientially with all the different types of terms, propositions, syllogisms, etc. Then at the end of these investigations he could construct the system called logic, within whose boundaries the process of "induction" would sooner or later be given some prominence. Here again we have a situation where x–the processes of induction–is an introduction to logic, and also a part of it.

Now "phenomenology" is related to the systematic science of Spirit as a kind of induction. For it is calculated to introduce one to the essential subject-object dialectic of Spirit on all essential levels. After this introduction has taken place, the writer is prepared to expound, and the reader is prepared to understand, an organized scientific system of the nature and operations of Absolute Spirit– within which system "phenomenology" (the appearance of spirit in and through the transcendence of immediate subject-object relationships) will certainly appear, as one of the operations of spirit.

b) Granting, then, that phenomenology can be both an introduction to Hegel's System and a part of that System, we still have the further problem: Why does Hegel's *Phenomenology* as an *introduction* consist of two parts (the Forms of Consciousness [*Gestalten des Bewusstseins*] and the Forms of a World [*Gestalten einer Welt*]), while that "phenomenology" which is included as part of the System is spoken of as consisting only of the first of these two parts (the Forms of Consciousness)?

To return to our example of the development of a science of logic: While using the inductive method in exploring the subject-matter of logic, one would come to "experiment with" both the inductive and the deductive methods of reasoning. Then when the "logical system" of logic is later completed, and the term "induction" is utilized to describe the process of experimental generalization,

the "induction of deduction"—which took place in the introductory explana-
tions—would be included implicitly, but probably not explicitly (since for purposes of systematization induction would have to be definitively contra-distin-
guished from deduction proper).

So also, Hegel, by a transition through a phenomenology of the various subject-
object distinctions dialectically germane to Absolute Spirit, arrives, at the end
of Part I of the *Phenomenology,* at the point where Spirit finally appears on the
scene as a transcendent unity of subject and object. But this transcendent *unity*-
in-distinction of subject and object can still be considered phenomenologically,
i.e., with the emphasis on the *distinction* of subject and object, self and "other."
This second process can continue on until we come to those aspects of distinction which prove to be no distinction, i.e., those which simply make the transcendent unity of Spirit as transparent as possible (cf. the phenomenology of art,
religion, and Absolute Knowledge, at the end of the *Phenomenology*).

But in the context of the *Encyclopedia,* which is a scientific system of all the
dialectic relationships of Spirit—when the phenomenology of finite subject/ob-
ject encounters is treated, it would be confusing to mention a "phenomenology
of the transcendent unity of Spirit," because the phenomenology (appearance in
distinctness) of Spirit is different in concept from the unity of Spirit in-itself. In
other words, the "phenomenology of unity" is not mentioned in Hegel's
Encyclopedia, for the same reason that the "induction of deduction" might not
be mentioned in a scientific system of logic.

In conclusion then,

a) The *Phenomenology* is an introduction to the System in the sense of being a
pedagogical means of supplying the manifold quasi-external[4] experience of
Spirit before expounding on the internal dialectics of Spirit.

b) It is also a part of the System, insofar as the appearance (phenomenon) of
finite objects to finite subjects is one of the essential moments of spirit (the
moment of consciousness of distinction—"phenomenology").

IV. WHAT IS THE SUBJECT—MATTER OF "PHENOMENOLOGY?"

It is difficult to discuss this problem without going very deeply into one of the
main problems facing the reader of the *Phenomenology:* namely, what is a
subject in the Hegelian sense, what an object, and what is the genesis of their
unity and division? For, as Hegel mentions in the *Encyclopedia,*[1] a "phenomenology" is germane to a state of consciousness in which the subject-object dichotomy is emphasized; and one of the main purposes of the *Phenomenology* is
to elucidate that relationship. Therefore, if "subject-matter" is an object in a
certain sense, it would behoove us fully to understand what Hegel meant by
"object" in order to come to a notion of what *Hegel* considered to be the
"subject-matter" of his treatise.

But leaving the discussion of this major problem to the next section for purposes of clarity, we will limit ourselves here to a consideration of "subject-matter" in the more conventional sense—with the result that the conclusions we draw may or may not correspond to the Hegelian sense of subject-matter. But, as we shall see, this consideration of subject-matter in the conventional sense will also have the merit of bringing us at least to the borderlines of the problem of subjectivity-objectivity which we will discuss in the next section.

In regard to the question at hand, we should note that it is in general quite difficult to distinguish accurately the object of a study from the way of studying it. As Heidegger points out,[2] we tend to think in terms of an objective being called "Nature," remaining as a self-identical subject-matter for all our scientific investigations. But *de facto* this "Nature" is the result of our own modern objectification techniques: It is permeated with our own subjective ways of looking at things, with the laws in terms of which we have chosen to examine it, with the constructs by means of which we have chosen to organize it. Nature nowadays is much different than it was in the Middle Ages or any other era.

When we come to the various "natural sciences," the same situation presents itself in miniature. Can we speak about a stable subject-matter in biology, as distinct from our progress in ways of viewing this subject-matter? If we bring in anatomical or cellular structure, or hormonal balance, or even the organic as opposed to the inorganic, we are dealing in large part with concepts introduced by human subjects at a certain point in history, and not with a pure, unadulterated "thing-in-itself."

It is evident, however, that we can at least make a distinction of *remote* subject-matter from ways of viewing it. For it is a fact of experience that various disciplines, with different points of view, or with different purposes, will converge upon some common area of research, which we might call their "remote" subject-matter. For example, the human body will be a common center of interest for biologists, art students, automotive safety engineers, pharmacologists, etc.—for very different reasons.

It is also evident that many different subject-matters could be studied for one selfsame purpose. For example, a Marxist might study Russian History, Hegel's theory of the Master-Slave relationship, economics, propaganda methods—all for the single purpose of coming to a fuller understanding of Marxism.

In view of these facts, we tend to think of the various sciences a) as ordinarily having something material, an objective subject-matter in some way publicly accessible to many individualities with many purposes and points of view; b) as having also ordinarily something formal, namely, the individual purposes, significations, and viewpoints that pervade the examination of this remote material.

But, as has been indicated above, when we come to a discussion of the *proximate* object of a particular discipline, it is hard to distinguish precisely some subject-matter which does not presuppose certain subjective modes of treating it, or to talk about individual intents without presupposing a certain conventionally intended subject-matter.

This difficulty significantly becomes an impossibility in the case of certain "objects" which are considered conventionally as being closer to the subjectivity. For example, if we conduct a study of feelings, ideas, human individuality, or intersubjectivity—any distinction we make between the "what" and the "how" becomes transparently arbitrary. We definitely have to keep the distinction. It would be impossible for us to consider anything subjective without making it objective. But it becomes increasingly obvious from such cases that the subject-object distinction is largely, if not entirely, our own creation, something which goes hand in hand with consciousness of the world and of oneself. And this is why these cases are "significant."

The *Phenomenology*, as Heidegger observed,[3] is one of those cases where the "what" is fully permeated with the "how." And thus it might be more accurate to say that the *Phenomenology* has a subject, than to say that it has an object.[4] Or, if it has an object, it is our own knowledge[5] —which is to say the same thing in different words.

But if it is true that the *Phenomenology* and any other scientific study of very subjective material are apt to give us significant insights into the true nature of subjectivity and objectivity—it is also regrettably true that they present extremely difficult problems of verification, problems which might diminish or nullify the value of these insights.

For example, at the end of this book on Hegel, I could write an appendix on "my purpose in writing this book." In the writing of this, I would have to separate apparent from real purposes, see them in terms of any hierarchical order they might have, make implicit purposes explicit, check them individually and as a unit against their expression through my actual writing, and so forth. The very fact that one who reads this has no reliable and certain way of either verifying or refuting what I have said, would hinder him from gaining from this type of subject-matter any worthwhile insight into the relationship between subjectivity and objectivity.

Let us consider one more example of a "subjective" type of subject-matter: If a philosopher by the method of introspection wrote a treatise on "The World of Ideas," describing ideas according to their genera, hierarchy, interrelations, genesis and clarity—one could neither verify nor contradict the philosopher's conclusions meaningfully, unless he had himself conducted just as elaborate and thorough an introspection as the philosopher had done. But even if he carried out such an introspection, and could verify certain of the conclusions of the aforesaid philosopher on the basis of his own experience—this verification would amount only to saying that two thinkers made the same type of primary mental "objects," or formed these mental "objects" in similar fashion, or ordered them according to the same hierarchical structure, etc.

The problem, then, is to find a "subjective" subject-matter which is more publicly accessible and verifiable, so that the potentialities of the subject-matter for clarifying subject-object dynamics will not be diminished or countermanded by its defective verifiability.

Fichte thought he had discovered such a subject-matter in Kant's transcendental investigations. He reasoned—and rightly, it seems—that if Kant had successfully uncovered the subjective grounds of objectivity, then the subjectivity of the transcendental ego is identical with the objectivity of objects. Thus if we dig deep enough into the roots of subjectivity, we find also the roots of objectivity, and thus *ipso facto* a subject-matter which is verified in and through the very act of being understood. And thus also we have a "philosopher's stone" which will enable us once and for all to define exactly and coordinate the relationship between the self and the world, between thought and being.

Hegel agreed in general that there was a fusion and identification of objectivity and subjectivity in and through the transcendental ego. But he did not quite look upon this discovery as a "philosopher's stone"—and mainly because it gave a one-sided picture. It elucidated the unity of subjectivity and objectivity, but not their distinctness, or, more precisely, not their unity-in-distinction. With Fichte's discovery we arrive at the abstract unity of the Absolute Ego incorporating objectivity in itself; but it is necessary to go beyond this to the concrete subjective-objective dynamism of the All.

In order to implement this latter goal, Hegel turned to a subject-matter which he looked upon as the "middle-term" between (i.e., *the* meeting-ground of) subjectivity and objectivity. This "middle-term" was what he called the Forms of Consciousness (the subject matter of Part I of the *Phenomenology*). These Forms of Consciousness, expanded into the proportions of *social* consciousness, became the "Forms of the World" (the subject-matter of Part II).

But it is very dangerous to pinpoint the subject-matter of Hegel's *Phenomenology* as being "the forms of Individual and Social Consciousness," without further explanation. For on the one hand, a "Form of Consciousness" might seem to be a very arbitrary thing (who is to decide what is to be a Form of Consciousness, and what not?). On the other, it has the connotation of something stable or static. Let us clarify these two points:

a) As Baillie points out,[6] Hegel does not choose just any Forms of consciousness. But he draws his "material" (1) from those individual forms of experience which are generally prevalent at some time in the development of individuals; and (2) from those events in history or in the history of philosophy which are typical of many others. Thus, for example, he chooses theories of sensation expounded by Plato for his chapter on sense-certainty; he recapitulates a stage in the development of a human being from infancy to childhood (from undifferentiated presence in the sensible world to differentiation of objects) in his transition from the chapter on sense-certainty to the chapter on perception; he recapitulates the transition of the adolescent from technical objective knowledge to self-knowledge in his own transition from the chapter on Understanding to the discussion of Self-Consciousness; in his representation of the transition from a custom-constituted society to a law-constituted society, he takes as his exemplar the passage from Greek civilization to Roman civilization; and in describing the passage from individualism to morality, he recaptures the historical developments leading to Romanticism and Idealism after the French revolution. Thus in a certain sense Hegel's *Phenomenology* might be compared on the surface to a developmental psychology, or to a philosophy of history. But he also goes beyond developmental psychology and philosophy of history, in that he judiciously presents his "moments" as stepping-stones to the experience of the Absolute, and in the context of their necessary internal dialectic.

b) This last point leads us into our second observation: These Forms or "moments" of consciousness could, very conceivably, be presented as static objective facts, or as static subjective conditions for experience. But they are not. They are considered as dynamisms giving rise to movements to higher states of individual awareness, or to higher stages of social consciousness. They are considered precisely in terms of the "logic of movement"—the dialectical progression from objective existence-in-self (the "thesis") to subjective existence-for-oneself (the "antithesis") to subjective-objective existence-in-and-for-oneself (the "synthesis").

Having made these latter observations, we are now in a position to assess the nature and complexity of the subject-matter of the *Phenomenology* in the light of the two factors mentioned earlier in this section—a) the intermingling of the "what" and the "how" especially in certain types of subject-matter; and b) the problems of verifiability with certain types of "subjective" subject-matter:

a) The Forms of Individual and Social Consciousness, as we have seen, are considered as meeting-grounds of the most central and essential "movement" taking place in the All of absolute reality—namely, that reciprocity between subject and object which is popularly expressed in terms of the "moments" of thesis-antithesis-synthesis. But this movement which is being considered is also considered *by means of* the same movement. As was mentioned in the preceding chapter, while Hegel's *Encyclopedia* is analogous to a systematic logical elaboration of deductive and inductive logic, his *Phenomenology* is analogous to a logical induction of deductive and inductive logic. But in the *Phenomenology* Hegel is not just striving to elicit intellectual assent to conceptual generalizations by organizing thought-processes (which would be the function of "a logical induction of deductive and inductive logic"); but to bring his reader to an experience, or rather, to bring his reader to the experience of the logic of experience by means of a "phenomenological" application of that logic of experience (the logic which supersedes—but also incorporates—the traditional logic of abstract thought-processes about static being).

Thus we have here, in the sense mentioned, a subjective-objective logic of subjective-objective logical processes—a complete merger of the "what" in the "how" and vice versa. Thus also it would be impossible to distinguish effectively an "object" of the Phenomenology, as contradistinguished from some subjective way of looking at that object. Its subject-matter is neither a material content nor a subjective modality, because it is both material content and subjective modality.

b) With regard to the problem of verifiability—a problem presents itself at the very beginning, in relationship to certain conclusions we arrived at previously. For we said that the *Phenomenology* in its general literary structure, might best be considered after the pattern of a novel using a "flashback" technique: insofar as Hegel seems to be striving to bring his reader to assimilate, to make-present, to himself, by a process of recollection *(Erinnerung)* of the experience of the individual spirit and of spirit-in-general—the experience of actual individuality in the actual world (which happens to be the point that Hegel actually started from). But in a novel when the writer strives to bring his readers to some presupposed experience, we do not adjudge the results in terms of the categories of "true" and "false." So, if the *Phenomenology* is essentially calculated to be the presentation of an *experience*—does the problem of verifiability even obtain, in regard to it?

The important point here is that the *Phenomenology* is not fiction, and is by no means calculated to provide an aesthetic experience. In lieu of aesthetic value, the reader will be prone to question whether the experience presented is truly the absolute philosophical experience-of-the-nature-of-philosophical-experience of the All — as it purports to be. How could one possibly judge this experience as true or false?

As we have said, Hegel takes his point of departure from types of individual experience, and types of historical experience. The statements he makes about these experiences are not statements about his individual intents with regard to them; nor are they statements about his own ideas of these statements, i.e., about "the introspective experience of the ideas of these experiences." And so the problems of verification will not be precisely the same as those we enumerated earlier in this section, with regard to such extremely subjective material.

But neither are his statements the type that could be corroborated or denied on the basis of a knowledge of empirical psychology, or history, or the history of philosophy.

In short, the propositions of the *Phenomenology* are of such a nature that they defy express verification procedures either on the basis of an objective knowledge of factual reality, or on the basis of a subjective knowledge of the internal conditions of knowledge itself.

In order to understand this seeming impasse, we must advert to the fact that—at least to the mind of Hegel and other proponents of German Idealism—something like a Copernican revolution in philosophy had taken place after Kant and Fichte. No longer would philosophy present a view of the world which entailed individual subjects encountering individual objects. This view had been superseded by the insight that the main reality in the world was existence of an Absolute Ego transcending and incorporating all facets of reality. Under Hegel's direction, this was elaborated into the insight that the main reality was the process by which Absolute Being was becoming Absolute Subject.

After the Copernican revolution had taken place in astronomy, it would be senseless and futile for astronomers to try to verify or challenge statements made from the vantage point of the new astronomy, on the basis of evidence collected from the vantage point of the old astronomy. If they wished to refute such statements, they must either refute the hypothesis of Copernicus or, although accepting it, show that it has been misunderstood or misapplied.

So also, those who would refute Hegel have this choice: either refute his pivotal concept of the dynamics of Absolute Spirit; or, while accepting this as a working hypothesis, show that it is possible to come up with a clearer notion of the dynamics of transcendence, with a clearer application of the dialectical logic, etc.

V. IS IT POSSIBLE TO CHOOSE A VANTAGE POINT WHICH IS NEITHER "SUBJECTIVE" NOR "OBJECTIVE"?

Carl Jung, in his *Psychological Types,*[1] includes a chapter on philosophy which gives an illuminating account of the consequences of a predominating orientation to the "objective" and to the "subjective," respectively.

The "objective" viewpoint, he says, characteristically is drawn to objects, facts, and events, as if to a magnet. It becomes totally immersed in these externalities, in all their fascinating multiplicity, and finds it difficult to see the forest for the trees, so to speak. This natural attitude is well illustrated in the philosophical movements of empiricism and positivism. When it is carried to an extreme, it becomes ludicrous in attempting to deal with very subjective material—e.g., poetry, art, religion, thought processes—in a factual, objective way.

The "subjective" viewpoint, on the other hand, seems to consider objects and facts and events a threat to the ego; and thus tends to withdraw from them to the citadel of its own ideas, from which vantage point it becomes engaged in drawing the confusing and threatening multiplicities in the external world into abstract thought-unities. When this viewpoint is carried to an extreme, it becomes ridiculous in a different way: by trying arbitrarily to force reality into the mold of its pre-existent mental schemata and rational laws.[2]

When we speak of the "possibility" of a viewpoint in the middle between these two aforesaid viewpoints, we are simply raising the question as to whether there is anything self-contradictory in the concept of such a viewpoint.

Before answering this question, we should make a distinction between two possible meanings which might be attached to "a viewpoint which is neither 'subjective' nor 'objective.' "

a) First of all, this might indicate a viewpoint which simply recognized the existence of, and seriously strived to do justice to, both subjective and objective factors in the material it was considering. There would of course be nothing self-contradictory here.

b) It might also indicate a viewpoint which tried actually to capture the interaction between subject and object. This would differ from the preceding type of "middle" viewpoint, insofar as it would of its very nature amount to the representation of a *movement,* or reciprocity. If we accept our terms here in a very univocal way, we would have to say that it would be self-contradictory to represent, i.e., to present in some sort of stable and delimited form, a movement in itself. But if we accept the fact that motion must be "arrested" and delimited for purposes of analysis, there would seem to be nothing inherently self-contradictory in such a viewpoint.

Hegel's immediate philosophical predecessors exemplified what we have called above the "subjective" viewpoint. As Hyppolite says,[3] they turned away from ordinary consciousness, in which the subject tends to disappear and give way to the object; and extolled transcendental consciousness, in which the object tends to disappear, and become just a projection of the transcendental ego.

Schelling, the most immediate of these predecessors, after the manner of a subjectivist who is constrained to make some concession to objectivity, tried to bridge the gap between freedom and necessity, thought and being, by the hypothesis of an absolute, incomprehensible transcendent unity uniting the two spheres. He explains the necessity of such a hypothesis in these words:

> Such a pre-established harmony [as we see] between objectivity (that which is conformed to law) and its determinant (which is free) would be incomprehensible except in the context of some superior term superseding both subjectivity and objectivity.[4]

For all practical purposes, Schelling squelches the subject-object problem by simply reducing it to his "superior term"—an undifferentiated, abstract "Absolute."[5]

Then, apparently to make up for the lack of conceptual definitiveness in the hypothesis of the absolute transcendent unity (it could be apprehended by "intellectual intuition," but in no way conceptually comprehended)—Schelling pointed to organic nature as a sort of aesthetic substitute for conceptual significance. For in organisms, he said, we have the epitome, in readily apprehensible form, of the synthesis of subjectivity and objectivity, freedom and necessity.

Hegel, perhaps because of an empiricist bent which would necessarily be stifled in such an intellectual milieu, was dissatisfied with these attempts of Schelling to make objectivity into an unsubstantial shadow of the Absolute. As far as Hegel was concerned, although subject and object as reciprocal poles are inseparably united, they are irreducible to each other. Therefore Hegel does not try to simply reduce the object to the subjectivity, or to resolve the subject into objective factors. He maintains the distinction in its rigor. He recognizes that there is something really objective, outside of and other than the ego, incapable of being simply reduced to the ego, *even if a perfect fusion of the ego with its other should be brought about.*

Hegel thus revises the absolute transcendent unity which Schelling spoke of, to envisage it as a marriage or transcendent unification of two distinct and indissoluble elements of Reality:

> That which appears [the Absolute in-itself, in Hegel's sense] alienates itself in the act of becoming apparent. By means of this alienation, consciousness attains to the ultimate extremity of its own being. But even so it does not leave itself or its own essence; and neither does the absolute, because of its alienation, fall into a vacuum of debility.[6]

Hegel also saw that the constant mutual coadaptation of transcendent being (the Absolute in-itself) to the transcendental ego (the Absolute for-itself) gives rise to the possibility of describing the process of unification of these distinct realities.

He does not, however, agree with Schelling that organic nature is the epitome of the fusion of freedom and necessity, subjectivity and objectivity. For as far as Hegel is concerned, organic nature does not reveal a fusion, but a dichotomy—the dichotomy of universal life from the universal individual (the earth).[7]

But if we turn to the manifold *forms of individual consciousness,* we have a proper "middle term" by which may be seen the fusion of free spiritual thought and necessary sensuous existence.

Being a scholar in history, Hegel was perhaps influenced by this fact to go on to consider the parallel process to the formation of individual consciousness, which was taking place on the larger scale, in social consciousness. And thus the Forms of the World similarly serve as a "middle term" for observing the fusion of the in-itself and for-itself.

If Hegel were predisposed to the "objective" viewpoint, he would no doubt have given prime importance to the forms of sense-stimuli, the laws governing their transmission and incorporation into percepts, etc., in considering the Forms of Individual Consciousness; and in considering the Forms of the World, he would probably have given most weight to considerations of heredity and environment, and political and social facts.

If he were predisposed to a "subjective" viewpoint, in considering the individual consciousness, he would focus on mental constructs, internal faculties, ways of assimilating objects, and the necessary laws of thought and volition; and in considering the social consciousness, he might be most interested in ideologies, the control of events through intelligence, the necessary laws governing political events, etc.

But *de facto* he tries to recapture the *movement between* the poles of freedom and necessity on both the individual and social level. In analyzing this movement he tries to show how the in-itself proves upon examination to be for-consciousness, and then upon further examination proves to be the concept both uniting, and maintaining the distinction of, the initial object and the empirical ego.

The fundamental hypothesis of Hegel in the *Phenomenology,* it should be noted, is that we should accept the objective as well as the subjective world and their immediacy, realize that they irresistibly meet and interact, and try to describe this interaction in order to come to a realization of this fundamental actuality which gives life to all of existence, whether subjective or objective. Or as Heidegger puts it, we must see objectivity precisely as appearing to subjectivity, if we would come to an appreciation of the be-ing of being.[8]

VI. WHAT IS THE MEANING OF THE "DIALECTICAL NECESSITY"
JOINING THE VARIOUS "MOMENTS" IN THE "PHENOMENOLOGY"?

In order to treat this complex question the more effectively, we will divide it
into the following relevant sub-questions:

a) How does Hegel come to make the transitions from one moment to the
next?

b) In what sense does the series of these transitional processes amount to a
"highway of despair?"

c) What is the "dialectic?"

d) Is Hegel's dialectical logic conformable to traditional formal logic?

e) Where lies the "necessity" in the dialectic?

VI. (a) *How does Hegel come to make the transitions from one moment to the
next?*

Merleau-Ponty describes the transitional processes in the *Phenomenology* as a
constant revision of imperfect intents:

> All of the *Phénoménologie de l'esprit* describes man's efforts to reappro-
> priate himself. At every period of history he starts from a subjective "cer-
> tainty," makes his actions conform to the directions of that certainty, and
> witnesses the surprising consequences of his first intention, discovering its
> objective "truth." He then modifies his project, gets under way once more,
> again becomes aware of the abstract qualities of his new project, until
> subjective certainty finally equals objective truth and in the light of con-
> sciousness he becomes fully what he already obscurely was.[1]

This description, insofar as it is in terms of a successive revision of purposes in
mankind in the course of history, would apply preeminently to Part II of the
Phenomenology, which draws heavily on historical movements to illustrate the
advance towards the goal of spiritualizing the world.

A similar process seems to take place in the development of individual consciousness: One comes to a relative degree of certitude about certain objects,
then in the light of further experience comes to revise these preliminary notions,
and in this way gradually approximates to concepts of reality which are so
satisfactory as to require less and less revision.

In terms of general structure, the transitions in Part I of the *Phenomenology*
take on the appearance of progressive movements in the development of individual consciousness, such as we have just described; and the transitions in Part II
take on the appearance of progressions in the history of mankind, such as
Merleau-Ponty describes.

But it is important to remember at this point that Part I does not just give a
historical or developmental account of the progress of individual consciousness
in knowledge; nor does Part II just give a sort of philosophy of history up to the
time of Hegel.

But rather, the prime purpose of the *Phenomenology* in Part I is to explore individual knowledge or consciousness itself as something actual and present and entire; while the purpose in Part II is to examine the actual state of the world as something similarly present and entire. And thus, for example, in Part I when we come to Reason, we must not understand this as some superior state that has been reached by means of passing through inferior levels, but rather as a state which even now, at this very moment, in any conscious individual, is being constituted by a progression through sensory awareness to understanding and vice versa. And in Part II, when we come to the stage of Revealed Religion, we must understand this as an actuality which even now, in the world as a whole, is being constituted by means of a dialectical progression from primitive familial and tribal mores through the moment of freedom extolled by Rousseau and others to natural and revealed religion—and vice versa.

In other words, the *Phenomenology* consists of a concatenation of "reminiscences," as Hegel put it, or "flashbacks," as we have termed it here in describing the *Phenomenology*'s literary form; but not reminiscences specifically of time, nor flashbacks specifically through time. Rather, the reminiscence or the flashback is taking place in the present, insofar as the individual spirit and the world spirit is striving to reappropriate, reassimilate the essential moments which are even now constituting its actual being. Being in the strict sense is only in the present; and, as Heidegger observes,[2] is represented in the *Phenomenology* as a presence.

And so, what happens more precisely in the *Phenomenology* is this: In Part I, consciousness applies the same method by which it has come to awareness to examine the present state of its awareness. It has come to awareness by formulating definite concepts, and then revising these concepts and refining them, in the light of an ever-widening context. It examines the present state of its awareness by formulating concepts *of* the various abstract facets of awareness, and refining these concepts in terms of the whole of awareness which becomes ever more explicit, as this process takes place.

In Part II consciousness, which is now understood to be fully aware, i.e., to be spirit, applies this same method (the method that we have described as the procedure fostering the development of individual consciousness) to an examination of *its* world, i.e., itself (since the self and the "other" have appropriated each other at this point), in terms of its dynamic structures, i.e., in terms of the currents of conscious intent that are even now contributing essentially to its actuality. So, while Part I might be summed up as consciousness' knowledge of the ever-present tension among the various aspects of consciousness, Part II might be called spirit's knowledge of the ever-present tension among the various aspects of its historical intents (in the sense in which Merleau-Ponty describes these historical intents).

Granted that this is the context and the general path of the transitions, three questions still remain unanswered: 1) How does time enter into the picture of the "movements"? 2) What precisely is the cause of, or the impetus to, the various transitions? and 3) Is there a terminus to such processes (or, in other words, what is the goal of the transitions in the *Phenomenology*?)?

1) In Part I the various abstract aspects of awareness are not considered to be the result of certain processes taking place at certain times in an individual's development; but as being even now actively constituted by their temporal antecedents, among other things. And similarly, in Part II, the various abstract historical intents are seen as being even now actively conditioned by their temporal antecedents. Note that, from a non-phenomenological point of view, these antecedents would not be present, but would be mere memories or mere history. Note also that if—as seems most probable—Hegel had in mind primarily his own state of awareness and his own particular milieu of European culture—there will necessarily be, from this very fact, an emphasis on certain types of biographical and historical antecedents, rather than others.

2) As to the cause of the transitions, we have seen that in the development of individual consciousness, our insights, after they have been well-defined and concretized, prove to be insufficiently comprehensive, to be one-sided, i.e., to be relatively false, in the light of the ever widening context of knowledge. This situation leads us on naturally—not just to any other insights—but specifically to those other insights which would tend to counterbalance the insufficiency of the former, i.e., to complement them. Those other insights are the result of what Hegel calls "determinate negations," negations determined precisely by the positive determinations accruing to former insights. This moment of determinate negation is, then, the springboard leading to the various transitions in the *Phenomenology*. At every point we will immerse ourselves in some insight, and exhaust its positive content; and then find certain "negative features" making their presence known amid the very process of explicating the positive features. And these negative features supply the impetus to look for counterbalancing or complementing insights.

3) As the individual develops in conscious awareness according to the process of continual revision mentioned above, the quietus to this incessant process would arrive at that point where one has such an extensive knowledge of things in their context that he no longer needs to make any more essential revisions in his concepts. As applied to Part I of the *Phenomenology,* the terminus of the process would come when the individual consciousness has explored and put to the test every known facet of its own awareness, such that every facet is seen in the context of awareness in its entirety. In Part II, such a terminus would arrive when spirit has conducted a similar investigation of the present intents extant in its world, and finally comes to see these isolated intents as a whole dynamism converging, as it were, into a single unified intent.

VI. (b) *In what sense does the series of these transitional processes amount to a "highway of despair?"*

Hegel writes figuratively in his Introduction[3] that "natural consciousness" will find the "Phenomenology" as a whole to be a "highway of despair." In what sense does Hegel mean this? From the preceding section, it should be clear that every determinate insight, as it becomes more determinate and fixed, leads in a sense to its own demise, in that as its limitations become explicit, doubts as to its veracity also become explicit. But if this process is what Hegel means by the "highway of despair," how does the "highway of despair" differ from ordinary scepticism, or from the "methodological doubt" of Descartes?

In order to answer these questions, we must advert first to the Hegelian dictum that consciousness is the concept of itself. If this is the case, then, as Hyppolite observes,[4] it follows that 1) the self of consciousness (the self of which it is the concept) transcends it; or 2) (to say the same thing in different words) the self of consciousness (the self which is the concept) transcends itself. (Note here the two meanings of "to transcend").

Before Hegel, Kant had demonstrated that the "objectivity" of objects was rooted in the transcendental consciousness; and thus that objectivity, while being "transcendent" to ordinary, determinate, empirical consciousness, is "immanent" to the transcendental consciousness.[5]

Transcendence, in the light of this doctrine, thus has two aspects: 1) It characterizes that which is external to the empirical ego—the "thing-in-itself," the Absolute Being; 2) It constitutes that which is more intrinsic to the empirical ego than it is to itself, i.e., it constitutes the transcendental ego, or the Absolute Self. The empirical ego itself, in this context, is the medium in which transcendence—in both its aspects—comes about.

In objective terms, we could say that the fundamental orientation of the "movement" of the empirical ego is to render Absolute Being (the transcendence "out there") immanent. In subjective terms, we would say that the orientation of this movement is towards making the empirical ego transcendent, i.e., towards bringing the empirical ego into unison with the transcendental ego.

If we regard reflectively the activities of an animal in seeking food, we could say that the particular determinate goals which appear to the animal (the determinate edibles) are not final goals, from the point of view of the organism. Rather, the organism has as its own goal, some final state of maturity, and illustrates this by continuing to seek food at other times in other ways. On this same analogy, we cannot regard any of the determinations of the empirical ego as final: but rather, the teleological impetus of knowledge is to come to the point where the determinate view of the empirical ego is a determinate view of transcendence (its own transcendence as reflected also in the transcendence of the object)—which would imply that the view is no longer "determinate" in the usual sense, nor is the ego "empirical" in the former sense.

If we consider subjectivity as a whole—that is, not the subject-object relationship, but the relationship between the empirical ego (subjectivity as appearing in objectivity) and the transcendental ego (objectivity as grounded in subjectivity)—we find that this single whole subjectivity is in a very real sense continually inflicting death upon itself. For this subjectivity is both determinate and determining; and its knowledge consists in the process of determining its determinate view—a process which reaches its culmination only when the view is shown to be limited, and false to the extent that it is limited, and is thereupon removed from its determinate "existence" (the privileged place it holds in the empirical ego).

Knowledge as a process, in other words, consists in continually "putting to death" the short-lived determinations of the empirical ego.[6] If it did not thus put them to death, the transcendental ego would be immersed in the empirical, i.e., there would appear for us no distinction between the two, neither the determined nor the determinant.

But here we also have "death" in a special, limited sense. For since the agent putting the various determinate views to death is the ego itself in its transcendental aspect—no cadaver is left behind, in the trail of the living agent. Rather, the dead existence is reincorporated in the new concrete insights of the ego (the ego in its empirical aspect). This is what Hegel calls an *Aufhebung*—a superseding which takes place through incorporation, and vice versa (an incorporation which takes place through superseding).

The *Phenomenology,* then, is a "highway of despair" insofar as the natural consciousness which takes the *Phenomenology* as its pedagogue must forfeit all hope of coming to any state or aspect of awareness at which it can take its rest; through which it can garner a reliable view of the All of subjective-objective reality; in which it can "live."

The attitude which thus readies itself to deal death to all determinate aspects of its consciousness, thus stands in marked contrast to the attitude of the sceptic. For the sceptic closes himself in the protective fortress of some determinate point of view, refuses to "die" to it, refuses to recognize that it itself is the result of the death of some determinate truth, and must sound its own death knell in order to come into continuity with the whole of truth. Thus the sceptic cuts himself off from truth, from the All, from transcending himself. (He implicitly recognizes the All, however, in standing apart from it, and allowing it to supply the conditions for his negations.)

This process also shows itself as something to be distinguished from the "methodological doubt" of Descartes. Hegel, insofar as he has roots in the transcendental idealism of his era, begins, as do his contemporaries and predecessors, from the Cartesian doubt about objective reality (that which the subjectivity is trying to transcend).[7] But Hegel does not want to produce just another transcendental philosophy, but a "metaphysics of consciousness."[8] Therefore, he is not satisfied with the theoretical doubting of Descartes—which impugns all sorts of metaphysical positions, but takes for granted various unexamined presuppositions (e.g., that we can "bracket out" all natural objects of certitude, to see what remains)—but introduces a type of doubting which was part and parcel of ancient metaphysics: namely, a doubting which calls all facets of what is taken to be "existence" into question, for the sake of elucidating them in the context of the All.[9]

VI. (c) *What is the "dialectic?"*

In his Preface to the *Phenomenology,* Hegel points to the *Parmenides* of Plato as the great example of dialectic among the ancients. In this Platonic dialogue, Parmenides urges the young Socrates to subject his own treasured insights to cross-examination, by striving to make out just as strong a case for the negative as for the affirmative of his doctrine. Then Parmenides proceeds to give an example of how the process of cross-examination would work in regard to his own doctrine. He takes his own pivotal contention—that Being is one—and asks if the One is existent. If so, it must participate in Being. If it does participate, there must be at least a duality of Being and Unity. And from this starting point he gets into such an extraordinary and elaborate dialectical disquisition that some modern commentators on Plato are still wondering whether this dialogue was simply a great metaphysical joke that Plato perpetrated by mimicking the art of the Sophists.

The thesis-antithesis pattern which we find in the *Parmenides* creeps up here and there in the history of philosophy—for example, in Abelard's *Sic et non,* and in the famous antinomies of Kant in his *Critique of Pure Reason.* If we would generalize about the use of dialectic, we could say that it seems to be elicited by certain very abstruse types of questions, in the consideration of which the reflective mind oscillates from one side to the other, perhaps because of a superabundance of *a priori* evidence for each side, or perhaps because of a dearth of *a posteriori* evidence for either side.

Fichte, applying the dialectic to his doctrine of the transcendental ego, elaborated it into a trialectic[10]—the third "moment" being a point of view which was not just a compromise between the two antithetical points of view, but superseded them while at the same time incorporating their essence. Thus in his "triadic" dialectic, we have the following fundamental pattern: the *thesis,* or self-identity of the ego; the *antithesis,* or encounter with its "other"; and the *synthesis,* or transcendent unit, in which the two former opposites generate the unity by mutually conditioning each other.

It should be obvious that to the mind of a rabid rationalist such an abstract triadic schema might seem to be a God-sent instrument for arranging the whole world into hierarchical sets of triads of thesis-antithesis-synthesis. And there was actually a definite trend towards this among the rationalists in Hegel's milieu. But Hegel, seeing the dialectic as an essential pattern of the interaction between the transcendental ego and the world, eschewed what he called the "dull formalism" of the subjectivist application of thesis-antithesis-synthesis. Instead, with scarcely ever any reference to thesis-antithesis-synthesis, he preferred to capture the spirit of thypattern by judicious use of the concepts of in-itself, for-itself, and in-and-for-itself—which were already in use in philosophy at that time.

If we would wish to have as mature as possible an example of the way in which Hegel applies this essential dialectic, we would have to go to the *Encyclopedia,* which is the embodiment of a systematic (but not necessarily formalistic) dialectical development.

But in the *Phenomenology,* to use an example we gave in Ch. III, we have something analogous to an "induction" of both deduction and induction. The dialectical deduction of categories does not appear there *as* a dialectical deduction, but is only picked up in an inductive way, as it were, in its various phenomenal appearances.

But although the dialectic does not appear *systematically* in the *Phenomenolo-*

gy, it is prevalent everywhere, and gives rise to exceedingly complex structures which are baffling to the uninitiated. For example, we have the "in-itself for us," the "for-us for us," the "for-itself in itself," the "in-and-for-itself in itself," etc. The understanding of such superstructures will depend in large part on an understanding of the basic structure of the dialectic, which we will now strive to elucidate:

First of all, it should be pointed out that Hegel ascribes the utmost importance to the principle of negativity (the moment for the for-itself, Fichte's "antithesis") for setting the dialectic dynamism in motion. And in this regard he has some precedents in the history of ancient philosophy.

Aristotle—taking into account the "void" of Democritus, Empedocles' "strife," Heraclitus' "opposite," and other examples of the power of the negative in nature—tried to arrive at a more sophisticated view of the principle of negativity, in the light of the state of science in his day. And thus 1) in order to describe the process of the becoming of material being, he developed the principles of matter, form, and *privation.* A material being having a certain form, could proceed to take on another form only if, *per accidens*, it was a non-being, i.e., only if it had a privation inherent in its matter, which gave it a natural appetite to assume other forms. 2) In order to describe the process of becoming in spiritual substances, he developed the theory of act and *potency,* potency being a relative non-being which is not simply nothingness, but a determinate capacity for taking on certain specific perfections.

Hegel, who is not concerned with describing the essential moments of physical interactions as were the ancients, but was primarily interested in the exposition of the interaction between subject and object, posited a new negative—the for-itself—as the movent principle in this latter interaction. Although the for-itself is not intrinsically more important than the in-itself and the in-and-for-itself, it is most important "for us," i.e., for us to come to an understanding of the dialectic, since it is, so to speak, the lever which raises up everything else.

With this in mind, let us examine what Hegel himself says about his dialectic in the Preface to the *Phenomenology.* Since the dialectic has three aspects—the movement of the object, the movement of the subject, and the movement of the totum—we will give quotations relevant to each of these three aspects.

1) Focusing on the object, or being, Hegel says

> The movement of a being [an in-itself] is 1) to become other [than it was in its immediacy] and in this way to become its own immanent content; and 2) to reappropriate to itself this unfolding of itself (which is also its existence), i.e., to reduce itself to this latter determinateness which has come on the scene (which is, for all practical purposes, to make its former existence in-itself just a *moment* in the process). In stage #1 the "negativity" consists in the self-differentiation, and the consequent positing of existence; in stage #2, the "negativity" gives rise to a determinate unity, as the being turns back upon itself.[11]

2) Focusing on the subject, or thought, he says

When the negative first comes on the scene as the non-identity of the ego with its object, it also implies that the object, or substance, is non-identical with itself. And the process of reflection which seems to be going on outside the substance, as an activity directed against it, is in reality the accomplishment of the substance itself—which shows itself by this fact to be essentially subjectivity. And when this process is completed, spirit, through the ego, will have made its existence equal to its essence: it will have become its own object.[12]

3) Finally, focusing on spirit itself as the totum created by the subject-object reciprocity, he says

Spirit [*das Geistige*] first is the essence, or being-in-itself; then it becomes other than itself, or for-itself, which is a determinate self-relation; then finally when in the midst of this determinate self-relation, in which it is outside itself, it remains simultaneously in-itself, we say that it is in-and-for-itself.[13]

Taking these quotations from Hegel as our basis, we will now strive to explicate the moments of the dialectical process as a whole, in the simplest possible terms:

a) First of all, consciousness and its "other" (substance, being, or the object) are in-themselves before confronting each other in "immediacy."

b) At the moment of confrontation, the being is in-itself and for-consciousness; while consciousness is still in-itself.

c) The being discards its preliminary deceptive appearances, and goes outside itself to reveal its true nature which is implicit in it. And thus in this movement it becomes for-itself (as a being which is no longer immersed in, and restricted to, its primal limitations). Simultaneously, consciousness goes outside itself and its own provisional concepts, to receive this revelation of truth; and thus is also for-itself, insofar as it is stepping outside the ambit of its former limited concepts to review them from without, so to speak.

d) The being assimilates the new aspects it has taken on, to its intrinsic nature, and thus becomes in-and-for-itself. Consciousness, on its side, incorporates this new revelation into its former insight, and thus likewise becomes in-and-for-itself.

In regard to this process which has just been described, it should be observed

1) that being or substance in offering itself to consciousness is innately oriented to becoming subject, to becoming consciousness itself. The whole world, even the inanimate, is oriented to becoming consciousness.

2) that the subjectivity or consciousness, in its turn, is innately ordered to becoming substance, a stable in-itself, by means of its immersion in being.

3) that the medium which makes it possible for substance to become subject and subject to become substance is the *concept,* the spiritual reality in which both come to existence. For our concepts are not just representations of being, but encompass being; and at the same time are not just possessions of ourself—but are our very self ("consciousness is its own concept"). Thus the possibility of existence in-*and*-for-self, both on the part of being, and on the part of subjec-

tivity—is a possibility fundamentally attributable to the concept.

4) that the task of examing the subject-object reciprocity, then, does not mean an attempt to get at the borderlines, and try to catch glimpses of subjectivity passing over into objectivity, and vice versa. For the concept is like the prime circular locomotion of Aristotle: It is an absolutely stable dynamism containing essential movement *in itself*—namely, the movement from certitude (the for-it-self) to truth (the in-itself), and vice versa.

The dialectic process as applied in the *Phenomenology* is unique, as Hegel points out in the Introduction to that work. It is unique because it is applied in a situation where the reflective consciousness (the in-and-for-itself) examines itself as an in-itself, with the purpose of becoming in-and-for-itself *for* itself.

As applied in Part I, the dialectic proceeds from the pole of subjectivity to examine various facets of its own awareness. These facets are considered as objects (in-themselves), and are allowed to prove their own one-sidedness and negate themselves (thus becoming for-themselves). The result of this process is that both awareness and the awareness of awareness are enabled to transcend themselves and arrive at a new level.

The terminal point of this process will come when consciousness is the concept of its concept (an in-and-for-itself which is in-and-for-itself).

Then, in Part II, consciousness proceeds again from the pole of subjectivity, to examine the totum of subjective-objective spirit (the concept in its full universality) which has risen up in the world. It examines this totum first as objective spirit (spirit-in-itself), then as subjective spirit (spirit-for-itself), and finally as absolute spirit (spirit in-and-for-itself). The knowledge of absolute spirit is what Hegel calls "Absolute Knowledge"—the subject-matter of the final chapter of the the *Phenomenology*.

VI. (d) *Is Hegel's dialectical logic conformable to traditional formal logic?*[14]

The consideration of this question will be based in large part upon Michael Kosak's article, "The Formalization of Hegel's Dialectical Logic," which appeared in the *International Philosophical Quarterly*, December, 1966.[15]

Traditional formal logic is grounded in certain axiomatic laws, among which the Law of Identity ($P \to P$), the Law of Contradiction ~$(P \wedge \sim P)$, and the Law of Excluded Middle ($P \vee \sim P$) hold a certain preeminence.

In regard to the Law of Identity, we might ask the question that Ludwig Wittgenstein proposed a number of times:[16] namely, is not the logical expression of identity (as in $A = A$, or $P \to P$) in a certain sense superfluous? If we start with any given object, situation, event, or idea, which we designate as "A," and we ask, what *is* it? the answer to this question will be the answer to "A=?"—but (if it is a meaningful answer at all) it will go beyond that immediately given entity which we called "A." In other words, the answer will bring out properties or aspects which were not included in the immediate "given," or were only implicit. And so, any meaningful answer to the question, "A = ?" will have to be supplied in terms of non-A, i.e., properties or aspects outside the positive ambit of the originally given "A."[17]

Nevertheless, the Law of Identity itself is not meaningless. For meanings have to be expressed in terms of stable, self-consistent structures. Just as in biology the various life functions are to a great extent conditioned by that static picture which the structure of the organism presents, so also in language the significance of our speech is largely dependent on that bedrock of static terms and relationships and contexts and areas of discourse into which rational man has divided the rational world.[18]

Thus when we say "P → P," we are pointing to that stable bedrock of rational discourse, and more specifically we are pointing out 1) that the terms of the proposition have to be used in a univocal sense; 2) that the "is" in the proposition P refers to some determinate completed point of time that we are considering, and not indiscriminately to all times; and 3) that the proposition as a whole is accepted in its givenness, exclusive of all deeper and ulterior meanings which may be part and parcel of the living significance that it holds for living subjects.

As regards the Law of Contradiction, when we say "∿(P ∧ ∿ P)" we are opting for consistency. We cannot extend our comprehension to all the variant connotations of P, or rise to very subjective insights about P, unless we assure ourselves from the outset that our extensions will have some stable cornerstone, our ascensions some stable foundation.

Finally, just as the Law of Contradiction assures us of unity and consistency in our mental constructions, the Law of Excluded Middle assures us that these constructions will be composed of distinct and recognizable parts. If we adhere to this law, we will not be continually faced with entities which are "neither fish nor fowl," contexts which merge confusingly into one another, etc.

In philosophy, however, a rigid adherence to these basic laws of traditional formal logic can be a liability more than an asset, and pose an obstacle to insight and intuition. For: 1) Philosophy in its discourse characteristically uses very equivocal terms. It discusses "being," "knowledge," "subjectivity," "unity," "matter," etc.—notions which are far from having determinate denotations, and become meaningful only if we explore and compare the many analogous senses in which they are utilized. 2) It is often concerned with making statements about the universe as the totality of spatial and temporal reality, such that even the "time" which it considers is not primarily any determinate time, but the movement of time as a whole. 3) It leads to an ultimate reflection in scientific knowledge about the world, which does not just try to recapture some area of reality in relevance to its contexts; but tries to capture the context of all these areas of knowledge precisely in the context of their totality (in other words its "subject-matter" is something formal—the context—which is considered as something material whose inner formality must be made explicit).

Hegel's dialectical logic, then, was a logic which was calculated to be optimally appropriate for philosophy: one which would take into account the equivocal use of words, the processes of time, and the subjective superstructures of thought-contexts. It was a logic of non-identity, which would not necessarily contravene the ordinary sentential calculi, but would merely go beyond identity to the movement which identity was unable to effectively encompass or denote

—the movements of subjects and objects meeting in and through time. Such a logic seems to be called for, at least in philosophy, by the very fact that the determinations we make in regard to reality are fully meaningful only if these determinations themselves are understood in the context of the questions,

1) what is considered objective, and why?
2) what are the alterations made by subjectivity on the original in-itself?
3) what is the history of the determinations made?

—and other questions related to these.

Hegel's logic is calculated to take into account such "ulterior" questions, and thus it depends largely on a new logical "constant"—the *"determinate* negation," the delimiting negativity which results from the very consideration of the implicit nature of the positive content. We will signify the "determinate negation" by the minus sign in what follows; while the elucidation of positive content will be signified by parentheses enclosing "P."

The basic theorem of the logic of non-identity is thus $P \to [(P) \leftrightarrow -P]$. (The constants, " $\to$ " and " $\leftrightarrow$ " must be taken here in the context of a logic of non-identity, in which a positive proposition can "imply" its negative, and/or a provisional proposition can "imply" its more sophisticated and accurate formulations.)

The most important prerequisite for the understanding of this "basic theorem" is an insight into the fact that $-P$ is not the same as $\sim P$. The difference can best be illustrated by some examples:

1) We could translate the non-identity theorem $F(A) \leftrightarrow -F(A)$ as "A is an American if and only if he is not an American."

In this case, "not an American" does not signify what it denotes literally. But in the context of its paradoxical formulation it means that one does not become truly American unless he gets beyond superficial Americanism; unless he is willing to oppose pseudo-Americanism; unless he thinks of the world-context, etc.

2) In $(P) \wedge -P$, which would be self-contradictory by the canons of traditional logic, no contradiction need occur in the setting of dialectical logic. For instance, if we translate this compound proposition as "sensation is an object," and "sensation is not an object"—in *dialectical* logic the terms, "sensation," "object," and "is" would be applied in different ways, in different contexts, on the basis of reflection—and in such a way as to bring out the differing applications and contexts.

3) In $P \vee (P) \vee -P \vee \sim P$, we have a disjunction that overtly goes against the Law of the Excluded Middle. But in dialectical logic this need not be so; because (P) is not the same as P, but denotes "the positive explication of the determinations of P"; and $-P$ is not the same as $\sim P$, since it denotes "the limitations of the statement, 'P,' " i.e., those considerations in view of which P would not suffice for presenting truth as a balanced totality.

For example, if we say, "a human being may be either male or non-male or something between these two alternatives,"—this goes against the Law of Excluded Middle, taken literally—but it provides for a more reflective grasp of humanity in the context of maleness vs. non-maleness—i.e., it would bring in considerations of hermaphroditism, homosexuality, the bisexuality of a 4-week-old embryo, the problem of the time in development at which it would be proper to predicate "human being," of an organism, etc.

After we have derived the first-level assertion $(P) \leftrightarrow$ -P from the zero-level assertion P in dialectical logic, we may then proceed to derive higher-level assertions from the first level. For example, a second-level assertion could be deduced in the following way:

The first-level assertion, P', would be $(P) \leftrightarrow$ -P. This could be translated as, "the determinate nature of P can only be understood in the context of the oppositions which create its limitations." But this opposition, $(P) \leftrightarrow$ -P is itself a *determinate* opposition; and as *its* inherent nature becomes explicated, we find the opposition to have a meaning from its temporal and semantic and reflective context, a context which can give rise to a reflective "determinate negation," of the form $-[(P) \leftrightarrow$ -P] .

To return to a previous example, if we discover true Americanism to consist in a reciprocity between "Americanism" in a certain sense and "non-Americanism" in a certain sense—our reflection upon the specific nature of *this reciprocity* may lead us to reflect 1) that it is *not* a reciprocity between two distinct attitudes, but a self-identity of some spiritual nucleus prevalent since Revolutionary times; 2) that it is meaningful only on the hypothesis that there is a universal impetus drawing all men out of their determinate national allegiances to international unity; 3) that it is possible only if there are separate poles or contingents or "parties" in a nation, which individualistically *refuse* to enter into reciprocity with their opposite; and so forth.

These latter insights would amount to a second-level reflection—P''—in the dialectic logic, which could be expressed symbolically as $[(P) \leftrightarrow$ -P] $\leftrightarrow$ $-[(P) \leftrightarrow$ -P] . This second-level reflection could be translated roughly as "the determinate reciprocity P' shows itself on reflection to be based in manifold ways on stable or isolated unities, or to be reducible to a stable and autonomous unity." This statement would be a specific mode of stating the perennial paradox of the interpenetration of unity and multiplicity.

A 3rd-level assertion based on this might possibly concentrate on the determinate nature of this interpenetration in the political and social spheres, showing perhaps that it is not a real interpenetration but only the external manifestation of irreconcilable philosophical presuppositions, etc.

And so we can see that we potentially have fuel here for infinite-level assertions.

We might fittingly conclude this treatment of the problem of the formalization of Hegel's dialectical logic by showing in a general way how it is applied in the *Phenomenology*:

The *Phenomenology* begins with "the unreflected subject" S, representing the initial state of a given persisting presence-to-self which contains in-itself the potential contradiction of being *both* itself *and* its "other" (which we will signify by "O"). The first reflection of this subject (on sensation) leads us in the following manner to the first-level assertion, SO: S → [S ↔O] → SO. In this process, sensation has passed from being itself to being its object, and thence to being a *reciprocity* between subject and object. If we designate the synthesis SO by the symbol S′, we can then describe in a quasi-intuitive manner the general process that takes place in the first sections of the *Phenomenology* which are entitled *"Consciousness."* In this process we move from S′ (which is itself a movement from the synthesized *subject* to a congruent object) to O′ (which is a movement [from *object* to interpreting subject] called "perception" by Hegel) and finally to S′O′ (a movement from the subject in a new sense to the object in a new sense, and vice versa—the movement of "understanding," which could be expressed graphically as SOOS).

This latter third-level assertion, expressing as it does a certain lucid interpenetration of subject and object, becomes the thesis for the next section on "self-Consciousness," and for the multi-leveled assertions which appear in and after that section. This process continues until we reach "Absolute Knowledge," a state of infinite subject-object interpenetrability.[19]

VI. (e) *Where lies the "necessity" in the dialectic?*

As was mentioned in the previous section, philosophy as a body of knowledge seems to be heir to a host of terms which are the furthest possible logical distance from univocity. "Necessity" is one of these terms. Hence the necessary difficulty in determining whether the many dialectical movements in the *Phenomenology* are necessary, as Hegel makes them out to be, or arbitrary. If we can be allowed to make some distinctions among the species of necessity, however, there seem to be five types of necessity which obtain in the *Phenomenology*'s unfolding. We will first differentiate these species from one another, and then discuss their applicability to the *Phenomenology*.

1) *Logical necessity*: From the syllogistic premises, $[P \rightarrow Q] \cdot [Q \rightarrow R]$ we might conclude that P "necessarily" implies R. By this we do not mean that there is something inherent to P that causes it inevitably to give rise to R. For if either of the premises were false, the truth of $P \rightarrow R$ would be problematical. But from the premises given, without making any commitment as to the truth of $P \rightarrow R$, we merely grant that P should imply R in view of certain *logical rules* (modus ponens, etc.) that we have *de facto* accepted. The "necessity" in this case can be reduced to the requirement of proceeding according to rules which we ourselves have freely assented to, and not withdrawn our assent from. It is the subjective necessity to admit those types of logical evidence that we have already deemed to possess validity.

2) *Natural necessity*: All physical bodies are governed by the laws of gratitation and inertia; and organic bodies are under the added necessity of moving, eating, and reproducing themselves. When we refer to such "necessities," we are indicating inner mechanisms without which physical bodies could not continue to exist and function. The necessity here is objective to the same extent that the laws we discern in nature are objective.

3) *Hypothetical necessity*: This obtains when a person decides upon a certain goal, and then tries to implement it. Only certain means are practicable, with

regard to that goal—and the person is "necessitated" to choose from among these means (on the hypothesis that he seriously wishes to attain the aforesaid goal). For example, if I were travelling from the U.S. to Europe, I could not begin from China, nor could I use an automobile. But I would be necessitated to start from some airport or seaport in the U.S., and to use more congruent means of transportation.

4) *The necessity of general historical situations and general individual experiences:* Kings, merchants, revolutions and religion are more "necessary" in *history* than nudists, witches, athletic contests and humor. Infancy, education, and pubescence are more "necessary" in *human development* than insanity and senescence. And in general, we tend to say that those types of structures and situations that are widespread and recur constantly in society are more necessary to the history of civilization; and that those stages or situations which most people normally pass through are more necessary to the individual.

5) *The necessity of transcendence*: Kant spoke about a seemingly inescapable "metaphysical" instinct which necessarily brings men to formulate tenuous speculative world views. Whether or not Kant was right in his pejorative estimation of metaphysical speculation, there does seem to be a tendency in thinkers to try to transcend all determinate insights to rise to some most-comprehensive view of this or that area of knowledge. This tendency is on par with ambition, love, greed, and the pleasure-principle—all of which lead men, in different ways, to become dissatisfied with every status quo and to delve onward to some goal which, they trust, will put them beyond such limitations as previously generated dissatisfaction in them. In the sphere of theoretical knowledge, the instinct of transcendence leads one to "set his sights" so high that every vista of certitude and truth is seen as just a stepping stone to some absolute impregnable citadel of certitude and truth—the counterpart in the theoretical realm to economic or emotional security.

The dialectical processes described in the *Phenomenology* exemplify the five types of necessity enumerated above:

1) *Logical necessity in the "Phenomenology:"* Here, of course, the logic that concerns us is not primarily the traditional logic, but a logic of non-identity (cf. section VI [d]). *If* one accepts the "rules" of such a logic—that a concept expands itself by generating its antitheses, etc.—he is under a subjective necessity to assent to the type of evidence he has allowed—i.e., all evidence which satisfactorily displays tensions of oppositions in conceptually elaborated reality.

2) *Natural necessity in the "Phenomenology:"* Just as organic and inorganic bodies are subject to certain necessary laws which govern their existence, so also the "species" of conceptually-determined objects in the world, according to the Hegelian hypothesis, is governed by the natural necessity of disregarding all initial immediate superficial aspects and becoming identified with the non-being of implicit hidden potentialities and inner relationships. Just as inevitably as the snake must cast off its outer skin seasonally, and the caterpillar cast off its outer form at some time in its life—so also a conceptually represented entity, if it remains present to the force of understanding, must successively cast off its

overt appearances and show all that it is not, or did not *seem* to be.

3) *Hypothetical necessity in the "Phenomenology:"* If a teacher wishes to bring his students to some insight, he is restricted by a "hypothetical" necessity as regards the choices he makes of procedures—in view of his purposes, the capacities of his students, the experience of the teacher himself, and the specific problems that present themselves as obstacles to the comprehension of the insight in question. In the *Phenomenology,* Hegel aims to bring his readers to the insight about individual and social consciousness that he actually possesses (or, more exactly, to the knowledge of self that consciousness actually possesses, through Hegel)—and he is restricted by a "hypothetical" necessity as to the procedures he uses for accomplishing this. In view of the goal he has set himself, and in view of the capacities of his readers, he cannot take Religion as his starting point, nor can he proceed from the Unhappy Consciousness to Perception directly. Rather, only a certain set of starting points, and a certain set of transitions at each stage, suggest themselves as practicable.

4) *The necessity of generality in the "Phenomenology:"*

As Baillie points out,[20] Hegel aims to present in the *Phenomenology* a self-reflection of consciousness upon its own experience. In order that he may truly present experience as experience, he makes much use of historical or biographical events or situations. But he is not interested in writing either a philosophy of history or a philosophical overview of his own intellectual maturation, but rather in presenting both individual and social experience in a scientifically comprehensible way. In order to accomplish this, he must make use of *universal* modes of experience. Thus as the "middle term" uniting the experiential substratum with the demands of scientific universality, he chooses those historical events which are typical of many others, and those individual forms of experience which are generally prevalent at some time in the development of individuals. In such a way he attains to the "necessary," running through the experience of man and mankind.

5) *The necessity of transcendence in the "Phenomenology:"*

If one is in despair about life, and wishes to persist in that attitude, he must adamantly keep himself from giving in to any chance feeling of optimism that comes his way.

The *Phenomenology,* as we have mentioned, is a "road of despair" which takes it for granted that it will never be able to find truth in any determinate viewpoint of consciousness. Therefore, at the risk of abandoning this attitude of despair which is axiomatic for it, the *Phenomenology* is under a necessity to transcend every finite viewpoint which seems for the moment to offer the solace of truth and certitude. Only by being uncompromising about truths can the *Phenomenology* arrive at transcendent truth itself.

Thus when Hegel speaks in his Introduction[21] and in many places in the text about the "necessity" obtaining in what he says, he would seem to have in mind one or more of the species of necessity we have distinguished above.

VII. WHAT IS THE MEANING OF "EXPERIENCE" IN THE
CONTEXT OF THE "PHENOMENOLOGY?"

The first title that Hegel gave to the *Phenomenology* was *The Science of the Experience of Consciousness.* This title was afterwards changed to *The Science of the Phenomenology of Spirit*; and this latter finally became shortened to *The Phenomenology of Spirit* in the final version.

The change in title was no doubt prompted a) by the fact that Hegel extended the scope of his original intentions, in order to consider universal consciousness (concrete spirit in the world) in Part II of the *Phenomenology*; and also b) by the fact that in the writing of the *Phenomenology* he came to perceive more and more clearly how it was to be related to his envisioned *Encyclopedia* (i.e., that "phenomenology" would later be included there as a moment of subjective spirit).

Nevertheless, the *Phenomenology* is still a science of the experience of consciousness. And, in a way, that first title has a certain advantage over the later one, in that it is more *descriptive* of the contents. For the *Phenomenology,* although leading on towards the elucidation of Spirit as its ultimate goal, is more immediately concerned with consciousness in all of its experiences.

"All of its experiences." In order to understand the import of this, we must first realize that "experience" is one of those equivocal terms that are used in manifold senses in science and in philosophy. Before discussing the precise sense in which "experience" is considered in the *Phenomenology,* let us make some observations on these equivocal uses:

a) All determinate types of experiences—e.g., the experience of sounds and colors, of beauty, of pain, of transcendence—can be reduced to the experience of being. That is, they are all primarily experiences of being or existence, and secondarily of some type of being or existence. For the object of experience must be pre-understood to *exist* (either in the physical world or in the mind) before it can be understood to have any determinate properties. And so, in a certain sense, all experiences, no matter what their species, are instruments for the revelation of being itself.

b) The experience of being is not found just in theoretical knowledge, but in any subject-object relationship. True, when we experience being in practical activity, in affectivity, in aesthetic feeling, etc., we do not experience it after the manner of something *understood.* But this is only to point out that the intellect is only one facet of our capacity for experience.

With these two observations in mind, we may state a) that the *Phenomenology* is concerned with experience in its primary, or exemplary, sense; i.e., as the experience of being. And all the various species of experience that are considered in the *Phenomenology* are considered *qua* experiences of being. b) —that the *Phenomenology* does not restrict itself to theoretical types of experience, but includes in its scope all possible manners of experiencing.

Thus the "experiences" that the *Phenomenology* treats of are not the theoretical kinds of experience that Kant was concerned with, but all kinds. And this wide expanse of experience is considered *qua* the experience of *being*.

What is the importance of a study of the experience of being? We should remember that it would be nonsensical for us to speak of something existing outside of, or aside from, human experience. In order for something to exist, it must be present to some consciousness; and the consciousness to which it is not present at least in some minimal awareness, has the right to say that its existence is in doubt.

"Existence," then, is not something absolute from thought, as if there were some border separating being and thought, or as if everything on one side of our tactile membranes was "consciousness," while everything on the other side was being. Rather, things exist precisely insofar as they are interfused with subjectivity. And a correlate: they can be known as *being* only if we understand the nature and operations of the subjectivity *making* them present.

Granted that being is constituted only as disclosed or revealed to us, then—as Heidegger points out[1]—the task facing the "ontologist" is to grasp being fully in its disclosure, i.e., to elucidate its elucidation, to know how it is known, and thus to come to a state of knowing-ness [*Wissen-schaft*], in which the light is seen in conjunction with the illumined.

But if being needs to be examined precisely as undergoing the alterations of subjectivity—a significant question emerges here: What subjectivity? The empirical ego? It would seem not. For the empirical ego is the "middle term" between subjectivity and objectivity; and it is able to function as such a "middle term" precisely because it is the subjectivity-made-objective. But subjectivity itself is always experienced by the empirical ego as something "behind the scenes," as the x-factor which in some mysterious way initiates and receives all experiences and endows them with its unity. This unifying ego which endows all discrete experiences with a transcendent unity is called by Kant the "transcendental ego," by Heidegger the "absolute self," by Hegel "pure subjectivity." But by whatever name we call it, this is subjectivity itself—and it is this we have to bring to light to understand being in its be-ing.

But how can we possibly gain any knowledge of this transcendental ego? By definition, it is always "behind the scenes," and never encountered directly, as an object. But it can be experienced indirectly, in the following ways:

a) By the experience of experience itself. Although the Absolute Subject cannot be experienced as a cognitive object, every experience of cognitive objects, or any object, is a presentation of the absolute subject, which unfolds itself and withdraws itself simultaneously through its representation. In a very real sense, "experience is the subjectivity of the absolute subject."[2] But when experience itself is made into a *positive object,* it is no longer experience. Thus we gain an experience of experience not in a positive way, but *per viam negationis.* We must make constant "determinate negations" of all particular experiences of being; transcending these latter by drawing them into the negative unity of universal experience (i.e., making manifest the unity of the transcendental ego in the very act of withdrawing from the particular). Thus in a certain sense it would be true to say that the presence of the absolute self becomes manifest to the same degree that its absence becomes explicitly realized.

b) By unfolding the *Concept,* in the sphere of theoretical experience. If we successfully transcend the sensuous aspects of the experience of being, and come to distinguish precisely the pure conceptual aspects of that experience—we are in a privileged position with regard to an apprehension of the presence of the absolute. For even though the absolute subject can never be apprehended directly, or as an object, or positively—still its negative presence drawing all things into universality is more readily apparent in and through the concept, than through any lesser medium in the theoretical sphere.[3]

c) By the overt manifestation of spirit *as* spirit, in the practical sphere. In the *Phenomenology,* this obtains especially in the rites of religious worship and in the creation of works of art.

All these modes of experiencing the be-ing of being, i.e., of experiencing the parousia of the absolute subject, are found in the *Phenomenology.* And in the final chapter, "Absolute Knowledge," they converge to form what Hegel conceived as the highest possible experience of the absolute self, i.e., the highest possible experience of experience itself.

VIII. HOW CAN CONSCIOUSNESS BE BOTH MEASURER AND MEASURED?

In his Introduction to the *Phenomenology,* Hegel states that in coming to a knowledge of consciousness itself, consciousness is both the "object" which is tested for truth, and the criterion according to which a pronouncement on truth is made; i.e., it is both measurer and measured.[1] In the light of the context here—where we are reflecting not upon some external object, but upon the reflective contents themselves—it is easy enough to follow the logic of what Hegel says, and to assent to it as a logical conclusion. But to possess the concept of what takes place with full certitude and truth—i.e., to possess it "in-and-for-itself"—is quite another thing. And since the whole of the *Phenomenology* is a measurement conducted by consciousness upon itself—it is important to come to a full appreciation of the significance and mechanisms of this process, and not just its bare logical possibility.

In order to do this, it is important first of all to note that in the examination of consciousness two processes are going on: a) the "extrinsic" process, in which the empirical ego (the subject being made objective) is faced with the phenomenon of the absolute object in-itself; and b) the "intrinsic" process, in which the empirical ego (the subject being made objective) is faced with the demands of the transcendental ego (the absolute subject for itself). At base, these two processes are one, insofar as the objectivity of objects is rooted in the transcendental ego. But they are still distinct. insofar as the world is really distinct from consciousness. The best way of putting it, is to say that they are a unity-in-distinction. But for purposes of examination, it behooves us to examine them in their distinction:

a) *Consciousness is both measurer and measured in the "extrinsic" process.* In order to explain this, it would be useful to draw an analogy to the dialogue that takes place between two people, X and Y. X makes a statement about reality to Y about which he (X) has great certitude; and is surprised when Y is unable to accept that statement as it stands. Y's inability to accept it is attributable to a number of factors: he has some prejudices which keep him from assenting to certain aspects of the statement; it is unclear how this statement can fit in consistently with his previous experience; the evidence for the statement seems tenuous; and X himself seems to have presented it in an extremely one-sided manner. At this point, we may say that X's statement stands as something true in-itself and seems certain to X; but must be reivsed if it is to seem true and generate certitude to Y. If the appropriate revisions are made, and the one-sidedness of the statement is made to disappear, then its truth will appear as something in-itself and also for-Y.

Then, considering just the context of the two people X and Y, the truth of X's statement will be something simultaneously in-itself, and "for" the both of them. Or, they will both assent to the statement because they have agreed on its concept, which is in-and-for-itself—which is to say the same thing.

In the encounter of consciousness with external reality, a similar dialogue takes place. Every appearance is for all practical purposes a statement: reality, in its appearance, is saying that it stands in such and such a way. To consciousness, however, this "statement" may seem unassimilable as it stands. It may seem to conflict with previously-held ideas; it may seem illustory; it may seem to be presented out of the context of the whole. And so consciousness challenges reality with these objections, and waits to see if reality can stand up to them. If reality is able to offer itself in a way more conformable to the demands of consciousness, it will be able to become simultaneously in-itself and for-consciousness, by means of its concept, which is in-and-for-itself.

In this case, we could say that consciousness has measured reality. But since reality is not some thing-in-itself forever outside consciousness' reach, but becomes *in-itself* precisely by consciousness' taking advertence of it, we could say also that consciousness' own awareness of reality is being measured. And so this is the way that consciousness would be understood to be both measurer and measured in the sphere of "extrinsic" subject-object encounters.

b) *Consciousness is both measurer and measured in the "intrinsic" process:* In order to understand this, we might best take an analogy from the moral sphere. For it is fairly clear that all the various aspects of morality and ethics in individual and social life are attributable to something very simple: namely, the internal conception of some ego-ideal, which the conscious individual feels himself compelled to live up to, or at least to make some sort of adaptation to. Kierkegaard calls this the "ideal self," Freud calls it the "super-ego." Whatever it is called, its function is clear to anyone who reflects on his own experience. He begins very early to formulate some ideal of what he wants to be. He revises this constantly as he develops and tries out his potentialities and comes to understand these potentialities better and better. Finally, with full maturity, there may come about a state in which both 1) his ideals are realistic, as compared with his potentialities; and 2) he approximates as closely as possible to these ideals (to the demands of conscience).

In the cognitive sphere, the transcendental ego performs a function similar to that of the ego-ideal in the moral sphere. Very early, we feel impelled to some ideal state of knowledge. If we tried to analyze the reasons why we are not satisfied with our determinate views of reality, but are urged onwards to more comprehensive views—we would face a difficult task. But this much we know: for some reason or other, consciousness is urged on (by itself) to come to some comprehensive view of the All of reality (the ideal vantage point will be envisioned differently, in correspondence with differing individual propensities).

The impetus to transcend every determinate view to come to some absolute view may not be as evident in some individuals as in others, but its operation is evident enough in general to justify us in positing a transcendental ego, or absolute self—the intrinsic potentiality of consciousness itself to become fully conscious. All the findings of consciousness are tested, challenged, and revised according to the demands of this transcendental consciousness. We could say, in this regard, that the empirical consciousness is measured, and the transcendental consciousness does the measuring. But the empirical and the transcendental are just two aspects of one and the same consciousness. And so the truth of the matter is that consciousness, in its own internal self-dialogue, is both measurer and measured.

IX. WHAT IS THE RELATION OF THE POINT OF VIEW BEING STUDIED TO THE POINT OF VIEW OF THE "PHENOMENOLOGIST?"

This is a more complex question than it seems offhand, because the *Phenomenology* is a reflection upon a reflection upon a reflection. Therefore, the question amounts to, "which reflection is which?" or "how are the reflections distinguished from one another?" The answer to this may not be hard to give; but it is hard to give it in such a way as to make the distinctions clear-cut and intelligible.

When Immanuel Kant in his *Critique of Pure Reason* speaks of the transcendental ego as the unifying focal point which draws the manifold of sense data into the schemata of the understanding—we may accept this as a valid hypothesis on the basis of our own intuition. For in all our activity we constantly presuppose that our consciousness is one, and that it is drawing the manifold of sense experience into its irreducible unity. But the reader of Kant might wish that the author of the first Critique had gone into this matter more thoroughly, and tried to make more explicit just how the transcendental ego functions as the great unifying force in consciousness. For a bare intuition that something must be the case is a far cry from an adequate comprehension of why it must be the case.

Hegel, coming through the doctrines of Fichte and Schelling to a realization of the pivotal importance of the concept of the transcendental ego for a philosophy of knowledge, tries in the *Phenomenology* to do just this: to show in elaborate descriptive detail just how the transcendental ego operates as the great unifying force in consciousness.

In order to understand the rationale of this task, we must recall once again that Hegel was not interested in just giving a history of the development of consciousness, proceeding from past stages to the present actuality, *via generationis*. He does not conceive consciousness as a present result of past temporal processes. Rather, consciousness is *the* living present, in which all the various stages of consciousness are constantly differentiating themselves, taking precedence one over the other, and intermingling to form one consciousness.

But how to present such a living actuality *as* a living actuality? The only truly effective re-presentation of this living actuality would be the production of the actuality itself in the readers of the *Phenomenology*. And this is Hegel's ultimate objective. But as for the means: in lieu of some superhuman powers of transforming other minds, Hegel had to settle for a descriptive word portrait. And a portrait cannot present a unified impression unless it has been artfully distinguished into distinct parts and scenes. Consciousness must, then, be divided up for purposes of description. But how divide up an inseparable, spiritual *totum*? By abstraction. Hegel divides up consciousness into its various abstract aspects, and prescinds from other aspects in dealing with them. In this way he comes to show the unity-in-distinction of all the various aspects—how they balance each other, lead into each other, etc. He also comes to refer to the historical antecedents of the "development" of the particular aspects—which gives the *Phenomenology* the character of a "flashback" literary style. But even these temporal antecedents are not considered as having "once" "previously" conditioned some aspect of consciousness, but as even now conditioning the living actuality of that aspect, and of consciousness as a whole.

But we have still not adequately described what Hegel was trying to describe. For he was not *just* trying to describe the actuality of consciousness by drawing a word-picture of the convergence of its various abstract aspects. He set out to make explicit the unifying function of the transcendental ego (the Absolute Self) in consciousness.[1] But if we take the transcendental ego as the unifying source, and the empirical ego as the manifold unified, and if we also assume that consciousness is a *unity* of this transcendental and this empirical aspect—we have as our conclusion that consciousness is a *unity* of a *unity* and a *manifold*.

Realizing this, we are now in a position to consider the question posed at the outset:

a) *The points of view being studied in the "Phenomenology."* These are the points of view of the empirical ego, involved and immersed in this or that abstract facet of consciousness itself. In other words, these are the reflections that the empirical ego makes upon the various aspects of its consciousness. These reflections may also include reflections upon the transcendental consciousness, and upon the unity of itself with the transcendental consciousness. In the *Phenomenology*, empirical reflections upon the transcendental consciousness take place in the chapters on Understanding and on Enlightenment; while empirical reflections upon the unity of the empirical and the transcendental consciousness take place in the chapters on the Unhappy Consciousness and Absolute Knowledge.

b) *The point of view of the "phenomenologist:"* This is the point of view of the *unity* of transcendental ego and the empirical ego. It is the point of view of Hegel, and of those of us who view the processes taking place in the empirical ego philosophically, i.e., not interested primarily in the appearances that engage the attention of the empirical ego, but more especially in the appearing of these appearances.[2] For the philosophical intent of the *Phenomenology,* as we showed earlier,[3] is to come to an experience of being; and this can only be accomplished if we come to the experience of the transcendental ego; but we cannot come to the experience of the transcendental ego directly, but only indirectly—by evolving the Concept in theoretical consciousness, by producing the experience of transcendence in the sphere of practical consciousness, and by recapturing consciousness' dissatisfaction with finite determinate insights. Of these three "methods," the third one is in a certain sense more important than the others, insofar as it is prevalent in the *Phenemonology* as a whole. And it is to this method that we refer, when we say that the philosopher is primarily interested in observing the "appearing of the appearances."

One appearance gives way to the next, in empirical consciousness. This constant "giving way" constitutes the essential dynamism of phenomenological experience. From the point of view of the empirical consciousness, a new object with a new content seems to appear to replace the former object. But from the point of view of the philosopher, a transcendence is taking place: the new object appears as the process of the movement of consciousness itself, i.e., as the process of the appearance of the Absolute Self in and through consciousness. If the reader of the *Phenomenology* does not himself explicitly have this philosophical point of view, he will fail to grasp the *Phenomenology* in its full philosophical import.[4]

In conclusion, then, the various "moments" of the *Phenomenology* take on the viewpoint of the empirical ego; while the treatise as a whole is conducted from the viewpoint of the unity-in-distinction of the empirical and transcendental egos. This unity-in-distinction which is elaborated into explicit form by Hegel, is the same unity-in-distinction that was apprehended implicitly by Kant in his doctrine on the transcendental ego.

It should be noted that we have not mentioned the viewpoint of the *transcendental* ego as being itself included in the *Phenomenology.* At the end of the *Phenomenology,* we (both the empirical ego, and the phenomenological philosopher) approximate to an ultimate viewpoint resulting from the ego's transcendence of all limited empirical points of view which present themselves. And it is precisely from that terminal viewpoint that the later investigations in the *Encyclopedia* seem to begin.[5]

X. WHAT IS A "PHENOMENOLOGY" IN THE HEGELIAN SENSE?

In the natural sciences, when there is doubt, obscurity, or inaccuracy, it is a common procedure to return to the "phenomena," to the immediately given facts, details, or events, and to set scientific conclusions straight on this basis. This continual return to the phenomena in all the various areas of natural sciences thus amounts to a criterion for truth in these sciences.

In philosophy, in a milieu of conflicting philosophers and conflicting systems, how does one overcome the inevitable doubt, obscurity, and inaccuracy of statement that ensues? It was natural that certain philosophers, on the example of the natural sciences, should think of "going back to the phenomena," checking them, revising their conclusions, and thus setting things straight once and for all.

But what are the "phenomena" which philosophy considers? Not just restricted areas, but the totality; not merely specific aspects of that totality, but its very being. Therefore, if one wanted to return to the phenomena in philosophy, he would have to return to the appearance of the being of the universe which he recognizes. But this being *appears* to us in *knowledge*. It is only when we know something, i.e., are conscious of it, that we give recognition to, and in a certain sense even constitute, its existence, or being. And so a philosophical "phenomenology" would require a study of the element of knowledge, and the processes of knowledge—the element where being appears.

There are, however, some unique difficulties which present themselves in a study of the knowledge of being: For one thing, if our knowledge of being is a total structure with substructures—the total structure is not the sum-total of constituent sub-structures; but rather, every distinguishable substructure would in a sense pervade the whole of knowledge. (Here is a sphere in which the ancient dictum of Anaxagoras—"everything is in everything"—applies literally.) For another thing, if the knowledge of being grows according to some process, still this process is not a "motion" in the usual sense, and cannot be analyzed by any of the methods employed in the empirical sciences for observing physical or psycho-physical changes. In short, the knowledge of being presents itself in general as a whole whose every part is not really separable from the whole; as a dynamism which remains essentially stable amidst its changes, i.e., whose growth is not measurable in any of the usual ways of measuring growth. What *method,* then, can be effectively employed for examining a phenomenon of such a sort?

Hegel considered Kant as one who used the phenomenological approach in philosophy, but utilized a defective method.[1] For although Kant assumes the aspect of the quasi-empiricist who goes back to the fundamental structures of knowledge of the appearing being to re-check them thoroughly—he does not approach this task in an empirical way. He brings with him all the ready-made presuppositions of the rationalist.[2] For he presumes a-priori that the structures he turns up will be conformable to the basic structures of deductive logic. And so he quite arbitrarily deduces the essential categories of phenomenal being by means of an analysis of the various types of judgement. Kant, is, of course, thoroughly conscientious about trying to make his a-priori conceptions apply "naturally" to the phenomena. But the upshot of such conscientious rationalistic applications is that the reader of the first Kantian Critique comes away 1) impressed indeed by the admirable systematic methodology of the treatise but 2) still troubled with a vague feeling of uncertainty as to whether he has really uncovered the primary structures of being as it appears to us.

The main criticism that Hegel levels against Kant is that he conducted his researches from an "extrinsic" point of view—i.e., from those rationalistic presuppositions which are extrinsic to the content being studied. If one is to conduct a "phenomenological" research enterprise more effectively than Kant, he must give up all presuppositions as to what he *should* discover, and simply abandon himself to the appearances as they show themselves.

Fichte, realizing the shortcomings of such an "extrinsic" investigation of knowledge, tried, in the "Deduction of Representation" in his *Wissenschaftlehre* to give a "pragmatic account" of the development of the human spirit to knowledge. Schelling also, in the "Epochs," in his *System des tranzendentalen Idealismus* attempted something similar. But both of them were hindered from the start from giving a truly "empirical" account.[3] For, although they did not have the presuppositions of Kant about finding traditional logical structures in knowledge—they had their own rationalist presuppositions. Fichte and Schelling both presupposed that their "pragmatic accounts" would serve to clarify the already established doctrine of the bare abstract unconditioned unity of ego and non-ego.

Hegel, agreeing with the insights of Kant, Fichte, and Schelling as to the importance of an investigation of knowledge as the appearance of being—proposed to conduct such an investigation once and for all without bringing along with him any ready-made rationalistic standards at to what he "ought" to discover in the inquiry.[4] His idea was to abandon arbitrary methodological procedures, as well as presuppositions as to what sort of an "Absolute" his investigations should result in—and allow the "facts" to speak for themselves.

Further, he wished, amid these investigations, to preserve the *paradoxical* characteristic which knowledge takes on—the general appearance it has of containing sub-structures which are interfused with one another, of being a dynamism which remains stable throughout all temporal fluxations. And so—eschewing both the inductive methods of the empirical sciences and the deductive methods of Rationalist philosophy, he chose—as his only "method"—a style of depiction roughly analogous to the descriptive methods of the novelist, the radio narrator of contemporary events, or the painter who tries to recapture the significant moments of an epoch on a single mural.

Such a descriptive method, as applied to knowledge itself, is bound to have some peculiarities. For one thing, if knowledge has in itself no spatial or temporal dimensions, what "side" can we begin with, what "scene" or "event?" But it is intuitively obvious that knowledge is a unity with multiple aspects. And so, on the basis of this simple intuition, Hegel addresses himself to this multiplicity of facets *as it appeared to him.*

Then another problem emerges: How can he pass in a descriptive procedure from abstract facet to abstract facet, if there is not the least bit of spatial or temporal contiguity prevalent in the material described? In ordinary descriptive procedures, the spatial or temporal context will suggest the transitions to be made. But here, in the *description* of *knowledge* itself, the transitions are suggested by a special kind of context—a context, namely, in which both the individual structural aspects and the individual dynamic "moments" are implicitly co-terminous with the structural dynamism described. The "logic" behind the descriptive transitions, then, is simply this: 1) Each feature of the manifold is seen in the context of the unity of the whole. And 2) as one brings out the positive determinate nature of any aspect, he comes to the "edges" of that aspect, so to speak, and his description naturally branches out into the widening context. As we see from this, Hegel tried to construct a "descriptive" phenomenology which would re-present effectively both the structures and the dynamisms obtaining in the knowledge of being.

Contemporary phenomenology stems largely from the approach of Husserl. How does Hegel's "descriptive" phenomenology differ from Husserl's, which also purports to be descriptive ("morphological")?

The following differences seem to obtain between the descriptive phenomenologies of Hegel and Husserl:

1) Husserl, like Kant, concentrates more on the structures in the knowledge of being than on the dynamisms. Admittedly, dynamic function cannot be conceived apart from structure, and vice versa. But one can concentrate on one over the other—as a description of the human body can concentrate on anatomical structure rather than physiological function. Such a viewpoint has both its strong points and its weak points. One of the weak points would be that it does not capture the subject-matter in "motion," so to speak.

2) Husserl concentrates on different structures than the ones that engaged Hegel's attention—e.g., on intentionality, reflection, and classes of essences, rather than on the triad of consciousness, self-consciousness, Reason, and on the other structures of conscious knowledge that Hegel deemed important.

3) Hegel strives to depict the Absolute Self as the successively presented "negativity" obtaining among the structures and processes of consciousness, uniting them while at the same time keeping them separate. Husserl, on the other hand, tries to present the transcendental ego—not as actually pervading the structures and processes of empirical consciousness—but in itself. He does this by a wholesale negation (phenomenological "epoché") of all the structures of natural consciousness. Once having attained, by this epoché, to the superstructure of the transcendental consciousness, he is then in a position to give a "pure" description of the truly essential transcendental structures of knowledge.

In this chapter we have concentrated on the very different approaches manifested in the phenomenologies of Hegel and the "father" of contemporary phenomenology, Husserl. If we tried to draw up a comparison between Hegel and others who are often referred to as "phenomenologists"—e.g. Heidegger, Sartre, Merleau-Ponty—the opposition would not be as clear cut. Phenomenology has veered in many directions since Husserl, sometimes falling under the influence of the Kierkegaardian "existentialist" reaction against Hegel (a reaction which at least modifies the definite epistemological orientation of Husserlian phenomenology). But it is interesting to note that Heidegger in one place propounds a notion of phenomenology which includes a methodological "reduction," and an eidetic analysis of the structures of the "pure psychic." This characterization is to be found in a draft penned by Heidegger shortly after *Sein und Zeit,* and included in the Husserliana (Band IX, p. 256) under the title, "Die Idee der Phänomenologie..." This was originally intended to be a joint statement (for the *Encyclopedia Britannica*) by Husserl and Heidegger regarding phenomenology. Husserl, however, refused to sign his name to the draft as a whole, and decided to publish his statement in the Encyclopedia under his own name alone.[5] If we could take this statement seriously, we might conclude that Heidegger concerns himself with the "structural" aspects of consciousness, after the wont of his predecessor, Husserl. However, in view of Heidegger's statements in *Sein und Zeit* and elsewhere about phenomenological method, it would seem necessary to conclude that Heidegger, instead of conducting a phenomenological reduction in the Husserlian sense, was more interested in scrutinizing the psyche in its interrelationships with the world, with a view to discovering the nature of Being. The fact that he was indeed diverging from the Husserlian approach became clearer, of course, after his *Kehre* or "reversal" in the 1930s. In comparing the phenomenologies of Heidegger and Hegel, one might say that, although there are patterns of dialectic in his thought (e.g. a dialectic of Dasein and the world), Heidegger certainly does not show the *ex professo* interest in subject/object dialectical methodology that characterizes Hegel's approach.

We began this chapter with a question concerning the nature of a Hegelian phenomenology. This question implies that "phenomenology" is a genus of sorts, which admits of various species. If we understood the nature of this genus, we might find a key to reconciling the divergent answers given to the question, "what *is* phenomenology?"

The difficulty in defining what "phenomenology" *is,* seems to stem in large part from the variety of procedures that might be utilized for conducting an analysis of *pure subjectivity* (considered as the elusive source of knowledge).

First of all, what is meant by the pure subjectivity? The term seems to indicate an area of the ego outside the empirical ego. This pure subject could mean: a) the unconscious, in the sense of depth psychology; b) the ego, insofar as it perdures throughout one's life and lends continuity to all the stages of conscious development; c) the ego insofar as it is a unity of all the different aspects of consciousness (sensation, perception, understanding, memory, etc.); or d) the ego insofar as it manifests certain characteristics in entering upon objectivity.

If we consider the pure ego in the sense of (a), then perhaps some research has been done on it, in the psychologies of Freud (with the "discovery" of the ego-ideal) and C. G. Jung (with the "discovery" of the archetypes) and others; if (b), then perhaps the best way to approach the pure ego would be through imitating the approach of Abraham Maslow, Rollo May and other humanistic psychologists; if (c), then perhaps Hegel's *Phenomenology* is the best approach; if (d), then the works of Kant, Husserl, Heidegger and others may be most useful.

If we accept the above-mentioned distinction among the connotations of "pure subjectivity" and if we allow that "phenomenology," in the generic sense, connotes any scientific procedure for exploring or discovering the pure subjectivity—then we might see many contemporary movements, including the revival of interest in Hegel, and including various movements in phenomenology and psychology, as further attempts to solve the problem first explicitly proposed by Descartes: what can we say about the *existence* of pure thought, and its relationship to existence in general?

NOTES TO THE QUESTIONS

Introduction

1. Immanuel Kant, *Prolegomena to Any Future Metaphysics*, Beck Ed. (New York: Library of Liberal Arts, 1950), p. 29.

2. *Ibid.*, pp. 28ff. Cf. also Kant's *The Critique of Pure Reason*, Norman Kemp Smith tr. (New York: St. Martin's Press, 1965), pp. 590f., B762-764.

3. "Die Wissenschaft des erscheinenden Wissens," *Phänomenologie des Geistes* (Hamburg: Felix Meiner, 1952), p. 564. N.B. the *Phänomenologie* will hereafter be referred to as "*P.*"

4. *Ibid.*, p. 47.

5. Cf. Hegel's *Wissenschaft der Logik* (Sämtliche Werke, Stuttgart: Frommanns, 1958:, IV, 1).

6. "Der Geistesweltumsegler, der unerschrocken vorgedrungen bis zum Nordpol des Gedankens, wo einem das Gehirn einfriert im abstrakten Eis." Quoted by Kaufmann, *Hegel* (London: Weidenfeld & Nicolson, 1966), p. 356.

7. "Wir sehen . . . den Grund des ganz bestimmten Vorwurfs, der ihnen oft gemacht wird, dass Mehreres erst wiederholt gelesen werden müsse, ehe es verstanden werden könne. . . . Die Meinung erfährt, dass es anders gemeint ist, als sie meinte, und diese Korrection seiner Meinung nötigt das Wissen, auf den Satz zurückzukommen und ihn nun anders zu fassen." *P., p.* 52.

8. Kaufmann, *op. cit.,* p. 141.

9. Findlay gives special attention to many of these misinterpretations in his introductory chapter to *Hegel: A Re-Examination* (New York: Collier, 1962).

Question I

1. Cf. *A Hegel Symposium,* Travis ed. (University of Texas, 1962), p. 133.

2. Cf. Hyppolite, *Genèse et structure de la Phenomenologie de l'Esprit de Hegel* (Paris: Aubier, 1946), p. 14: Chez Fichte, dans la partie de sa *Wissenshafts-lehre* dont il voulait faire une "histoire pragmatique de l'esprit humain," et qui se nomme Deduction de la representation, se trouvait un premier modèle de ce que sera la *Phenomenologie de l'esprit* de Hegel. Dans cette deduction de la representation Fichte se propose en effet de conduire la conscience commune du savoir sensible immédiat à la soi philosophique.

3. Cf. Hyppolite, *op. cit.*, p. 44 (N.B. The *Genèse et Structure* . . . will be referred to simply as "Hyppolite.") Cf. *Schellings Werke* (Munich, 1927), II, 590.

4. Although Hegel, a good friend of Goethe, would not have been familiar with *Faust* in the final 1808 version, he would have access to the earlier edition of *Faust: a Fragment*, to which the Walpurgis Night was added in 1797. But the "classical" Walpurgis Night was not added until 1832.

5. *A Hegel Symposium*, p. 133.

6. *Ibid.*, p. 136.

7. Hyppolite, p. 14: La conscience de soi philosophique est déjà présupposée, et cette histoire, malgré son intention très voisine de celle de la *Phénoménologie* de Hegel, reste encore assez artificielle.

Question III

1. Hyppolite, p. 55 ff.

2. "Part I" of the *Phenomenology* refers to those sections which Hegel designates by Roman numerals I-V. "Part II" refers to the remaining sections.

3. Hegel seems to have gradually altered his plans concerning the length and content of the *Phenomenology*, while he was writing it. For an analysis of the evolution of Hegel's intentions regarding the *Phenomenology*, see Otto Pöggeler, "Zur Deutung des Phänomenologie des Geistes," in *Hegel-Studien* I, 1961. Pöggeler here refutes those who claim the latter parts were added to the *Phenomenology* abruptly or as a departure from plan.

4. Hegel eventually began to refer to the *Phenomenology* as an *"äusserlich"* treatment of spirit, in comparison with the *Encyclopedia*, which offers an intrinsic consideration of spirit in the element of pure thought. See Otto Pöggeler, *op. cit.*, p. 291f.

Question IV

1. See *The Philosophy of Mind*, Wallace tr. (London: Oxford, 1971), §415, 418.

2. Heidegger, *Holzwege* (Frankfurt: Vittorio Klosterman, 1952), p. 176. An English translation of the essay in the *Holzwege* on Hegel's Introduction to the *Phenomenology* has been published under the title of *Hegel's Concept of Experience* (N.Y.; Harper & Row, 1970).

3. See Richardson, *Heidegger* (The Hague, Nijhoff, 1963), Ch. IV.

4. *Holzwege*, p. 185.

5. *Ibid.*, p. 154.

6. Hegel, *The Phenomenology of Mind*, Baillie tr. (London: George Allen and Unwin, Ltd., 1931), Translator's Introduction, p. 45ff. (N.B. this work will be referred to hereafter as "Baillie.")

Question V

1. H. Baynes tr. (London: Routledge and Kegan Paul, 1964), pp. 372 ff.

2. The "necessary" opposition of philosophical viewpoints is considered by Hegel in terms of "realism" vs. idealism. (Cf. *Lectures on the History of Philosophy*, Vol. III, pp. 161-162; German edition, p. 270.)

3. Cf. Hyppolite, p. 24.

4. Schelling, op. cit., p. 600.

5. Baillie, Translator's Introduction, p. 38.

6. Heidegger, *Holzwege* (Frankfurt: Vittorio Klostermann, 1952), p. 176: Das Erscheinende entaüssert sich in sein Erscheinen. Durch die Entaüsserung geht das Bewusstsein in das Aüsserste seines Seins aus. Aber es geht so weder von sich und

seinem Wesen weg, noch fällt das Absolute durch die Entäusserung in das Leere seiner Schwäche.

7. Hyppolite, p. 37 f.

8. Heidegger, *Holzwege*, p. 172.

Question VI

1. *Sense and Nonsense*, Dreyfus tr. (Northwestern, 1964), pp. 65-66. (Toute la *Phénoménologie de l'Esprit* décrit cet effort que fait l'homme pour se ressaisir. A chaque âge historique, il part d'une "certitude" subjective, il agit selon les indications de cette certitude et il assiste aux conséquences surprenantes de sa première intention, il en découvre la "vérité" objective. Il modifie alors son projet, s'élance à nouveau, reconnaît encore ce qu'il y avait d'abstrait dans le nouveau projet—jusqu'à ce que la certitude subjective soit enfin égale à la vérité objective et qu'il devienne consciemment ce qu'il était confusément. [Cf. *Sens et non-sens* (Paris: Les Editions Nagel, 1948), pp. 113-164.]

2. *Holzwege*, p. 185.

3. Baillie, p. 135.

4. Hyppolite, p. 21.

5. *Ibid.*

6. Merleau-Ponty, *Sense and Nonsense*, p. 67. Hegel in an early writing, *Glauben ist die Art,* describes the development of knowledge as a process in which the apparently solid and independent objects we believe in, prove upon analysis to be unworthy of our faith, and thus provide the impetus to adopt further, more sophisticated beliefs, and so on. See H. S. Harris, *Hegel's Development: Towards the Sunlight 1770-1801* (Oxford: Clarendon, 1972), pp. 314, 321.

7. Hyppolite, p. 17ff.

8. This seems to be the best practicable way of describing Hegel's endeavors at this point. We will attempt to describe them in a more precise, meta-philosophical way, in the conclusion to this study, where (in Ch. II) the notions of a "Critique," a "phenomenology," a "metaphysic," etc. will be critically examined.

9. Hyppolite, *Ibid.*

10. Kant had already given Fichte his basis for this, by developing a method of "Triplicity." But Kant did not realize the import of his own discovery, and does not expound it explicitly. Cf. *Lectures on the History of Philosophy*, Vol. III, p. 477; German edition, p. 610.

11. *P.*, p. 44: Die Bewegung des Seienden ist, sich einesteils ein Anders und so zu seinem immanenten Inhalte zu werden; andernteils nimmt es diese Entfaltung oder dies sein Dasein in sich zurück, d.h., macht sich selbst zu einem *Momente* und vereinfacht sich zur Bestimmtheit. In jener Bewegung ist die *Negativität* das Unterscheiden und das Setzen des *Daseins:* in diesem Zurückgehen in sich ist sie das Werden der *bestimmten Einfachheit.*

12. *Ibid.,* p. 32: Wenn nun dies Negative zunächst als Ungleichheit des Ichs zum Gegenstande erscheint, so ist es ebensosehr die Ungleichheit der Substanz zu sich selbst. Was ausser ihr vorzugehen, eine Tätigkeit gegen sie zu sein scheint, ist ihr eigenes Tun, und sie zeigt sich wesentlich Subjekt zu sein. Indem sie dies vollkommen gezeigt, hat der Geist sein Dasein seinem Wesen gleich gemacht; er ist sich Gegenstand. . . .

13. *P., S.* 24: Das Geistige . . . . ist das Wesen oder *Ansichseiende,—*das sich *Verhaltende* und *Bestimmte,* das *Anderssein* und *Fürsichsein—*und [das] in dieser Bestimmtheit oder seinem Aussersichsein in sich selbst Bleibende,—oder es ist *an und für sich.*

14. See also the conclusion of this book, section II. In both places, the following symbols are used: → (implies); ∧ (and); ∨ (or);∼(not).

15. In view of the fact that the formalization of Hegel's dialectical logic is not, strictly speaking, a formalization of abstract logical entities, it might be best to characterize it as the "formalization of the non-formalizable." This should not be understood as a contradiction but as a sub-paradox referable to the fundamental paradox that, from a *dialectical* point of view, traditional logic and dialectical logic are complementary opposites. (See *infra*, Conclusion, II B, n. 25; see also my article, "El Futuro de la Erudición Hegeliana," in *Teorema* (University of Valencia), pp. 47-49.

16. Cf. e.g. his *Tractatus Logico-Philosophicus,* Pears tr. (London: Routledge & Kegan Paul, 1961), #5.5303.

17. Kosak, *op. cit.*, pp. 610 f.

18. As Hegel puts it, we must make logical statements about sense phenomena, finite situations, facts, objects. And this is the sphere in which the "logic of identity" is our primary criterion. Cf. *Enzyklopädie,* 1st ed., p. 39, Paragraphs 21, 22.

19. Kosak, *op. cit.,* p. 626. Kosak has done studies of the formalizable aspects of dialectical logic, and the application thereof, in *Telos* V and VI, 1970, and in a paper, "The Dynamics of Hegelian Dialectics and Non-Linearity in the Sciences" presented at the Boston University Symposium on "Hegel and the Sciences," 1970.

20. Baillie, Translator's Introduction, pp. 45-50.

21. Baillie, p. 144.

Question VII

1. Cf. Richardson, *Heidegger,* pp. 348 ff. Heidegger defines Hegel's task in the *Phenomenology* in his own terminology: the task is, he says, to make explicit the dialogue between the "ontic" dimension (where concepts are formed through awareness) and the "ontological" dimension (where the concept behind all concepts is conceived, i.e., where awareness itself becomes a well-delineated object of awareness).

2. Heidegger, *Holzwege,* p. 171.

3. Cf. *Lectures on the History of Philosophy,* III, p. 525; German ed., p. 662; also *P.,* I(C).

Question VIII

1. Baillie, pp. 140-141.

Question IX

1. See Section VII *supra* for a discussion of the motivations which would lead Hegel to take on this task.

2. Heidegger, *Holzwege,* p. 172 f.

3. Cf. Section VII *supra*, passim.

4. Hyppolite, pp. 29-30.

5. Hyppolite, p. 67, 24, 29.

Question X

1. Hyppolite, p. 13, p. 15.

2. On the "subjectivism" of Kant, see also the *Lectures on the History of Philosophy,* p. 443 (German edition, p. 573).

3. *Ibid.,* pp. 14-15.

4. Cf. Baillie, p. 141.

5. For further details on the background to Heidegger's draft, see the Introduction to Heidegger's "Idea of Phenomenology," by Deely and Novak, in the *New Scholasticism* XLIV, 3, 1970, pp. 325 ff.

ANALYSIS

HEGEL'S PREFACE TO THE "PHENOMENOLOGY"[1]

An author, in his preface to a philosophical work, would accomplish very little by comparing his system with other systems, or by giving a preview of what may be expected in the way of conclusions. For systems of philosophy contradict one another and supersede other systems as the blossom negates and supersedes the bud; and to give a sketchy outline of conclusions makes no contribution to full and living philosophical truth. There are some who would justify such a sketchy outline on the grounds that the result of philosophy is the reconciliation of the general and particular. Therefore (they reason), when we present a general outline of the aims of a philosophical work, we are doing justice to the particular as well as the general. What they mean is that they are doing justice to particularity, not to the particulars. These latter are incapable of being presented in a summary outline form. In order to present the particulars of philosophy, the experience of these particulars must be presented in all its detail. There is no shortcut.[2]

In our time there has been much noise and discouragement in the camp of philosophy. But we might best compare this distress to the gasp of breath taken by the newborn babe—a breath which presages a breaking away from former life processes, and a qualitative "leap" to a new existence both encompassing the quantitative progressions formerly made and negating them.[3] And we may optimistically look forward to a "blessed event"—the elaboration of philosophy as a *science* [4] and indeed as a science so lucidly and systematicaly presented as to be publicly accessible—and not just the concern of the "initiated." Of course, we have not yet reached this stage. So we must resign ourselves, in the interim, to speak esoterically.

In the beginning of philosophy, the tendency was to look up to heavenly essences, and almost lose sight of the earth.[5] Now, however, our orientation is in the opposite direction. We see the earth much more clearly than the divine. As a result men, with their high aspirations, become dissatisfied, and are apt to grasp at any crumb of "edification" that is offered to them by modern thinkers.

Thus the general trend among modern thinkers is to extol substance in its aloof unity; essences in their impressive depth; intuition in its satisfying immediacy.[6] But what they forget is that substance, e.g., a monolithic divine substance absorbing all,[7] lacks reality unless it undergoes the conflict and negation and differentiation of a subject; that essence is most truly itself only when fully and adequately expressed in proper *form*; and that intuition by itself can be only impressive and edifying, but lacks the character of solid and true knowledge until it undergoes the negations and elaborations of mediation (mediated knowledge).[8] In other words, philosophy can justify itself only when, in addition to proving that it is a proper result of the external processes of time itself,[9] it is internally justified by the scientific accuracy and clarity with which its basic principles are elaborated.

We should note that God Himself—if He is a subject rising above the mere immediacy of substantial being—must undergo a certain (mediating) negation by the objectification of Himself. Thus the word, "God," must be reexamined and impugned, if we are to get beyond the sterile concept of a God who is taken for granted as subject, but loses the dynamism and activity of subjectivity in the very static way in which various attributes are predicated of Him.

Following the same line of thought, philosophy must not rest in substance, intuition, etc.; but rather should be prepared even to negate its first principles, however true they may be, for their very one-sidedness and hence relative falsity:

> A so-called "basic proposition" or "principle" of philosophy—even though it be true—is nevertheless also false precisely in so far as it is [just] a basic proposition or [just] a principle. [10]

Realizing this, philosophy will be best disposed to extend itself to the whole truth, whose prerequisite is that the underlying principles be expressed and elaborated and mediated in the fullest possible and most scientific way. If philosophy accomplishes this, it will have succeeded in expressing the Absolute as Spirit, as Subject fully conscious of itself, fully objectified, and fully conscious of its own objectivizing; as knowledge which is fully existent, and being which is fully intelligible; as the inner being of the world presented in the form of true reality, through cognition.

The individual spirit is only incomplete spirit, comprising in itself some moments in the unfolding of universal spirit, and manifesting in itself some predominant characteristics which are but partial facets of the complete perfection of that universal spirit. The individual spirit and the universal spirit advance towards science in different ways. For the final object of all science is the understanding of knowledge itself. [11] The advancement of the individual spirit towards this goal takes place through the organic assimilation of what is presented inorganically to the mind.[12] The advancement of the universal spirit towards this goal is accomplished through the elucidation of knowledge in all its departments through the scientific culture of any particular era.

In former times, the main task seems to have been the separation of the universal, the unelaborated essence, from the bare existent as sensuously presented.[13] This necessary task is happily completed. But a more strenuous assignment still faces us: namely, the elaboration of these rather vacuous essences and universals through the power of mind, to the point where they are systematically presented in their dynamic interrelationships (not just familiarly bandied about, and accepted in a haphazard and eclectic fashion).

Although the process of minutely analyzing sense data into concepts is often deficient insofar as it merely breaks up the familiar into its familiar components —nevertheless, even this process is important. For it is a manifestation of mental activity; of a mental unrest which begins by tearing apart what is established, but which ends (or should end) in a reflective, speculative analysis of the concepts which resulted from the previous analysis. If this second analysis is successful, it will restore movement and life into such abstractions as "being" and "substance" and "essence" and "universality"—which can very easily become static, dead notions connected in a rather habitual way with some rather conventional content. Ultimately this process will take the form of the *systematic exposition* of the dialectical interrelationship of abstract concepts.[14] But in a more immediate and proximate way this process will lead to a direct confrontation and opposition between science, which from its citadel of truth regards self-consciousness with some disdain for its subjective certainty and self-possession; and self-consciousness, which suspects science of having lost possession of itself in the elaboration of its mental equipage. When these two opposites are reconciled,[15] science will for the first time possess the complete and certain self-knowledge of true consciousness; and the fixed concreteness of the ego, and the fixed distinctions of the ego's thought, will for the first time be effectively subsumed into the ever-moving circle of spiritual culture. And each will gain new being by the sacrifice which has been made.

The scientific method of triplicity, which has been restored to recognition by Kant,[16] is nevertheless being often misused to support a dull formalism in which determinations and schemata can be predicated of one another *ad infinitum* in circular fashion. But rightly understood, it should lead to true (philosophical) experience, in which

> the immediate, the unexperienced, i.e. the "abstract"—whether it be a sensuous object or a simple abstraction conceived in thought—becomes alienated from itself, and thereupon is restored to itself out of this alienation: and at this point first becomes established in its reality and its truth, to the same extent that it now becomes the property of consciousness.[17]

This "method"[18] is the only one which gives satisfaction and certainty. Other methods, which may seem paragons of precision and certitude, are deficient because of the external and material way in which they elaborate their proofs. History, for example, uses the process of mere external comparison of events, persons, dates, books—to produce its evidence; which still gives you no reasons for the internal necessity behind historical events. Even mathematics is deceptive. It totally ignores the esssential determinations which give life and meaning to existence, and contents itself with accounting for some proposition in terms of lifeless, identical (i.e. not internally differentiated) quantitative forms. What is more, after having thus made arbitrary choices of quantitative structures as its "principles," it goes on in "proof" to apply these principles in such a way that there is no truly internal, necessary connection between that which is proved and its evidence. As a result, the drift of the mathematical proof acquires intelligibility only at the end; and this intelligibility is not in terms of the "why," but only of the "how." And thus, under the tutelage of mathematical methodology, triangles are partitioned up into other figures which do not necessarily relate to the truth of the triangle; propositions are accounted for in rigid spatial terms; and even the negative dynamism of time is described in terms of a sequence of numerical units.

The activity of consciousness is, of course, somewhat evident in such proofs. But the most obvious significance of such methods of proof is that the mind has to have *some* proof, some evidence, and therefore often rests at the minimal, external type of evidence.

The attitude of Formalism in philosophy, which occupies itself with applying the schemata of the mind in mere external fashion to things, without going out of itself to enter into the dynamism of the thought-content—or which creates a rather vacuous Absolute[19] to give impressive unity to sense-data—must endeavor to take the "leap" to true systematic philosophical knowledge. That is, it should learn to immerse itself in the determinate nature of being, discerning the simple definiteness which is self-identical and hence abstractness. Here they will find the νοῦς of Anaxagoras (or, as they later put it, the form[20] the specific nature, of a thing). This determinate quality of the content, this logical existent, seems at first to be merely externally determined by other beings, while "in itself" it remains unchanging and stable. But on further consideration it is seen to have *otherness* in its own internal makeup, from the very fact of the abstract simplicity of its own auto-determination (since the abstract is essentially that which is separated from, and hence other than, the particular concretion to which it happens to be related—which, in this case, happens to be itself). Hence in itself it is in process—a process which in its resolution is nothing but concrete existence. Thus it is true that "being is thought," since the internal *ground* of determinate concrete existence is abstract simplicity.[21]

True conceptual thinking, therefore, of which we have a foretaste in the metaphysical insights of Aristotle and the magnificent dialectic of the *Parmenides* of Plato—is not something which depends on external proofs and demonstrations, or which utilizes propositions arbitrarily compacted from transcendent subjects, universal content, and predicates and accidents applied in a rather formalistic way. Still less is it the leisurely exposition of common-sense truth, or the truths of Revelation; or a haphazard collection of lofty inspirations. Rather, it is the disciplined adherence to that conceptual content which is the *life* of cognitive objects, and thus an inner union with the self, so to speak, of being. It is a union in which predicates become metamorphosed into their subjects; in which the determinations given are spontaneously supplied by the nature of the cognitive content; in which the proposition consisting of subject-plus-predicate is superseded by a higher type of thought-entity, a pure dialectic unity comparable to rhythm in music—which is a harmony of metre and accent; in which, finally the negations involved result internally from the very specific determination and negation of the conceptual content itself. In this last aspect, it is sharply contrasted with the formalistic persuasion (which concentrates on pure external negativity, i.e. all that tremendous sphere of negativity which is outside those few finite modes which it deigns to admit into its own brand of thinking: and thus tends to a hyper-critical attitude, and negations *ad infinitum).*

Admittedly, the dialectical-conceptual thinking we are opting for here involves much labor—both on the part of the thinker and on the part of his audience. When it is practised, we are bound to hear complaints about having to read every line of this or that philosopher over and over again (since his statements, made on the basis of substantial conceptual exigencies, and resulting in the identification of differences, are paradoxical as compared with the common usage of words). But it is worth such labor, if we can arrive at the state where the subject is more than just a name passively receiving predicates and accidents; where philosophy is organized in its true scientific form; and where all the sciences are vitalized by the truth which only philosophy can lend to them.

> That which, even as regards content, in any given species of knowledge or science, is "truth"—can only be worthy of such a name when it has been engendered through philosophy; . . .the other sciences, though they might prefer to pursue truth by ratiocination without the help of philosophy, . . .cannot, on their own, appropriate for themselves their life, their spirit, their truth.[22]

It is thus the task of philosophy to enter into the basic determinations and moments of our conscious world, elaborate them from within by being obedient to the spirit which they manifest, and thus render them lucid and publicly accessible by dint of the processes of true conceptual thinking. When this has been accomplished, the universality of a philosophical system will cease to be a universality apprehended only by certain individual philosophers. And gradually but inexorably—in keeping with the more universal orientation prevalent in the spiritual life of mankind in our times—the public also will dispose itself to accept the form of paramount universality towards which philosophy is directing it.

HEGEL'S INTRODUCTION

Offhand, one might suppose that the best way to make an effective and prudent approach to true reality, would be to examine first what seems to be the *instru-*

ment for this approach—namely, knowledge itself. After we have mastered the intricacies of this "instrument," we will be in a better position to come to an understanding of that which is dealt with by means of this instrument—namely, the absolute reality. But then, problems begin suggesting themselves: for example, knowledge, as an instrument working upon outside objects, *alters* them for purposes of assimilation. Would not this fact prevent us from reaching absolute reality in itself? No, someone will object. For we are saved if we know just what the limits of knowledge are;[1] since then all those horizons of unassimilated reality, just beyond these limits, will be known by contrast to be the "absolute reality." But to those who make this objection we may simply reply that the unassimilated reality is not *illumined* at all by such a realization of our limits. It still remains the "Great Void." And further, we might also ask, just why do they have such a distrust of the ability of knowledge to grasp onto absolute reality as it is in itself? Should they not, with equal reason, distrust this very distrust they show? Or, if they are really serious about distrusting knowledge, what would be their epistemological criterion of "truth?" To trust truth while distrusting knowledge of truth would seem to be a marked inconsistency.

A possible means towards the resolution of these problems appears, however, if we take note that there is one type of knowledge which is unique, which is an exception to the above-mentioned "rules." And this "limiting case" is our knowledge of *consciousness.* For in the case of consciousness-of-consciousness, we are not simply faced with an assimilable *ansich*[2], an inorganic otherness which has yet to enter into the realm of consciousness, where everything of its very nature *(an sich)* is *für sich.*[3] Rather, when consciousness is its *own* object, the *ansich* (consciousness) is at the same time a *fürsich* (a becoming-consciousness). And thus it happens that in our examination of consciousness, the "object" *is* some notion of the mind, and the mind's notion *is* an object; that is, the notion is identical with the object. For the precise object which is to be examined here, is not the "first object,"[4] i.e., the object as yet *ansich* but not *für sich* through conscious representation—but rather the "second object," i.e., the Experience,[5] the appearance of the first object as the notional possession of consciousness.

But how are we to judge of the truth of our knowledge about consciousness? Generally speaking, in establishing the truth of anything, we appeal to outside criteria, to which our doubtful notions are compared. The "truth" of our notions is impugned, when they do not correspond to these criteria. However, it is inconceivable that our knowledge of consciousness could be called into doubt in this way.[6] For whatever knowledge there is *in* consciousness, *is* consciousness.

Of course, there could possibly be some shuffling about, with a view to bringing about a more explicit and extensive view of consciousness. And then again, we will never be able to get a "view from behind," so to speak, since the essence of consciousness consists in the very process of *becoming* immediately-produced knowledge, and thus cannot exist previous to, or be in any way held aloof for viewing by, the consciousness wishing to grasp it. But, admitting that these factors are inherent in its nature, we can still affirm that the criterion for truth in the case of consciousness is purely the internal criterion of its own psychic existence.

[And thus we should be led to suspect that] the true nature of science in its full actuality, will be revealed when consciousness is itself unfolded to consciousness explicitly,[7] in such a way that all its moments are aptly delineated, and in such a way that every incomplete and therefore false point of view is not eschewed superficially by a negativistic scepticism, but is seen in the internal dynamic negativity of its own temporal determination, and thus is allowed to take its congruent place in the total scheme.

The representatives of self-consciousness in its uncritical self-possession, however, will look upon this path to science in an unfavorable light, since they are smug in their own "knowledge" (which in truth is only the beginning of, the movement towards, knowledge). Also others will be hyper-critical, holding fast against all authority, and requiring every truth to be the truth only as they see it themselves. And though this latter view may at first sight seem admirable, it is nevertheless quite possible and probable that its exponents will sooner or later be expounding opinions purely out of conceit.[8]

To avoid the Scylla of smugness and the Charybdis of hyper-critical scepticism, the best prophylactic is a healthy, serious *progressive scepticism,* which

> unlike hyper-critical scepticism, directs its interest to the whole compass of forms and stages of consciousness, and braces spirit for the first time to ferret out the truth, by bringing about a thoroughgoing inquisition into the so-called "natural" attitudes, ideas, and opinions.[9]

This is the only laudable approach, the only one which of its very nature is prepared to challenge all the notions one holds, with the express purpose of bringing them to the full light of consciousness.

This reflective process, rightfully carried out, will gradually bring knowledge to its inevitable goal; namely,

> to the stage where it is no longer constrained to go beyond itself, where it encounters only itself, and where concept coincides with object, and object with concept.[10]

At this final stage,

> appearance becomes equal to essence; the expression of consciousness becomes the expression of this final stage in the authentic science of spirit; and finally in thus comprehending its own essence, consciousness will *ipso facto* point out the nature of absolute knowledge.[11]

Consciousness, by successively negating all one-sided "appearances" of knowledge, will at the end come finally to some absolute standpoint which—precisely because it is the expression of the determinate negation of all possible limited standpoints—is itself the one standpoint that can not be negated constructively.[12] [In climbing a mountain, if one refuses to repose at any intermediary point, he must eventually arise at a summit.]

Attempts to prove that this is the nature of science to the partisans of incomplete knowledge would be unwarranted and futile. Accordingly, without attempting any definitive preliminary justification of this position, we will now approach straightway the problem of showing science in its true life, by means of a phenomenal exposition of the incomplete forms of knowledge in their progressions and dialectic.[13] If the exposition is successful, it will throw light on the way that natural consciousness is groping its way to true knowledge.

SENSE-CERTAINTY

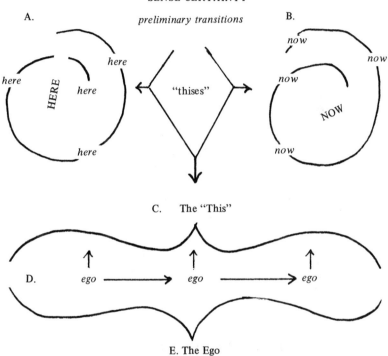

A.   *preliminary transitions*   B.

C.   The "This"

D.

E. The Ego

A. Every particular "here" proves itself to be the negation of some previous "here." Thus there emerges the notion of a universal Here, produced by the negation of every particular here.

B. A similar process takes place with regard to particular "nows."

C. All in all, the particular "thises" come to manifest the *universal* This, as the object of sense-certainty.

D. Attention is given to the ego, which is thought to be the source of the universal notion of "This."

E. But an ego that is formulating universal notions at "this particular time" is different from the ego, or the moment of the ego, which happens to be formulating universal notions at another particular time; and so forth. From this process, we come to concentrate on the *universal* Ego, which draws *all* the particular states and stages of the empirical ego (the ego which notices this or that, and formulates universal notions about what it notices) into that unity which we refer to as the "I."

SENSE-CERTAINTY (cont.)

overall transitions

A.   B.

object ⟵ ego   object ⟶ ego

C.

object ⟷ ego

A. The ego, in investigating its experience of "thisness," focuses upon the object ("thisness" as something extrinsic to the ego) as the essential thing.
B. Then the ego itself seems to have the essential function in noticing and even creating thisness.
C. Finally, consciousness (the relation of the ego to otherness or objectivity) realizes that the really essential thing in sense experience is the constant interaction and reciprocity between ego and object, or ego and otherness.

PART ONE. THE FORMS OF CONSCIOUSNESS[1]

A. *The Attitude of Sense-Certainty*

There are those who say that the truest and most certain foundation of knowledge is the givenness of sensation—the *sine qua non* of all thought, since we must come into immediate *contact* with the world, before we can exercise our consciousness in regard to it. By means of sensation, then, it would seem that we are enabled to return to being in its unadulterated form, i.e., in its immediacy, just at the moment when the indeterminate otherness of the world converges upon our faculties, and appears to us as a simple "here" or a simple "now." At this moment of consciousness we are dealing with mere "thisness," before it has undergone any elaborations by the conscious self. And thus it would seem to present us with an unassailable criterion for checking the accuracy of our knowledge about the world.[2]

Those who look for truth and preeminent certainty in sensory givenness, however, would lose some of their optimism, if they would subject their own viewpoint to reflective analysis. For such analysis would lead them to the very uncomfortable conclusion that there is the *barest minimum of both truth and certainty*[3] in our immediate sensory contact with the world:

First of all, the "immediate being" with which we seem to come into contact by sensation, does not present itself to us as immediate being; but rather as a particular instance of a dialectical existence which breaks up into two poles—ego and object. But still, as the "this" presents itself, the ego takes on a passive stance, and the object seems to be the actual, the important, the essential aspect.

"Thisness"—the "now" of presence in time, and the "here" of presence in space—accordingly becomes related to the ego as the *essential* to the *non-essential*. The ego here takes on the aspect of a mere supervening conscious element, the entrance into which would amount to an exit from immediate truth into some mediated aspect of truth.

But upon further examination, the "here" and the "now" seem to lose their aspect of essentiality: For if "here" is a tree, and subsequently "here" is a house—"here" can be a house only in virtue of not-being the tree. Every particular "here" exists only as a rejection or negation of preceding "heres"; and itself is subject to rejection. Thus it develops that the only "here" that has any stable existence is the *universal* "here," which is precisely the rejection of all particular "heres." And likewise, the only "now" that has any stable existence is the universal "now" which is neither nighttime nor daytime nor noon nor two o'clock—but can be applied to all "nows" precisely because it is not any particular now.[4]

Our analysis thus brings us to a complete turnabout. In coming into primal, immediate contact with a particular segment of the spatial or temporal world, we only *seem* to be confronting a bare particular. We actually are meeting the *universal,* the product of consciousness.[5]

In the present context, the "here" and "now" are universals in the sense that our concepts of space and time result from the successive negation of particular "heres" and "nows."

In the light of this universal concept of "hereness" and "nowness," sensory givenness no longer appears to be as preeminent and essential as it had seemed before. In fact, the conscious ego now looms on the horizon as the most important, most essential determinant of sense-data. For it is the ego that subsumes sensory immediacy into the universal "here" of space and the universal "now" of time, and gives it negative significance, or "particularity," in context of this universality.

But the "essential" ego turns out to be at the mercy of the same vanishing process as the "heres" and the "nows." The "I" that sees the house becomes such, only in virtue of the fact that it is not the "I" that sees the tree. And the "I" can notice daytime only if it is not the "I" that is noticing nighttime. And thus the only "I" that remains stable and essential in all the various sensory encounters is the *universal "I"* which sees *simpliciter,* and notices *simpliciter,* but is not particularly engaged in seeing or noticing any particular thing.

Thus consciousness, having first revised the impression that the object is dominant in immediate sensory experience, must now revise the subsequent notion that the universalizing ego is dominant. If it is not to end up with a static opposition, with universal ego at one extreme and universalized otherness at the other, it must take a stance which will do credit to the dialectical process taking place in primal sense experience. It does this by raising its sights, and recognizing that the *truly* "essential" thing in sense awareness is the totum of the process taking place amidst the two poles. Thus it is the reciprocity *between* object and ego that is the essential, immediate datum in the attitude of sense-certainty. And furthermore, it is a very restricted reciprocity that we are considering here. We confine our attention to the empirical interaction in which a single "here" or a single "now" is being noticed by the ego in one of its single aspects. We abstain from considering the universal "this" as a product of successive negations of particular "thises," and from considering the universal ego as the negative unity of ego in all of its particular states.

But Hegel advises us to submit this notion of an immediate reciprocity in sense experience to a simple test: We know what we *mean* by the single "now" or "here" which the ego encounters immediately at one of its moments. But let us try to indicate what we mean, by language. This is a sobering test. For if we try to express the "now" that we mean, our expression points out something that only "has been." But that which has been, *is* not. Thus we can call it a "now" only in virtue of the fact that we are negating its "having been." Thus the "now" that we are *speaking* about, is the *negation of the negation* of the "nows" that were meant. And likewise, in regard to the "here," which can only be meaningful in a context of "above," "below," "beyond," "right," "left," etc., we find that

> the "here" that is *meant* ought to be a point. But it doesn't exist as a point. Rather, as soon as the existent "here" is indicated, it becomes evident that this indication itself is not the immediate knowledge that it purported to be, but a movement away from the "here" that was meant, into many other "heres," and ultimately into the universal "here" which is a simple manifold of "heres" .... [6]

At this point, the fundamental paradox of the attitude of sense-certainty becomes lucidly clear: Whatever is meant by an immediate situation-encounter with the sensible world—it is not amenable to conscious expression, in language. For language can express only the universal.[7] And if we would assess the truth of the contents of consciousness, we must bring these contents into the sphere of universality.

PERCEPTION

initial transitions

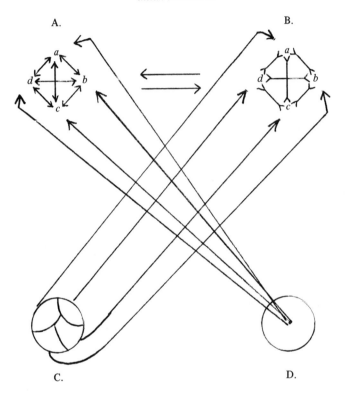

A. The perceptual object, consisting of many "thises" (i.e. sensuous properties, represented by a,b,c,d) seems on the one hand to be a unity of these thises. (The unity here is represented by the double arrows.)

B. On the other hand, the same perceptual object seems to be a multiplicity of sensuous properties, each of which remains distinct from the other and repels it from itself. (The mutual repulsion and differentiation is represented here by the inverted double arrows.)

C. The ego, insofar as it has a multiplicity of faculties and sense powers, seems to be responsible for the multiplicity of distinctions which it "notices" in the perceptual object.

D. On the other hand, the ego, insofar as it is a basic unifying force, seems to be responsible for the unity which it attributes to the perceptual object.

PERCEPTION *(cont.)*

final transitions

E.

E. Consciousness realizes that in perception the object is both a unity and a multiplicity, and that the ego is involved simultaneously in unifying the multiplicity of the object, and differentiating its unity.

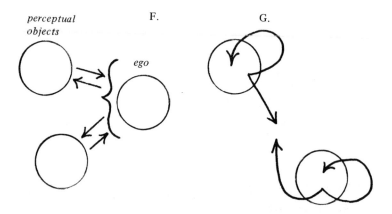

perceptual objects

ego

F.

G.

F. Consciousness begins to see perception in terms of a dialectic movement, in which the ego returns to itself after emerging outside itself into the perceptual world; and the object, correspondingly, manifests a movement of "going outside itself" and "returning to itself."

G. The dialectic interplay of "going outside self" (existence for-another) and "returning to self" (existence for-self) becomes manifest not only in the relationship of perceptual objects to the ego, but also in the relationship of one perceptual object to another perceptual object.

B. *The Attitude of Perception*

The primary object of consciousness is now seen to be a universal "here" giving context to all particular "heres" and a universal "now" giving context to all particular "nows." And it is also manifest that this object is mediated into universality by universal subjectivity. Subjectivity, in its turn, has now gotten beyond the illusory attitude of sense-certainty, and refuses to become immersed in the moments of particularity that had previously commanded its respect. Thus also it is now oriented primarily and necessarily to the universal.

But its universal object is not apprehended directly and immediately, but only by mediation of sensuous content. And as consciousness goes about the process of mediating the manifold sensations that impinge on it at various times in various places, the mediating process itself produces a world of distinct *"things."* For sense data are not merely distilled or obliterated by consciousness, but organized into concrete expressions of the universal—i.e., into thinghood.

Thus, being, as explicit universality, shows itself as focal essences in which, in various ways, the colors, sounds, smells, movements, etc., which are given in sensation, converge and cluster into the unity of distinct "things." And the attitude of perception, which is alone capable of recognizing "things" as unities-in-diversity of sense data, tends to view this world of thinghood—which, unlike immediate sensory experience, is amenable to conscious expression in terms of universality—as the true foundation of human knowledge. This is a "common sense" attitude, which accepts objects, in the conventional sense as "given"—and proceeds to ascribe properties and relations to these objects. It is up to us to immerse ourselves in this standpoint, and investigate the claims that it registers for the truth.

In a cube of salt the various qualities which are perceived by my various senses converge into a unified thing. This salt is white and also pungent, and also cubical in shape, and also of a certain specific weight, etc. The object of perception is one "here," but it comprises many "heres." (There is whiteness here, pungency, etc.)

If we analyze the perceptual object further, we see its distinct properties are *universal* qualities, universal "thises" which happen to become particularized in that object. For example, the whiteness of the salt is a universal datum of the sense of vision, a quality which happens to obtain in the salt, where it also interpenetrates with the other sensory qualities. Thus, in respect to these universal qualities, the "thing" takes on the aspect of an "also," a passive universal medium keeping a host of determinate properties in negative relationship to one another. But then again, insofar as each determinate property is opposite to and exclusive of other determinate properties, and insofar as the "thing" does not *just* keep them apart, but brings them together in their distinctness, the thing seems to have another aspect. It is a unifying agent, a "one," as well as a passive medium, an "also." The attitude of perception thus finds itself encountering, at its own level, the "paradox of the one and the many."

It tries to clarify this paradox by bringing in the ego to the reckoning. Perhaps the object, bare and unadulterated, is a mere multiplicity of sensuous universals, of universal properties which are compacted into the unity of thinghood by the subjectivity. Or perhaps, on the other hand, the object is a simple and undifferentiated "given" unity, which the universalizing ego, by means of its multiple sense faculties, differentiates into the state of "also-ness." But then it slowly comes to dawn on consciousness that *both* the ego and the object are performing *both* these functions. For—as was demonstrated in the attitude of "sense-certainty"—neither the subject- nor the object-pole is more "essential" than its opposite; but consciousness, in its various attitudes, seems to be a totum resulting from the dialectical reciprocity between both poles. Thus the ego returns to itself from its inspection of the perceptual object. And just as the ego returns to itself as a universality with self-identity, so also the object returns to itself as a manifold "also" which is nevertheless a unity. Thus the sense-conditioned universality of the perceptual "here" and "now" proves itself at this point to be a universality affected with an intrinsic opposition or paradoxical dichotomy, a universality conditioned by its very components.

Perceptual consciousness now arrives at the distinct recognition of the advantage that it has over immediate sensory consciousness: It need not remain in immediate unity with the object as a necessary condition. Rather, it arrives at a considerable degree of universality and of truth by a process of continually withdrawing from encounters with objects to reunion with itself. For by dint of this process it is enabled to check and re-check just what falls to itself,[1] and what falls to the object; and thus to gradually approximate to the simple unadorned being of the object.

Having returned to self-unity, then, the ego notices that it itself is a unity which is universal, an in-itself which is for-itself and a for-itself which is for-another; and that the dialectic relationship of *ansichsein* with *fürsichsein* and *fürsichsein* with *füreinanderesein,* is an intrinsic, necessary dialectic in terms of which its own unity-in-multiplicity may be understood. On the basis of this insight, the ego again ventures out to re-examine the perceptual object, to determine whether the unity-in-multiplicity of the object can also be clarified in terms of some such intrinsic dialectic, which is not simply a sense-conditioned bifurcated universality. Accordingly, it now separates itself from concentration on a single perceptual object, and attends to such objects precisely in their inter-relationship. It sees that the individual perceptual object cannot "return to itself" as a self-identical "for-itself,"[2] except in the context of other objects, from which it is distinguishing itself. Thus in the very condition of being for-itself, it is related to other objects by negation, i.e., it is for-another *(füreinander).*[3] Or, to analyze the relationship of *fürsichsein* even more fundamentally, when an object is for-*anything,* that "anything" must be conceived as an "other," if a *relationship* is to be set up; and thus the perceptual object is related to itself *as an other* which is other than the rest of the perceptual objects, but yet shares with these latter the character of being other than the immediate existence in-self of the perceptual object.[4]

When we have arrived at the point where we can see the two moments of *fürsichsein* and *füreinanderesein* operative as an essential unity-in-opposition in perceptual objects, we have attained the goal we set out to reach: We have gotten beyond mere sense-conditioned universality to an *unconditioned absolute universality*, one which explains the essential perspective which obtains in the attitude of perceptual consciousness, and at the same time brings consciousness into the realm of the understanding, which is oriented to formulating the world in terms of truly necessary relationships.

Those who fail to rise to this realm of the understanding, and are "arrested" in the attitude of perception or "common sense," must necessarily become involved in the sophistry which guards the "rights" of these faculties. They have to strive to keep the opposite moments of singleness and universality from contradiction, and to salvage the self-identity of things by resorting to all-embracing abstractions like "essential," "single," "necessary," etc. Such concepts are, indeed, controlling ideas, and even the guiding force behind philosophy; but in a living philosophy they do not reveal themselves as stationary and tangible entities here or there. Neither are they revealed in themselves as the truth; but rather they only reveal the truth in moments which are not explicitly themselves. Thus common-sense, by regarding them as stable truths, needs to resort to all kinds of qualifications, exceptions, rationalizations, etc.—and in the end succeeds not in establishing the truth of anything, but only in demonstrating its own untruth.

C. *The Attitude of Understanding*

1. THE FIRST UNIVERSAL

Consciousness, at the terminus of the attitude of perception, enters into a new realm, where it is no longer immediately involved with individual objects, but rather finds a world of wider significance spread before its eyes; a world whose existence and truth seems to consist in a dialectic movement taking place in objects and among objects. We are now at the standpoint of the Absolute Unconditioned Universal, where existence-for-self *(fürsichsein)* is seen only in the context of existence-for-another *(füreinanderesein)*; and where otherness itself becomes an incentive to self-possession and self-sameness.

The dialectical unity-in-opposition of existence-for-self and existence-for-another is at one and the same time *both* content and form, insofar as it is the incipient Concept[1] which (as we shall see later) admits no intrinsic distinction between "form" and "content." But since the Concept is merely incipient now, it takes on the aspect of an *external* oscillation between the two opposite moments. And the dialectic between these two moments, insofar as it is presented as an external object *distinct* from consciousness, presents itself also as a distinction of form from content (since consciousness itself has the aspect of "that which gives form to the universal object," and there will be, consequently, some aspect of the universal object attributable to, or received from, consciousness— the "formal" aspect).

In the context of this distinction between form and content, the "content" becomes the dialectical oscillation between (a) the One (the unification of things

UNDERSTANDING

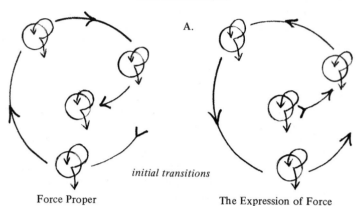

A.

initial transitions

Force Proper   The Expression of Force

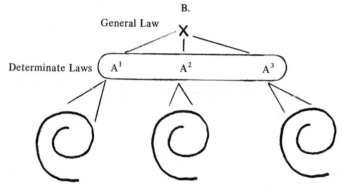

B.

General Law ✗

Determinate Laws (A^1 A^2 A^3)

A. The dialectic interplay of existence-for-self and existence-for-another which took place in individual perceptual objects becomes manifest in the relationship of Force which pervades perceptual objects. Force has two aspects: on the one hand, it is a simple unity continually returning to itself (Force Proper); on the other, it is an outward movement, continually manifesting itself or expressing itself in the sensuous manifold (The Expression of Force).

B. The differences and polarities in various "forces" are expressed in determinate physical laws; but these determinate laws are synthesized into a single "general law" (X) which purports to express the unity of all physical existence.

Transition to the "infinite concept"

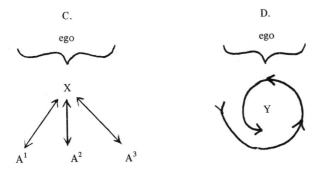

C.   D.

transition to Self-consciousness

E.

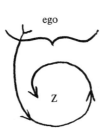

C. A certain ambiguity between the two aspects of law (law as unifying [X] and law as differentiating [A^1, A^2, etc.]) draws attention to the *ego* as the *source* of law.

D. Out of the subjective reciprocity of unifying and diversifying aspects of law, the ego becomes aware of the "infinite concept," which is the concept of unity-in-diversity, or unity-in-opposition (Y).

E. As the ego becomes cognizant of its power of creating conceptual unities-in-diversity, it likewise becomes cognizant of the fact that, in a certain sense, it itself is creating a unity-in-diversity with objectivity (z). It now turns in upon itself, to explore the ramifications of this creative function.

or materials which happen to share a single property or activity) and (b) the universal medium (a multiplicity of things or materials in which a single property or activity is manifested). The "form" then becomes the dialectical relationship between (a) "existence-for-self" and (b) "existence-for-another," taking place in individual objects and among sets of objects.

From *our* point of view, however, the moments (a) and (b) of form appear in correspondence with moments (a) and (b), respectively, of content. And so for the present we can take the liberty of expressing both form and content in a *composite* way as the dialectic of (a'), or unified existence-for-self, and (b'), or manifold existence for-another.

2. THE FIRST UNIVERSAL AS FORCE:

In order to understand the totality which results from this composite dialectic, we should pause to recall that, as mentioned in the preceding section (p. 68 and n. 4), the perceptual object, in becoming for-itself, becomes for itself-as-other, and thus immediately becomes for-other "selves" (for other objects). In this latter "moment," it is essentially relating itself to a manifold of objects and entering into that manifold. But the former moment, the moment of being for-self, as the spark or impetus which sets this whole process into motion, is the *sine qua non* unity, the focal point to which the manifold of processes must keep "returning" (in the same sense that the water in an artificial fountain might keep returning to its source).

Now the understanding, catching sight of this reciprocity between the for-itself and for-another in an *object,* forgets about the particular object in which it took place, and begins to see the reciprocity of for-self and for-another as a universal "object" pervading the world of objects. The understanding calls this universal-ized object "Force," and therewith attributes to Force itself the reciprocity of for-itself and for-another.[2]

This understanding of Force becomes exemplified in the various physical laws—the laws of the acceleration of falling bodies, Newton's three laws of motion, the laws of electricity, the laws of the rotation of the earth around the sun, etc. Each of these laws takes on the aspect of an oscillating movement between the "moments" (a') and (b').

Let us take just one of these laws—Newton's law on the reciprocity of force and mass ($F=MA$)—as an example, to comprehend concretely the transition that the understanding has just made.

In the perceptual sphere, consciousness has come to a simple notion of the interaction between distinct things by observing the carom-effect caused when one body hits another and that other body starts moving. Perceptual conscious-ness sees that the existence of the first body for-itself must be expressed, by the effects it has *on-another.* From this and other similar instances, consciousness rises to the understanding of the reciprocity of force and mass which prevails among particular bodies or materials.

But subsequently the two aspects of existence-for-self and existence-for-anoth-er are applied to Newtonian Force itself as an object. The moment in which this

Force is conceived as for-itself is the moment of its self-unity, a point of intensity gathered together within itself and abstracted from all extension and measurable expression. (And *de facto* we do seem to consider such "Forces" as force and energy and electricity and gravity as purely qualitative inner mechanisms governing thing-like and quantitatively measurable bodies.) But the moment in which this force is conceived as for-another is the moment when it enters into the manifold, and exerts empirically observable effects such as the carom-effect mentioned above.

Thus in the formula F=MA, "F" represents Newtonian force considered as existing for-itself, while the compounding of, and reciprocity between "M" and "A" is the same force considered as existing for-another, i.e., in the context of the manifold.

It should also be noted that the "MA" in this equation amounts to a sublated incorporation of the previous perceptual data which gave rise to the understanding of Force in the first place: For "mass," as the only variable which expresses the properties of a determinate thing, denotes the perceptual object for-itself; while "acceleration," a variable expressing of its very nature a relationship to a manifold, denotes the perceptual object for-another.

Therefore, if we take the equation, F=MA, as a whole, "F" would be force as a unified for-itself, "MA" would be Force as a manifold for-another, "M" would be the perceptual object for-itself, and "A" would be the perceptual object for-another.

It should be noted that the two major moments, (a') and (b'), whether they become instantiated as MA and F or as the components of some other equation, are characteristically self-cancelling moments: the unity passes into the manifold, and the manifold is the Expression of (objective) Force: while the unity-reflected-back into itself is Force itself, or Force Proper. Every type of force—whether it be Newtonian force, or gravity, or electricity considered as force—pertains to some unique unity-in-distinction which prevails among objects. The individual force appears as something objective, bringing about the unity of objects (although implicitly, as we shall see, it is a concept gathering together the perceptual manifold into unity). But it is never *expressed* as a unity. It is expressed only through its manifold instances. Thus "force" and the "expression of force" appear as two interdependent moments which are continually breaking off from each other, and cancelling each other.

The interdependence and *unity* of the moments of "unity and manifold expression" is the "First Universal"—the appearance of the *Absolute Unconditioned Universal* in an objectified form. In other words it is the Concept, which has not yet appeared *as* the Concept. In order to appear as the Concept, the intrinsic dialectic of its constituent moments must become manifest.

3. THE BIFURCATION OF FORCE

Force at this stage seems to be a circular, self-perpetuating movement. But this movement seems to require some impetus, an "Other," to get it started. For example, magnetism as a force requires a substance such as iron to serve as a "vehicle" for it. This vehicle is taken to be some outside Force, which incites Force into activity. But are we to presume that such an external substance really has the power to condition the activity of Force? If there is any *power* in this external substance to condition Force, this power might be best described as a second force which incites the first force (the first force which we were considering) into activity. In the case of magnetic force, this power could be one of the polarities—North or South—which seems to incite the other—South or North—into activity. Thus the circular movements (a') and (b') of Force can now be differentiated—in view of this new consideration—into the movements of "inciting" and "incited" forces; and in place of Force as a single circular oscillation we have a continual reciprocity between two forces, in such a way that the "Other" is no longer something *other than* force, but simply an *other* force.

One of the most general ways of understanding this bifurcation would be in terms of the physical concomitance of attraction and repulsion in various forces. More specific manifestations of the bifurcation into inciting and incited forces would be, for instance, the conception that every action conditions an equal and opposite reaction, or the distinctions between positive and negative electricity, North and South magnetic poles, centripetal and centrifugal force, the opposing attractions of the earth and the moon on the tides, and so forth. In each of these cases, even though we know that there is a simultaneity and continuity between the opposed forces, and that the "inciting" force is not prior to the "incited" force and is, in fact, itself incited by the so-called incited force—we tend to think of force in terms of this relationship between a force and its counterpart or "other."

4. THE "SECOND UNIVERSAL"—THE *DISSOLUTION* OF THE PREVIOUS DISSOLU-
TION-INTO-TWO-FORCES

Reciprocal forces—such as positive and negative electricity—*must* coincide because they are reciprocal. When they do coincide, one of the forces takes on the aspect of the "inciting" force, and the second force becomes the "incited" force. The inciting force (A) as the "Other" which gives rise to the incited force (B) is considered in the first instance to be some actual "manifold expression" of force, as far as its content is concerned. The incited force (B), correspondingly, becomes force repressed within itself, which must be excited to its expression. *But* the inciting force (A), like any force, consists in the oscillation between manifold expression and repressed unity. Therefore, its own manifold expression must be incited by its repressed unity. And, in still another sense, its own unity must be incited by its manifold expression. In this way the "distinctions" of content vanish into each other, and all that we have left is the distinction of the inciting (active) existence for-self and the incited (passive) existence for-another—distinctions which turn out to be merely formal distinctions which can be applied indifferently to force (A) or (B), or to the moments (a) or (b) of the content of force (to use the symbolism introduced earlier). As purely formal distinctions, they vanish into each other, and in fact their whole function is to disappear into each other.

Thus the distinctions of both content and form are superseded—but in different ways. The distinctions of content are dissolved insofar as they proved to be purely "formal" distinctions. (The distinctions of form, (a) and (b), which formerly were attributable to (a) and (b), respectively, of content, are now *just* as attributable to (b) and (a), respectively of content, thus bringing about the disappearance of "content" in the former sense.) But the distinctions of form are *also* dissolved, since the existence of "form" without content is meaningless. In fact, the distinctions of form and content merge here into each other, and we begin to see the dialectic in terms of a pure oscillation between existence for-self and existence for-another—an oscillation which is no longer attributed to Force as an objectified content, but now becomes manifest as a polarity *in* the concept of the *Understanding*.[3]

When we fix our attention on *this* concept, we have arrived at the *second universal*, i.e. force no longer as an objective reciprocity of (a') and (b'), but as the *thought* of the dialectical disappearance of (a') into (b')—the thought which was implicit in the first universal, but needed to be explicated.

5. THE APPEARANCE OF APPEARANCE

A syllogism develops: the inner being of force (that is, the objective referrent of the concept of Force) is comprehended by the conceptualizing Understanding through a middle term: *Appearance*.[4] Appearance is a semblance *(Schein)* which is not *just* a semblance. It is the semblance which bridges the gap between the understanding and the inner being of things and (as we shall see) reveals the latter to the former.

The emergence of Appearance marks the emergence of Understanding in the strict sense, and also of the proper object of the Understanding, which is "the inner being" of Force.

The inner being of Force is the context or basis for the mutual self-cancellation of phenomenal distinctions, and—when we think of this phenomenal world as something present to us *(Diesseits)*—the inner being takes on the aspect of a "beyond" *(Jenseits)*, a suprasensible world containing no positive reality in itself:

In this inner truth—i.e. the Absolute [Unconditioned] Universal which has emerged into a unity out of the opposition of universal and particular, and has become [an object] for-the-understanding—we conclude to a suprasensible world, which now establishes itself as the true world, out of reach of the sensuous world of Appearance.[5]

As something which is just beyond the boundaries of what appears and is experiencable, it is considered to be a void, whose essential characteristic consists in being just "on the other side" of all positive phenomenal content. But this void, this empty thing-in-itself, is not unimportant For it gives us the first glimpse of the development of Reason:

This in-itself is the first, but as yet imperfect, manifestation of Reason.[6]

Reason, as the full dialectic synthesis of inner *and* outer, will develop into prominence much later in Hegel's phenomenological analysis (see Part III, *infra*). But the apprehension of the "inner world," which has emerged just now, is the necessary and sufficient prerequisite for that fuller understanding.[7]

6. APPEARANCE *QUA* APPEARANCE

Seeing that this "beyond" is a void, some may decide to say that only the world of appearance is true. Others may try to fill up the void of the suprasensible world with an arbitrary content—dreamings, imaginings, or artificially produced "appearances." But the true solution to the "emptiness" of the suprasensible world is to be found only when one arrives at the full realization that it has given rise to the phenomena, to the world of appearances; in fact that it relates *essentially* to that world, and that its essence is precisely to give rise to appearance. In other words,

Appearance *is* the essence of that inner world and, in fact, the "filling" of the inner world.[8]

If and when we realize this, we have found the proper "filling" for the "beyond," and in doing so, we have arrived at the proper notion of appearance—appearance not as the positive being of sense-data, but precisely as *the appearance-of the inner being of Force*. At this point, we have attained to the perspective of appearance *qua* appearance (appearance apprehended in its essential function and its proper context).

7. THE FIRST SUPRASENSIBLE WORLD·LAW EMERGES FROM APPEARING FORCE

The fact that the inner world is not just an empty void, and that the *positive* meaning of this inner world becomes manifest to us in and through the mediation of Appearance—must now be made explicit.[9] The Appearance of Force is the appearance of pure change (i.e. pure difference—an "incessant process of permutation and transposition"[10]—which emerges from the "inner being" of things. This "inner being," on the other hand, is the stable universal essence, which supplies the basis for pure change. The unity of Appearance and the inner being of things becomes explicit as "universal difference"—or the stable universal expression of the movement of change of phenomenal particulars. We may also call this universalization of difference—and we do call it—law.[11] The suprasensible world "behind" the phenomena has been transformed into the kingdom of laws present within the phenomena, and concomitant to all the transactions of force which take place.

8. THE "GENERAL LAW" SUPERSEDES DETERMINATE LAWS' AND A QUASI–BIFURCATION OF LAW RESULTS

Law as universality *should* be able to subsume and completely transform the determinate aspects found within appearance. But this observation only applies to law-in-general. What we have most to deal with are particular, determinate laws, e.g. the law of falling bodies and the laws of electricity. Each of these laws manages to transform some part of the independent aspects of phenomenal flux into universality; but not all. There is still some measure of unassimilated independence "left over" in appearance.

In order to overcome this defect, and bring about a complete subsumption of appearance into universality, consciousness tries to formulate a *single general law* which will unify all laws and embrace the totality of appearance. This results in Newton's *"law of universal attraction."*

9. THE SEARCH FOR "NECESSITY" IN LAW

The law of universal attraction has great importance, insofar as it represents the final step in the effort to unify and universalize and control the instable flux of the world of appearance. However, it also has some defects: For one thing, it is so abstract and superficial that it does not say much about the phenomenal world. It can be reduced to the rather superfluous statement that "everything has a constant distinction with reference to every other thing."[12] Likewise, as a determinate law standing above other determinate laws it in a sense stands above law itself. At least, it is not the kind of law which is concerned with determining the relationship between individual aspects of phenomena, and unifying these individual aspects. To be sure, the law of universal attraction brings about a unity—but a unity which obliterates all difference and individual subsistence. It seizes upon the necessary unity at the core of all phenomenal change, but brings about this unity so sweepingly that no individual differences remain. And thus this ultimate inner necessity and absolute unity of the law of universal attraction is a defect of sorts.

Thus we have the law in a twofold form, and this twofold form betrays a vacillation with regard to the nature and context of law itself. On the one hand, law (the general law) seems to be a pure unity which dissolves all differences. On the other hand, law (each particular law) seems to be referred to differences which have no *real* necessary unity among themselves (and are certainly not "dissolved"): For example, although positive and negative electricity seem to be necessarily related to each other, the "necessity" here is purely verbal (i.e. the necessary relationship of two terms which are grammatical reciprocals).[13] We cannot say that the law of electricity necessarily must express itself in this polarity. The case of motion is even clearer: Although the law of motion is expressed in terms of certain "necessary" factors—space, time, distance, and velocity—these factors patently are not related in any necessary unity among themselves, and (as compared with the case of electricity) it is even more obvious that the law of motion need not be expressed as a necessary relationship of these factors.[14]

10. THE NECESSARY DISTINCTION OF LAW FROM FORCE

If distinctions such as "positive and negative" in the case of electricity and "space and time and velocity and distance" in the case of motion are rather arbitrary distinctions, what is a real, truly necessary distinction? Hegel answers that

> The Understanding *does* have the concept of such an intrinsic distinction: the intrinsic distinction [results from the fact] that the law is from one point of view the inner nature [of force], the in-itself; but from another point of view is a distinction residing in the concept itself.[15]

In other words, the vacillation regarding the notion of law is symptomatic of an incessant and inevitable oscillation *between* the inner being of the world of appearance (represented as something "out there" beyond phenomena) *and* the concept of the understanding (represented as the subjective pole which is observing force and formulating laws about the various manifestations of force).

11. "EXPLANATION" EMERGES AS A PROCESS WHICH IS BASED ON AN INCOMPLETE UNDERSTANDING OF THE DISTINCTION BETWEEN LAW AND FORCE— "TAUTOLOGY" RESULTS

This dual character of law leads to the process which we call *Explanation*:
We start with a particular event, e.g. a flash of lightning. We formulate this occurrence in terms of a law—in this case, the law of electricity. We then relate the law to the appearance of force, which we consider to be the "ground" or referrent of the law, i.e. the element in which the law is incorporated and which the law controls. In this case, the "ground" happens to be the incessant circuit existing between positive and negative electricity. Conveniently enough, positive and negative electricity, as polar opposites of force, just happen to disappear into each other and cancel each other out, leading to pure unity. In other words, force, which thrives on dynamic *difference* (inciting force, incited force, etc.) is for all practical purposes considered to be identical with law, which is the ultimate manifestation of the *unifying* power of the understanding. A reputed objective entity is identified with a reputed subjective formulation. But officially, in reflection upon the relationship between law and force—Understanding considers the former to be *distinct* from the latter.

It is true to say that law is distinct from force, since the Understanding is *distinguishing* law from force. But the statement here is a mere tautology: x is distinct from y because x is distinguished from y by the Understanding. It is also true that an electrical *force* creates a unity of opposites just as the *law* regulating electricity creates such a unity of opposites. But here again, we have a tautology: Force and the law of force display the same characteristics because, in *practical application,* they are usually identified. If x and y are identical, it does not add much to our knowledge of affairs to observe that x and y display the same characteristics. Thus we see that the vacillation of understanding as to whether force and law are identical or distinct leads, one way or the other, to tautological processes.

12. DIALECTICAL MOVEMENT IS TRANSFERRED FROM FORCE TO THE CONCEPT
OF FORCE (i.e. TO THE LAW REGULATING FORCE)

But one very important development takes place as a result of these subjective
processes: The incessant oscillating *movement* which was previously attributed
to the Appearance of Force, now becomes noticeable within the understanding,
or more precisely within the concept of law—which was previously thought to be
the paragon of unity and stability. Conversely, the stability and unity which
were formerly attributed to the understanding, are now transferred to the object
of the understanding—the Appearance of Force, which takes on the aspect of a
passive entity to which laws must be applied. Thus, as Hegel puts it,

> Our consciousness has made a transition from the inner being [as that
> which became manifest to us in Appearance] as an object to the opposite
> pole—the Understanding—and now possesses movement and change within
> the Understanding of itself.[16]

13. EMERGENCE OF A "SECOND SUPRASENSIBLE WORLD," THE INVERTED
WORLD

Once the understanding begins to possess this movement and change within
thought itself, immediately the act of thinking about the phenomenal world
becomes not just a unification of sense data but a constant infusion of "movement" and dynamic opposition into that which is understood. And correspondingly the "law of the phenomenon," which had had a unifying function, takes
on the aspect of a self-sundering movement between opposites. The "first suprasensible world"—the kingdom of changeless laws which governed changing phenomena—now is transformed into the second suprasensible world, which might
best be described as a topsy-turvy or "inverted" world [*eine verkehrte Welt*][17] —
a world of paradox, in which determinations which previously were thought to
be self-identical are now seen in the light of oppositions inherent in their nature:

> The stable kingdom of Laws which previously constituted the "suprasen-
> sible" world by providing an immediately intelligible portrayal of the per-
> ceptual world, now reverts into its opposite. The [former determinate]
> Law of Force was on the whole a self-stabilizing sort of thing, as also were
> the distinctions which it comprised. But in the *new* legislation that which
> is selfsame nudges itself away from itself, and that which is distinct estab-
> lishes itself once more in selfsameness . . . This second suprasensible world
> is thus an inverted world.[18]

In this new world of paradox (to mention some of the examples given by Hegel),
that which seems to be sweet becomes the sour, the oxygen pole in electricity
becomes the hydrogen pole,[19] the act of punishing a criminal becomes a kind of
self-punishment and the reconciliation of the criminal with himself is accomplished through castigation by his community.[20]

It is important to realize, however, that the insight which now begins to
perceive the primal movement and opposition which takes place among *elements*

and aspects of law, is but an extension of the basic insight (which has just emerged) that there is an incessant movement taking place between *law and the phenomenon,* between the world of thought and the world of sensuous appearance.

14. THE INVERTED WORLD BECOMES THE INVERSE OF ITSELF—i.e., NO LONGER A "SECOND" SUPRASENSIBLE WORLD

When we attain to the perspective of this "second suprasensible" world, however, we must not look upon it as just a new relationship between inner and outer. In other words, we must not think that we have merely passed from a situation in which the inner world of law presented a static, unchanging picture of the changeable world to a new situation where the *inner* world is seen to be the inverse or opposite of the *outer* world. This would be a misleading representation, says Hegel, since

> such a dichotomy between inner and outer, between appearance and the suprasensible—seen as paired independent realities—would no longer be apropos. For now the distinguished differences are no longer separated into two entities which would supply the foundation for these distinctions and give them an independent subsistence. . . .[21]

Another way of explaining the transition that takes place here would be to say that the second suprasensible world, which creates a dialectical unity-in-opposition from the unifying laws of the first suprasensible world, carries this dialectical function to an ultimate logical conclusion: it makes a *unity*-in-opposition of the *very relationship between* itself and that other world, so that they are no longer viewed as two worlds (although, from the point of view of the *Understanding,* they may still *seem* to be two distinct worlds which need to be unified by the power of the understanding). In other words the second suprasensible world—the inverted world, the world of unity-in-*opposition*—becomes the inverse of itself, the *opposite* of *itself*—i.e. no longer a world distinct from or opposite to the "straightforward" world where the abstract unity of law cancels out the abstract distinctions of appearance.

15. EMERGENCE OF THE CONCEPT, i.e. LIFE AS INFINITY

At this point we have relinquished the accoutrements of the Understanding— the finite concepts which draw phenomenal distinctions into thought-unities (laws)—and have arrived at *the* Concept, i.e. the *infinite concept* which is *prius natura* to all finite concepts—the concept of the *unity* of the *unities* of thought with the *manifold* sense data of appearance.[22] Since this latter Concept comprises *all* thought-unities (finite concepts), it cannot itself be a thought-unity. It is unity in a higher sense. Likewise, since it comprises *all* the distinctions which are "thought about" in the phenomenal world, it itself cannot be such a distinction. It is distinction in a higher sense. Expressed in a rather formalistic way: it is the unity-in-distinction of all unity with all the distinction which is "found" by being *created* at the heart of consciousness; and it "creates" a special kind of unity-in-distinction which (since it is a pre-condition for consciousness of the world) is *found* to be already there.

The standpoint of this Concept of Infinity is the standpoint of Life—not life merely as a quality of individual physical organisms—but life in a primal and preeminent sense:

> This simple infinity (the Absolute Concept) is the enunciation of the simple essence of life; of the soul of the world; of that universal lifeblood which in its all-pervasive presence remains undisturbed and unbroken in the midst of distinctions; which itself is the totality of distinctions in superseded form; which pulsates without changing, and trembles without losing composure.[23]

16. THE DISAPPEARANCE OF "APPEARANCE" AND THE EMERGENCE OF SELF-CONSCIOUSNESS

The absolute Concept is an "infinity," in contrast to the finite, determinate laws which it supersedes. Its own finite *unity* consists precisely in being self-*distinguished,* self-divided. And so its finite unity proves itself *not* to be a finite unity; to be, rather, an infinite circular oscillation. But the distinctions which it gives rise to are identical with its own intrinsic selfhood; the oppositions which it sets up contain the opposed contrary implicitly in their very act of opposition; and what we call the state of pure undivided "unity" (finite unity) proves to be just a *moment* resulting from such oppositions—namely, the moment of simplicity which stands in contrast, as an abstraction, over against distinction. Those who fail to grasp this latter truth, says Hegel, will be hard-pressed to give any satisfactory account of "how multiplicity can ever result from unity."

At first this second inverted kingdom of dialectical speculation seems to be confined to the inner world of the mind. As we advance in pure conceptual activity, we become more conscious of this "inner world." It still seems to be distinct from the inner being of things, as revealed to us by Appearance. But as the activity further develops, it proves itself in a final way to be the dissolution of all distinctions. For the distinctness which the mind apprehended is a self-created distinction which, like all distinctions in this second kingdom, has no isolated reality, and is in organic continuity with the unity that created it. And so gradually the "veil of the temple"—Appearance—begins to withdraw itself as a *middle term,* and we come to view the merger of the pure inner region of mind with the inner being of things in the world.[24] And this is simply to say that consciousness becomes aware of the reflection, the projection, the distinction of *itself* in and through the objective-appearing "beings" of the world. That is, consciousness, following through completely on the attitude of Understanding, becomes *Self*-Consciousness.

> When the Concept of "Infinity" itself becomes fully objective to consciousness, consciousness becomes thereupon a consciousness of distinction as immediately *ipso facto* superseded. Consciousness (as an in-itself, distinguished from the world) becomes *for*-itself; it exists as the distinguishing of the undistinguished—i.e., as self-consciousness.[25]

Consciousness thus turns abruptly away at this point from its examination of objective knowledge, and returns to itself to begin to plumb the depths of self-consciousness, which has sprung up as a harbinger of the truth which is to come.

SELF–CERTAINTY

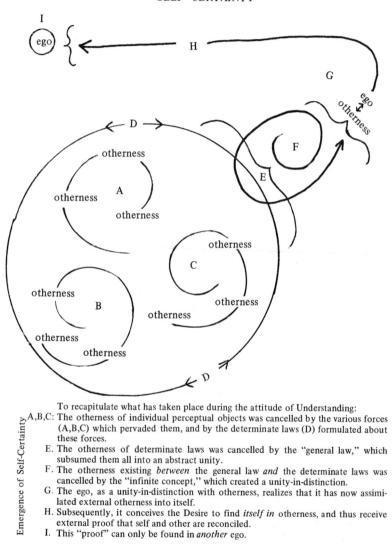

To recapitulate what has taken place during the attitude of Understanding:

A,B,C: The otherness of individual perceptual objects was cancelled by the various forces (A,B,C) which pervaded them, and by the determinate laws (D) formulated about these forces.

E. The otherness of determinate laws was cancelled by the "general law," which subsumed them all into an abstract unity.

F. The otherness existing *between* the general law *and* the determinate laws was cancelled by the "infinite concept," which created a unity-in-distinction.

G. The ego, as a unity-in-distinction with otherness, realizes that it has now assimilated external otherness into itself.

H. Subsequently, it conceives the Desire to find *itself in* otherness, and thus receive external proof that self and other are reconciled.

I. This "proof" can only be found in *another* ego.

Emergence of Self-Certainty

PART TWO. THE FORMS OF SELF-CONSCIOUSNESS

A. The Immediacy of Self-Certainty

The necessary, infinite, and absolute Concept of Law which is produced by the understanding, brings it to the first notion of *self-conscious ego* as the departure point of Force into the world. And the ego now "drops everything" and turns to self-consciousness itself as the "philosopher's stone" for arriving at the truth.

The "knowable object," having been raised from the state of sensuous immediacy, differentiated in the regions of perception, and reunified by Understanding—now again returns to itself, becomes reflected upon itself, simultaneously as the ego begins to return upon its own self-consciousness.[1] But the knowable *object* has now been altered. For just as consciousness is the generic (distinction-unifying) Concept for-itself, so also the true object of consciousness at this moment is the genus in-itself, as endowed with the life of consciousness. In other words, the object is *Life,* made immanent in the world, and parceling itself out in time and space:

> The essence of Life is the "infinity" which sublimates all distinctions, that pure circular process whose repose is the absolute restlessness of the infinite Concept; it is that autonomous process in which the distinctions lose their own autonomy; it is time in the state of essential simplicity—a time which from its vantage point in this autonomous process also contains the tri-dimensional features of space.[2]

It might be useful to stop here for a moment, to dwell on the Hegelian Concept of Life-as-infinity:

Hegel often uses the term, "life," in a special sense, or—better yet—in what might be considered to be its ultimate sense.

In the present section, we see that the Understanding, having gotten beyond perceptual immersion in particular objects, begins to see various "laws" operative among these objects and then, after subjecting its concepts of these laws to examination, realizes that in dealing with the world through the medium of these laws, it is in a very real sense dealing with a projection of itself. And the world, on its side, becomes a manifold transfused with the intellective life of consciousness.

In later sections of the *Phenomenology,* we will encounter still other uses of the term, "life," which are likewise at odds with our usage of that word in the ordinary parlance.

For example, 1) in the section on the Master-Slave relationship, individual self-consciousness will come to "find" its full and autonomous life only through another self-consciousness which assumes a subservient role with relationship to it.

2) At the conclusion to the section on Observation, Reason, having failed to find an adequate reflection of its life in the external world, decides to *make* for itself an adequate reflection of itself—by its deeds and its works.

3) In every section, we find that some immediate "other," which seemed offhand to be opposed to consciousness, and to resist its efforts, finally gives way and becomes subsumed into, and transformed by, the life of consciousness.

4) In the section on the ethical substance, in Part II (Section (BB) in Baillie) the unconscious and immediate *existence* of a nation gives rise to conscious individualized life—but still remains outside the ambit of this life as something "divine" or "transcendent."

All such usages of the term, "life," are obviously in marked contrast to the common usage, in which we think of life as something peculiar to individual plant, animal and human organisms—and terminating more or less at the bodily surfaces of these individual organisms.

If we would try to pinpoint how Hegel's usage differs, we might sum up his esoteric usage of "life" as follows: 1) Life is the process by which beings are drawn into the unity of consciousness and/or become conscious themselves. 2) Life is the process by which subjects come to find themselves in the otherness of their world by objectifying themselves in that world, and by projecting aspects of themselves onto the objects of that world. 3) These processes take place simultaneously and mutually generate each other—so that there is really only one process taking place in the whole scheme of things.[3]

Consciousness, perceiving that the different objects which it apprehends have only the truth-content which it gives to them, has come to realize that the "other" accosting it has become revealed as a modality of self. Thus the true otherness it has to deal with is not any otherness outside itself, but the otherness of its own ego, considered as object. And ego-constituted otherness, as an in-it-self, has the paradoxical characteristic of being a self-sameness, since it is also simultaneously for-itself. But this self-sameness must still become more explicit.[4] And so consciousness comes to a state of *Desire*—desire, that is, for complete conscious unity with itself as other.

An obstacle to this Desire appears, however, in the form of external otherness which continues to impinge on the ego and require assimilation. For consciousness has only *incipiently* realized that its Life is the all-pervading force behind objectivity. Thus the ego is driven on to strive for complete satisfaction of its desire for self-unity—a satisfaction which will be obtained only when all external otherness has been cancelled, so that the *only* otherness facing it is internal, conscious otherness.

This "cancellation," at present, means a simple affirmation of the ego-pole over the objective pole in consciousness—not a withdrawal from, or a negation of, external reality. Thus it is a process which must take place not by a leveling-out process in which all individual objectivity is extinguished, or ignored, but in such a way as to give the heightened significance of the ego to all "subsumed" individual forms:

> Universal Life . . . insofar as it *includes* the "other" in itself, cancels its own essential simplicity; that is, it sunders its simplicity; and this sundering of (simple) indistinct flux amounts to the *affirmation* of individuality.[5]

Conscious, intellective Life cancels its own simplicity, and becomes (implicitly) individual; and in like manner it proceeds to cancel the simplicity which has been given to individual forms under the aegis of Law, and to explicate their *diversity* ever more perfectly, i.e., now in "living" form.

But individual existence even in this new sublated form still has an aspect of external otherness to self-consciousness. For in a certain sense consciousness is dependent on the contingency of distinct perceptual objects *presenting* themselves to be sublated into true individual existence out of the unity of Law. How can consciousness get beyond this subordination to external contingencies? The only possible way for canceling *this* subordination would be to bring certain actual perceptual objects to *cancel themselves*. If this could be arranged, there would no longer be any doubt left about the mastery of self-consciousness over otherness. Thus under impetus of its own Desire, self-consciousness proceeds to search out a special kind of individuated "living" object—namely, *another self--consciousness which will negate its own distinct "given" existential orientations at its (the first self-consciousness') own bidding.* Here will be an "object" which will not really be an object in the sense of an opposed, external thing; but will give nothing but an echo of one's own subjectivity. And then finally, if this "object" will agree, at the bidding of the first self-consciousness, to take upon itself the task of dealing directly with those other external objects which still seem to retain their independence—self-consciousness will have completely attained its goal. It will have completely cancelled, for present purposes, the threat to its own self-certitude, with which external otherness previously confronted it.

This new concentration on self-conscious "objects" leads us to the next phase of self-consciousness—the "Master-Slave" relationship among consciousnesses.

Consciousness thus now first enters the realm of *spirit*—a mediating flux properly taking place only amid discrete subjectivities. The individual spirit, which becomes aware of its independence from the unpredictable contingencies of the world only through another self-consciousness, needs now to examine and perfect its relationship to other self-consciousnesses. As a result of these maneuverings, it will eventually step into the realm of spiritual daylight—the confrontation with Absolute Spirit itself—which unifies and supersedes all distinct individual spirits:

> Absolute Spirit . . . through the processes of the development of the freedom and self-subsistence of its opposite (the plurality of distinct self-consciousnesses existing for-themselves), comes on the scene precisely as their unity: The "I" manifests itself as a "we," just as the "we" manifests itself as an "I." [6]

THE MASTER-SLAVE DIALECTIC

Transitions

A. ⃝   { ego   Self-consciousness seeks for a reflection of itself in the external world (otherness).

B. other } >——< { ego   It seems to find such a reflection only in
   ego   another ego, which appears different.

C. other }   { ego   It tests the other "ego" to determine whether that other is just a sensuously existent object, or a free self-consciousness like itself. It carries out this test by challenging the sensuous being (body) of the other.

D.   { ego   If it completely cancels the sensuous being of the other, however, it cancels the other ego.

E. object- } recognition { subject-   It finally settles for a more practical arrangement, whereby it is satisfied with an external reflection of its own freedom in the other.
   ego   } ——————————→   { ego
   (Slave)   (Master)

F. object-ego }   { master   The object ego, forced to give recognition to the subject ego, comes gradually to recognize his own subjectivity, by a negative rebound.
   becoming }
   a subject }

G. slave = } Self-   { master =   The object ego, fully aware of his self-conscious freedom, ceases to be an object-ego, ceases to be a Slave. The subject-ego must therefore also cease to be "Master" of the Slave.
   master   } recognition) slave

All the preceding transitions should be understood in terms of the following ultimate transition:

ego { ←——————————————→ } ego

H. In this transition, which does not take place until the end of the first part of the *Phenomenology*, the mutual recognition of egos replaces the various kinds of one-sided recognition; and intersubjectivity in the fullest sense ensues.

B. *From Intrasubjectivity to Intersubjectivity*

Self-consciousness, in its moment of simple self-certainty, conceived the Desire to make all otherness into self-conscious otherness. The true fulfillment of this Desire could only arrive when

its own proper existence-for-self had established itself as an independent object which it encounters; or, what amounts to the same thing, when its object had presented itself as this pure certainty-of-self.[1]

In other words, it was implicit in that initial Desire which it conceived that 1) self-consciousness should "find" itself in an other self-consciousness objectively recognizable; and 2) the "objectivity" self-consciousness is dealing with, must cease to be simply passively interfused with conscious Life, and actively assume the form of self-consciousness itself.

Thus, as we have seen, this very desire to make its internal otherness objective has led the initially solopsistic self-consciousness to seek out special kinds of "objects"—other self-consciousnesses. Thus we pass now from the consideration of self-consciousness' attempts to become related to itself, to a consideration of its relationships to other self-consciousnesses. This intersubjective relationship, however, should not be understood as a simple distinction amid subjectivities, but precisely as a union of one subjectivity with itself, *through* others. For we have just come to the point where, under the impetus of the infinite Concept, which cancels *all* distinctions, *individual distinctiveness cancels itself,* to become *other*-than-a-distinct-ego, i.e., to become a union of egos.

Self-consciousness and its "other" thus initially find themselves face-to-face in objective, sensuously existent form; a form, nevertheless, in which they do not just see an "object," but an echo or reflection of themselves. A dialectic begins to take place, which can be expressed in terms of simple "moments:" 1) Self-consciousness, giving recognition to itself *as* objective "other," *ipso facto* sublimates the mere "being" of that other. 2) But for the purposes of self-certainty it has sublimated *its own* objective "other." And thus, it has also sublimated itself. 3) It thus "gets itself back." And in the process of doing this, it gives otherness *back to the other.* This is "the other side of the coin," in regard to one and the same process.

But how can one self-consciousness, encountering another, be sure that it is indeed encountering the same spirit whose certainty it finds within itself? How can it be certain that it is not merely continuing the activities of the attitude of Understanding—where it endowed alien objects with its *own* conscious Life? There of course would be a difference of *degree*: another self-consciousness would be *more* endowed with Life, *less* alien or inorganic to consciousness. But is it merely a matter of degree? Or is (self-) consciousness now truly encountering a different *kind* of "object"—an objective subjectivity endowed with an independent existence-for-self such as it senses within itself?

The question here is one of *freedom.* For freedom, as existence and activity for-self, is the distinctive characteristic of self-consciousness. And it is difficult to discern the presence of this freedom in a context which seems to take on the aspect of merely "living" objectivity.

The ego must accordingly set itself to find proof; it must "test" the alter-ego to adjudicate the presence of freedom. And this test will involve the negation, disregard, and destruction of life. For

> it is only through disregard of life that we have proof of freedom—proof that the proper province of self-consciousness is neither a province of being, nor of the immediate modality under which being presents itself, nor of conscious immersion in the elaboration of Life; proof that self-consciousness is a for-itself that has nothing present to it except vanishing moments of reality.[2]

In other words, the only way that a self-consciousness can show that it is something independent, existing for-itself—is to somehow demonstrate that it is not immersed-in the world of objectivity. Especially must it show that it is not immersed in the objectivity "closest" to it—i.e., its own immediate bodily existence.[3] To achieve this goal, it has to "remove" itself from this objectivity. But it cannot remove itself directly (since it does not yet comprehend itself in definite form, and thus cannot "lay hold" on itself to remove itself). And so it removes itself indirectly, by removing the signs of its immersion in its immediate sensuous existence. Thus it must "risk its life."

Now, the immediate goal of self-consciousness at this point is to find out whether its "other" is free. It itself shows freedom by a recklessness about life. Correspondingly, it must also bring its "other" face-to-face with death, since *recognition* of the other as a free self-consciousness is impossible unless this latter also shows *its* independence from mere existence. Thus self-consciousness initiates a life-or-death conflict, a war, in which its "other" must risk his life, pitting his freedom against the freedom of self-consciousness.

The result of this war, however, is a sobering realization. Forfeiting one's life is, to be sure, a sign of freedom, insofar as it is an abstract negation of immediate existence. But in order for this negation of existence to *perdure* concretely among self-consciousnesses, there must be a continual *return* to existence (to negate it). In other words, the concrete freedom of self-consciousnesses in the world *requires* existence, in order to be "free" of it. The maintenance of life is a condition *sine qua non,* if the "infinite" dialectical process is to flourish at all among self-consciousnesses in the world.

Self-consciousness, therefore, must resign itself to a living relationship with an "other"—a compromise relationship in which it will strive to induce the other to give independent echoes of self-consciousness' own activity. In other words, it must get the other to "do what it is doing," on the other's own impetus. In return for this, it gives him "recognition."[4]

It is inevitable, however, that in a milieu of individual self-consciousnesses, each trying to attain mastery and a recognition of their freedom—many individual self-consciousnesses will to a greater or lesser extent find themselves giving recognition of the freedom of others, without *receiving* corresponding recognition of their own freedom by those others. Thus this latter type of consciousness, whose freedom is not recognized, takes on the aspect of a "Slave" consciousness—interacting in dialectical opposition with the type of consciousness which gains recognition of its freedom (the "Master" consciousness).

The impetus of self-consciousness towards its "truth" thus at this point takes on the character of a master-slave relationship, in which certain consciousnesses manage to get other consciousnesses to actively contribute to their own self-conscious purposes, by their work in and upon the objective world of things.[5] The Master consciousnesses, happy to see every manner of self-conscious adherence to their free determinations in the objective world around them, give a minimal response to the Slave consciousnesses, but not much opportunity for enjoyment of their own freedom. The Masters are not about to diminish their own self-enjoyment by affording objective recognition of the freedom of their Slaves.

In the relationship obtaining between Master and Slave, however, neither does the Master come to the truth of self-consciousness through the subservience of the Slave, nor does the Slave ultimately lose his freedom to the Master. For:

1) *The Master,* in apportioning to the Slave the task of dealing directly with objectivity, and in reserving the unadulterated enjoyment of the Slave's work to himself, has come to see the Slave as an object, not precisely as an "other" self-consciousness. That is, he is not *doing* what the slave is doing, and thus fails to find a true echo or reflection in the slave's activity. And what is more, the Master seems to forget that it was precisely in dealing with the world of objects that he himself had first conceived the "Desire" of coming to an objective self-consciousness. So in a certain sense, he has left behind him the mainsprings of his own peculiar existence. He started out searching in the world of objects for a true reflection of his own self-conscious activity; but now is satisfied with looking down, from his citadel of self-certainty, on some objective self-conscious activity which is not his own, which is not the truth of his own self-consciousness.

2) *The Slave,* seeing self-consciousness as an external entity in the Master, is overcome internally by an all-pervading, absolute fear of death. This fear would be a paralyzing fear, if it were not negated. And the only way to negate it—in view of the demands of the Master—is through work. The Slave is driven on, then, by the internal incitement of a "fear of fear," to negate fear, by reworking external objects under the surveillance of the Master. But the paradoxical upshot of this process is a) that this "fear of fear," which thrives as a negation of negation, is *ipso facto* a form of reflective self-consciousness (since it is precisely by a negation of conscious negations or distinctions that consciousness arrives at self-consciousness); b) that the Slave actually comes to incarnate his self-consciousness *in* the production of re-formed objects—i.e., he finds his own self-consciousness in an objective form (as products which are reflections of his own free *creativity*)—which brings him nigh to the objective the Master had started out with. [6]

Thus the Master-Slave relationship is a temporary symbiotic relationship which is continually tending towards its own reversal: That is, the Slave is continually finding his self-consciousness in objectified form, and thus is continually receiving proof of his freedom in and from the objects which he negates and sublates. The Master, on the other hand, who set out to attain such proof of his own freedom in the first place, has become *dependent* on the compliance of the Slave for receiving *any* objective corroborations of freedom, and still does not receive truly objective corroborations of his *own* freedom. Thus the Slave, without starting out from the certainty of free self-consciousness, continually produces the truth of free self-consciousness, along with the possibility of concomitant certitude; while the Master, starting out from this certainty, produces the mere semblance of freedom and self-consciousness, without actually attaining to its objective truth.

Now self-consciousness, caught in the paradoxical turnabout of the Master-Slave relationship and unable to completely resolve these contradictions, begins to look for some other way to render "otherness" truly self-conscious and to make itself into something truly objective.

C. *From Intersubjectivity to Personality to Supra-Personality*

The pure awareness of abstract ego which the "Master" self-consciousness attained to, does not result in its acquisition of unity as a self-subsisting, self-identical, permanent ego. Rather, it is unable to find any real content in itself, and in the distinctions it makes through the "infinite" Concept. And thus it must remain established, for the time being, in its relationship with the Servant self-consciousness, if it is to attain any self-unity with true existential content. However, two extreme tendencies begin to reveal themselves eventually, in the Master and the Slave, respectively:

1) The Master, as the dominating and self-asserting and strictly self-conscious aspect of consciousness, has a tendency to assert its own independence by fortuitously and haphazardly engaging in the processes of abstract thought. For it can easily acquire a facility in emphasizing the distinctions and negations that can be made about a concept—without reference to the concept's dependence on objects. In this way, it would simply ignore the fact that the very *determination* of a concept implies a relationship to distinct objects. And as a consequence, it would begin to belittle or misdirect the activity of the Slave.

2) The Slave, on the other hand, as that self-consciousness which toils upon objects and re-forms them, gives objects the form of consciousness. It raises them to the level of concepts, the level at which to deal with objects is equivalent to dealing with oneself (since concepts at one and the same time incorporate objectivity and the self). Thus indirectly the Slave self-consciousness is enabled to become object to itself, and indeed to become the personification of the objectification of self-consciousness. Realizing this fact, the Slave begins to show a tendency to take delight in its own power of drawing the determinancy of particular forms into the unity of its concepts—of subsuming the particular into the infinity of the universal (that otherness which is implied by the very nature of determinateness). If this tendency takes root, the Slave will start acting on its own in its "work," without submitting to the more universal insights of the

STOICISM, SCEPTICISM, AND THE UNHAPPY CONSCIOUSNESS

recapitulation

A. Master $\Big\}$ *Slave*

transition to Stoicism

B.

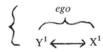

C. transition to Scepticism

A. Recapitulation of preceding chapter: The Slave consciousness, assimilating the otherness of the Master, comes to find otherness within himself, and is correspondingly set free from external otherness.

B. The Master-Slave dichotomy becomes transformed into a dichotomy or duality existing *within* the individual personality. The duality exists between X, the self-identity of the ego; and Y, the otherness of the ego, manifested through its power of forming multiple determinate concepts, all "other" to one another.

C. A dichotomy emerges between X', the abstract self-identity of the ego; and Y', the otherness and contradiction which the sceptical ego produces in the empirical world through the power of intellectual negativity.

STOICISM, SCEPTICISM, AND THE UNHAPPY CONSCIOUSNESS (cont.)

The "Unhappy Consciousness"

D.   *Self-Consciousness* Y^2 $\Big\}$ X^2

E.   *Self-Consciousness* Y^3 $\Big\}$ $\Big\{$ X^3

                              $Y^4 \longleftrightarrow X^4$

F.

                              The Rational Self

                              (Reason)

D. The empirical ego (Y^2), conscious of its own changeability and self-contradiction, seems to lose sight of its unchangeable self-identity and unity. It begins to project this unchangeable unity (X^2) into a vague "beyond," conceived as something objective but indefinable.

E. The "Unchangeable" unity which transcends consciousness, takes on some determinate form (X^3), and becomes more readily intelligible to the Unhappy Self-consciousness (Y^3).

F. Self-consciousness, coming into reconciliation with the Absolute Unchangeable, becomes absolutely reconciled with itself (i.e. it brings about a reconciliation of self-identical unity and self-differentiating otherness within itself). The resulting *unity* of unity and otherness in consciousness, is a new stage of consciousness–Reason.

Master. In other words, the Slave finds that it no longer need depend on the Master to instill universality *and* the aura of self-consciousness into its determinate activity: for in the very act of "producing" determinate concepts from particular forms, it can gain both universality and the certitude of self-consciousness for itself.

Stoicism, which is also a historical event, represents one temporary impasse in the drive towards the final resolution of the conflict between Master and Slave. In this attitude, the two aforementioned tendencies towards independence are "brought to a head," and a new type of self-consciousness appears in the world.[1] For the stoical self-consciousness is one that

> finds its essence neither in its "other," nor in the pure abstraction of ego; but rather in ego which contains otherness within it—under the form of the distinctions of thought.[2]

1) The stoical self-consciousness does not "find its essence in its 'other,' " since the Slave disregards the wishes of the Master, and re-works objectivity into that conceptual form which suits him best.

2) Neither does it "find its essence in the pure abstraction of ego." For although the Master can boast of a certain perfection as the self-identity of ego in abstract isolation—it is nevertheless imperfect, insofar as it has a covert dependence on the Slave's compliance with its demands.

3) It finds its essence, rather, "in ego which contains otherness within it—under the form of the distinctions of thought." That is, it goes one step beyond the Master-Slave duality. The abstract ego of the *Master* now need no longer depend on the Slave in order to come to unity with otherness—since it discovers essential otherness, and essential objectivity, in its own determinate concepts. The otherness-to-ego of the *Slave* now need no longer depend on the more universal rulings of the Master to come to unity with self-consciousness, because it has realized one of the characteristics of the "determinate concept"—namely, that the determinate concept *is* self-consciousness with all its power of universal negativity. Stoical self-consciousness, then, both from the side of the Master and of the Slave, finds its essence in the determinate concept, which is a union of self-conscious "content" with the "otherness" of the universal context of objectivity. Thus otherness now arises from the very *determinateness* of self-consciousness as incorporated in its concepts:

> The determinate. . .has nothing stable in itself, and *has to* vanish before thought; since when something is "distinct" it *ipso facto* does not subsist in itself, but has its essence only in another.[3]

Self-consciousness thus now comes to find a new infinitude of freedom (existence-for-self) in its power of making thought-constituted distinctions, and becomes intrinsically related to otherness (existence-in-self) as these distinctions disappear into one another, to reveal objectivity-in-general.

But the stoical self-consciousness has certain rather obvious deficiencies: For one thing, insofar as it concentrates on purely conceptual distinctions, it lacks tangible content, and does not apprehend reality explicitly, in all its details.[4] For another thing, it has not fully negated otherness, but simply takes on the role of an indifferent observer who "allows determinate otherness to negate itself."[5]

Self-consciousness at this point ignores the former deficiency and concentrates on the latter; and in so doing carries stoicism to its logical extreme—to *scepticism*.

The "sceptical" self-consciousness goes a few steps further. It does not simply produce "*self*-negating" distinctions (distinctions which come into relationship with their "negative" from the very fact that they are determinations set in the context of their delimiting milieu)—but begins to produce distinctions *only* for the purpose of negating them through the power of conscious activity.

The stoical self-consciousness had been content to come into union with otherness by the very act of producing determinate concepts. But the sceptical self-consciousness desires to make this union complete by actively *creating* otherness, by actively concentrating on the determinate limitations of concepts, and *making* them disappear into their negative.[6] In this way the sceptical self-consciousness hopes to acquire full experiential knowledge of the freedom of thought (freedom from the contingency and apparent autonomy of objectivity or "otherness").

> In Scepticism, the negative dialectic process is now a moment of that peculiar self-consciousness to which it does not merely "happen" that— without knowing how—its truth and its reality disappear; but which itself, with full certainty of its freedom, "permits" any "other" which pretends to reality to vanish before its sight.[7] ... Let self-sameness be shown to this self-consciousness, and it points out difference; but then again, let this difference, which it had just pointed out, be held up before its eyes, and it passes over to the other side to point out sameness.[8]

But as Scepticism goes about its vocation of negating every determinate content that shows its head, and even of negating any negations that gain prominence—it cannot help but notice that it also has an empirical ego, and that this empirical ego is continually presupposing and coming into contact with ideas or entities which Scepticism had supposedly brought to naught. And so the otherness which it had purportedly brought under its complete control is continually making inroads upon the life of self-consciousness, and showing itself to be as yet unassimilated. The sceptical self-consciousness finds itself caught in a transparent self-contradiction.

And thus the dichotomy of self-and-other, which had been partitioned among two separate consciousnesses in the Master-Slave relationship, and had apparently dissolved into a thought-unity in the individual Stoical self-consciousness, now with the maturation of the Sceptical self-consciousness, shows itself to be just as rampant as ever—albeit now relegated to one self-consciousness rather than two. And the dichotomy as it now appears is just this: On the one hand, self-consciousness,[9] establishing itself in full-blown freedom, shows that it is negativity itself, negative universality itself, and thus objective otherness-to-self. On the other hand, the empirical ego immerses itself in the natural world in such a way as to posit an otherness which does not seem to be assimilable to self-consciousness, and in such a way as to negate the negations made by self-consciousness. And so, while the sceptical self-consciousness hoped to station itself at a vantage point of negativity which would render it forever impregnable and unchangeable, the empirical ego is caught in the midst of changeable objects which seem to resist being caught up into the negative universalizing activity of self-consciousness. Thus the conflict which is now taking place in the individual soul is a conflict of unchangeable self-subsistence versus self-alienation in a changeable world. Thus also we pass to the next stage of self-consciousness—the *Unhappy Consciousness*—i.e., the alienated soul which has become cognizant of its duality.

This Unhappy Consciousness is straightway beset by a paradox: The opposition or duality which it feels, is taking place within *itself*. Thus there is an immediate and implicit *unity*, which brings it about that the "unchangeable" self-subsistent consciousness and the "changeable" empirical ego are both referred to a single (self-alienated) soul. For as the Unhappy Consciousness first appears it

is itself the gazing of one self-consciousness into another, and is both of these self-consciousnesses at once, while its *essence* is to unify them; but it is not yet explicitly this its essence, it is not yet a *unity*-in-duality.[10]

Thus the Unhappy Consciousness encounters its own unity as something not *de facto* realized, not made objective in consciousness itself. And it therewith rises to the challenge, and takes the merely *projected* state of explicit or objective unity as the *goal* at which it can finally come to rest from its condition of disunion.[11]

The progress of the Unhappy Consciousness toward its projected transcendent unity takes place in three stages:

Self-consciousness, [in proceeding to make explicit the unity of its unchangeable, universal self-transcendence with its changeable and particular empirical ego] passes through the following moments: 1) the Unchangeable opposes itself to particularity in general; 2) the Unchangeable takes on the aspect of a particular opposing itself to self-consciousness as another particular; and 3) the (universal) Unchangeable is effectively united with the particular.[12]

1) THE STAGE OF THE OPPOSITION OF THE UNCHANGEABLE TO PARTICULARITY:

In this stage, the Unchangeable is an external, alien being, a transcendent "beyond" vaguely apprehended but hardly graspable. Self-consciousness,[13] which is continually involved in a seesaw between the contradictory poles of change and changelessness, comes to look upon the Unchangeable as essential stability, unaffected by that apparent contradiction between change and changelessness. Self-consciousness, on its side, correspondingly takes on the aspect of the "unessential," as regards its relationship to the attainment of unity with the Unchangeable.

If the Unhappy Consciousness is ever to lay hold on the essential, it must free itself from the unessential. But it itself *is* the unessential. Therefore it must strive to free itself from itself. Unable to do this on its own, it turns to the Unchangeable, looking for salvation. But the Unchangeable is a vague "beyond," without form, nameless, not in any way accommodated to the conceptual comprehension of consciousness. Consciousness could tend decisively and effectively towards the Unchangeable only if the latter were a thought-constituted particularity (which it is not).

2) THE STAGE OF THE ASSUMPTION OF PARTICULAR FORM ON THE PART OF THE UNIVERSAL UNCHANGEABLE:

(a) Self-consciousness, not finding the Unchangeable in any definite way, in any definite direction, under any definite form—finds itself in a predicament analogous to the situation of a man with the power of sight who is searching for something in a dark room: He must forget about trying to find his objective by sight, and start to feel around for it. So also consciousness, seeking out the Unchangeable, must now suspend its conceptual faculties, and revert to the immediacy of *sensibility*. It strives, therefore, to draw near to the Unchangeable through feeling and devotion and infinite yearning.[14]

In these efforts, however, self-consciousness does not attain much in the way of objective results; the "results" are predominantly subjective: It begins only to be conscious of its own nothingness as it pits its existence against the transcendence of the Unchangeable; and it begins only to be acutely aware of its own particularity, as it strives to elevate itself to the universality of the Unchangeable. And since the Unchangeable "appears" only in the transitory guise of a sensuously-constituted imaginative projection, and does not, strictly speaking, have any stable conceptual form—consciousness also comes to realize that it is involved in a continual vanishing process. Consciousness, precisely because of its sensuous orientation, is constantly preparing for itself a "grave of existence," i.e., a pseudo-transcendence which, because it is *essentially* a vanishing process, is death.

(b) Consciousness now sets itself the task of finding the Unchangeable in more stable form,[15] i.e., as a universal particular, as a thought-constituted particularity. It becomes related to the Unchangeable in the attitude of *hope*—since it is always a contingency whether or not the Unchangeable will reveal itself, or continue to reveal itself, to consciousness, in some definite form.

When the Unchangeable begins to reveal itself, consciousness takes its stand as an *active present* which assimilates and nullifies *passive reality,* bringing the latter, so to speak, into the "light of Day." (In the context here, "active present" means that which consciousness seems to do freely and autonomously, while "passive reality" means that which seems to be done for, or done to, consciousness, or presented to consciousness *ab extra*.) But both poles in this relationship—the active and the passive—begin to dissolve into one another. The passive reality which consciousness seems to be actively forming into particular universality, is, from another point of view, something being actively and spontaneously offered to consciousness by the Unchangeable, which supplies the conditions for a union with passive reality in the first place. Then again, the active force, the existence-for-self, which consciousness is continually making use of in sublating reality—is, from another point of view, a passively received gift (a talent, a faculty, a power), an object existing in-itself, given to consciousness by the Unchangeable.

Thus a dichotomy appears in both the passive reality and the active force—a dichotomy which is a symbol of consciousness itself, as "a reality broken in sunder." If consciousness "gives thanks" for the revelation of the universal in the particular, it immediately afterwards comes to realize that in a very real way it is just giving thanks to itself (the one who has brought the revelation to the fore in himself). Consciousness consequently, after having attempted to lose itself in its enlightened strivings, paradoxically finds itself, and only itself, as the genuine reality. It returns to itself, then, puzzled, and with the apprehensive intimation that it is hemmed in by its own determinate self.

(c) As a result, consciousness takes a negative attitude towards its own *particularity*, which prevents its activity and enjoyment from having any universal significance. And since its particularity seems in a special way to be epitomized in the functions of animal life which human beings are subject to, and in the various sensory operations—it turns against these, and negates them (through asceticism, Rationalism, etc.). But in doing this, it gives these functions and operations a fixedness of being and meaning which they had not had before. In accentuating them the more, it only succeeds in giving them the greater significance.[16]

At this point, being aware of its utmost destitution and misery, consciousness chooses the only possible "step forward:" a nullification of its own existence, through a conscious sacrifice to the will and counsel of the Unchangeable.[17] It thus tries once and for all to make explicit the relation which it has suspected all along to be implicit in the dynamics of self-consciousness.

The *relation* which consciousness then proceeds to establish with the Unchangeable, insofar as this relation is the conscious "middle term" which mediates between the individual and the universal—is itself a new type of consciousness, a conscious "mediator." Or, to put it another way, when self-consciousness relates its own self decisively to its own absolute "other" self, the "mediator" comes on the scene—i.e., the mediated relation itself, which is also a consciousness. Hegel gives an adumbration of this "moment" in the Preface to the *Phenomenology:* "That which returns upon itself is a self; and the self is precisely a unified self-sameness *relating* itself to itself."[18] Self-consciousness then transfers to this mediating consciousness[19] its guilt, its freedom of decision,[20] its self-certainty, and its equipage and possessions. Thus in a negative, roundabout way, by negating its own proper will, and executing what it does not understand—it begins not only to negate its own particularity, but also to affirm its will as other, i.e., as the *universal* will.[21]

3) THE STAGE OF THE UNION OF THE ABSOLUTE "OTHER SELF" WITH THE DE-
TERMINATE INDIVIDUAL SELF:

As consciousness thus abandons itself to the action of the absolute "other," a
new kind of object and a new kind of action merge in a new kind of unity for
consciousness—all of which is a harbinger of a coming reversal of the self-alienation of the Unhappy Consciousness. For the individual consciousness has now
risen to the state where it is no longer at dialectical odds with internal otherness,
but implicitly (i.e., in a negative way, through renunciation) has made the action
of the universal "other" into its own action. It will not, however, be responsible
for absolute action explicitly, until it arrives at the fullness of spirit—i.e., that
stage where it no longer even considers this absolute action as an "other," but in
the strictest sense is able to posit it as its *own*. But nevertheless, in this absolute
action, posited implicitly in its particularity, consciousness has *ipso facto* likewise come to an implicit realization of *Reason.* For Reason is just the faculty for
seeing "otherness," the "beyond," as expressing itself universally and immanent-
ly in the world, and in self-consciousness.

PART THREE. THE UNIFICATION OF
CONSCIOUSNESS AND SELF-CONSCIOUSNESS[1]

A. The Dawn of Reason

1. "THE RATIONAL IS THE REAL": REASON SEEKS THE TRUE MEANING OF THIS
INSIGHT

Self-consciousness has passed through the preliminary stages of sensory awareness, perception, and understanding, where it negated otherness as something
existing in-itself. It has also followed the path to and through the unhappy
self-consciousness, where it came to negate otherness as something existing just
for-consciousness. Now it finds itself at the vantage point at which it has certainty that

> that which is—or the in-itself—only "is," insofar as it is an object *for*
> *consciousness*; and that which is for-consciousness, must also be something
> in-itself.[2]

Thus self-consciousness, now in union (albeit a negative union) with absolute
objective-subjective otherness, had proceeded through a demonstration of the
dialectics of its own processes to the immediate and bare certainty of the truth
that "consciousness is all reality."[3] This is the standpoint of Reason;[4] and
consciousness, as "Reason," is the consciousness which is implicitly all things,
and which comprehends in itself all difference (insofar as it has come to an
immediate comprehension of absolute difference in itself, "before" it has been

initial transitions

A.   Reason

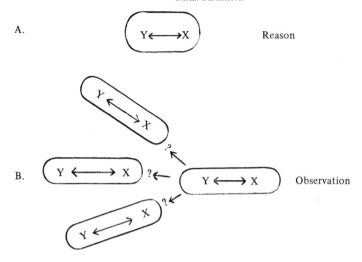

B.   Observation

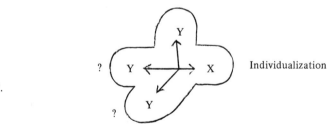

C.   Individualization

A. After the Unhappy Self-Consciousness has overcome its alienation, there is an implicit union of ego and otherness, thought and being, subject and object, inner and outer. This union is Reason.

B. Reason is (subjectively) certain that it is the union of these opposites. However, it has the desire of seeing this union as an (objective) truth. Thus theoretical reason begins the process of "Observation," in which it searches in nature for evidence of the union of "inner and outer." It begins with inorganic nature, proceeds to organic nature, and terminates with inquiries into the psychic and physical nature of man. But it is not quite successful in finding the evidence it was looking for, in any of these observations.

C. Practical Reason then realizes that, in *self-expression* it brings about some kind of union between inner and outer, subject and object, etc. It then proceeds to examine various kinds of self-expression, including erotic love, moral egocentrism, and moral idealism. All it finds in these observations, however, is an abstract union of inner and outer.

final transitions

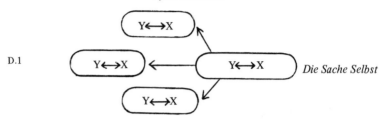

D.1   *Die Sache Selbst*

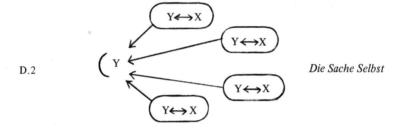

D.2   *Die Sache Selbst*

D.3   *Die Sache Selbst*   Union with the Ethical Substance

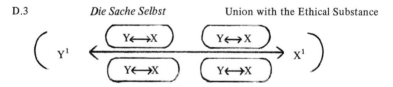

D.1 Reason then begins to see that the concrete union of inner and outer is to be found in *human activity and work.* First of all, it examines how an individual consciousness, in expressing itself in work, comes into a relationship with the expression which other individual consciousnesses give to *themselves* in work.

D.2 Then it examines the function of Law as a general or universal expression resulting from, and produced by, individuals.

D.3 Finally, however, in the process of testing the various laws for self-consistency, it discovers that the basic "law" is not an expression or operation of individuals at all, but a pre-condition for all "concrete" human operations. This basic law is the union of the individual with the universal "ethical substance," or social consciousness. And with this final union the reconciliation of inner and outer, subject and object, etc. is complete.

elaborated into a plurality of differences).

This appearance of Reason as the equation of reason with reality, is itself the basic or generic *Category*—on which basis other specifically different categories can now be further deduced or elaborated. But the fact that Reason at this point appears only as the generic Category, also implies that it is here at the merely abstract moment of its existence, where

> it does not yet comprehend how the unity of self-consciousness is *Being* in its absolute *negativity*—a comprehension which of its very nature would need to comprise in its scope negation itself, distinction and difference itself.[5]

In other words, Reason has just arrived at the stage where it realizes the unity-in-difference of the "unity of apperception" with the "manifold of presentation," of thought and being, of subject and object, of inner and outer.[6] The "difference" of the opposites at this immediate stage is a difference which is immediately dissolved in their transparent abstract unity. If Reason wishes to fully comprehend the significance of this immediate insight, it must go on now to show just *how* thought is related to being in all particular types of cases, or derived categories.

In order to arrive at this latter comprehension—which would amount to its full "truth"—it must abandon its sense of immediate certainty, and, by a painstaking process of *reflection,* show how the pure generic category is related to the specific modes of subject/object unity which are implicit in it:

> Since the manifold subordinate categories are species of the pure generic category, we would have to say that the latter, as their genus or essence, is by no means set in contradiction to them. But still, the subordinate categories come on the scene as an ambiguous type of being which, because of the very *multiplicity* of its specific modes, implies an *otherness* set up over against the pure Category. Thus *de facto* there is a certain contradiction here, because of this multiplicity; and so the pure categorical subject/object unity must go on to assimilate these species to itself, thus bringing about a higher negative unity-in-differences.[7]

Thus the immediate task facing Reason is to confront its different particular categories in their multiplicity, and to demonstrate in what sense it comprehends in itself the absolute unity of all such differences. Each specific mode of subject/object unity-in-difference must be examined on its own merits, and then brought into a higher unity-in-difference with the first category. As this process takes place, the first category of the unity-in-difference of thought and being will thus lose the abstract character of its first formulation by Idealism, and become individualized and concretized by means of the orderly deduction of its various species.

Idealism, as the philosophical insight which has risen to comprehend the meaning of the first generic category, must beware of becoming arrested at this abstract insight, without going on to comprehend it in the fullness of its concrete applications.

Thus true Idealism must be distinguished from that abstract, pseudo-idealism which, without *demonstrating* the absolute intrinsic unity of the self with the other, merely reposes in its intuitive certainty that reason is all reality, but then forthwith is immediately faced with an otherness opposing the individual reasoning consciousness—an otherness not effectively sublated: For

> the *Category* . . . consists precisely in this, that self-consciousness and being are one and the same reality; but not "one and the same" in the sense of similars which invite comparison. Rather, the sameness of each with the other is something intrinsic now to the significance of each. It is only a one-sided, unsound, erratic idealism which would establish the unity of the in-itself and the for-itself in consciousness, and then obliviously allow the in-itself to come on the scene again in its pristine aspect of unassimilated opposition.[8]

Such an "unsound" idealism thus has to backtrack and deal once again with opposing otherness. It begins again to treat objects as if it were still immersed in the attitudes of sensation, perception and understanding; as if it were still investigating some immediate otherness external to itself, and not sublated by consciousness. Thus also it ends up trying to overcome the abstract nature of the basic insights of Idealism by combining idealism with a bastard empiricism. In other words, it begins again to consider objects in a pre-"rational" context, and then uses such objects—which it admits to be non-truth—to contribute to the "truth" of the certainty of Reason. In so doing, it is merely filling up its empty ego-certitude with a purely arbitrary content.[9]

Finally, true Idealism must also be distinguished from the (Kantian) brand of idealism, which never rose to the insight concerning the necessary unity of being and thought: and thus deduced "categories" which fell short of necessity, and indeed were created in a rather haphazard way—on the basis of the various types of judgement which just happen to be distinguished in logic.

True Idealism, on the other hand, both possesses the authentic Category in its necessity, and has the proper orientation towards the "phenomenal" world. It faces the variegated otherness of the world of nature which it *knows* to be rational, although it still *seems* to be something alien to Reason; and it prepares itself to observe and test nature, to find out just exactly in what sense its certainty about the rationality of nature is to be taken. It therefore begins with an examination of nature, although it might conceivably have taken some other tack to transcend its immediate abstract state as unity-in-division.

Reason begins gropingly to tap the mines of nature, searching for veins of conscious life. It strains itself to appropriate the manifold diversity of the world of nature, by molding it into the patterns of Reason—in the fond hope that after it has proceeded far enough, nature will begin spontaneously to manifest its intrinsic rationality.

The upshot of this stage of conscious rational *Observation* will be that Reason will discover only its *imprint* in nature—not its very self; not the Concept in some sort of sensuous expression; not Reason's implicit identity with nature as something finally made explicit. For these latter goals can only be attained at the end of consciousness' voyage of discovery, when and if substance has become subject, and is known explicitly as such.

a. *Reason's Observation of Inorganic Nature:*[10] The instinct of Reason in its immediacy now proceeds to draw the world of inorganic nature into something of a conscious unity, and to render it more accessible and familiar by classifying and arranging its material elements. But in the beginning of this process it is immersed in sensuous phenomena, and has not come to complete knowledge of its own nature; and thus it tends to consider the unifications and classifications which it makes—the laws of chemistry, physics, geology, etc.—as immanent in sensory data, and as if drawn from these latter. It fails to recognize that, if it were consistent, it would have to go through all individual cases before making any particular "law"—*if* the necessity and validity of the law did really arise purely from its empirical basis. It justifies the procedure of induction, on the basis of the *analogy* of unexamined cases to examined cases, and on the basis of the *probability* that this holds forth for the investigator. But no probability is tantamount to truth. And thus inevitably Reason meets problems at the "limits of universality"—i.e., at those misty, exceptional individual cases which are always showing up and disproving universal laws.

The proper avenue of approach for Reason would be to recognize that the "universality" of law is purely its own creation. Even when it is seemingly approaching the singular instance for the sake of observation, Reason is doing this in conformity to its *own* universal law. For the universal laws of positive and negative electricity, acids and bases, etc.—do not possess any stable foundation in the sensory world. They are neither determinate bodies nor the determinate properties of perceptible bodies (e.g., negative electricity is not a property of resin, although it might be discovered through experiments with resin). In short, the laws do not appear to us at all as a sensuous or corporeal "other," but as an otherness constituted in and through consciousness itself, i.e., the otherness and objectivity of the *concept.* Thus these laws pervade the appearance of things, without *residing* in any of them. Far from being the laws of the appearances, they are the laws of disappearance, i.e., the disappearance of the different types of matter—e.g., acidic matter—into their opposites.

Reason can only come into full effective control of these its own laws, when it recognizes this "disappearing" characteristic of the universal structures which are denoted by the laws. For only then will it cease to deal with these laws as if they were mysterious, erratic, mutually conflicting, largely unpredictable, "thing-like" entities, offering a certain irresistible opposition to the efforts of consciousness to control them.

Reason should also realize that the various types of "matter" which it deals with by means of its laws, are likewise constructs of the mind[11]—determinate predicates which the necessary notions of law endow with a separate subsistence from sensuous facts, which supply the adventitious conditions for their investigation.

Those, however, who view physical law as that which "ought to be," but may not-be, are simply getting lost in the wilds of terminology. For

> what is universally validating, is also universally valid; what *ought* to be,
> *ipso facto* is. And if something should be, but is not—its truth is not.[12]

In other words, both the necessity and the *existence* of a law are intrinsically found in, and attributable to, consciousness itself: and thus, in every true law, to say that "it ought to be" is identical with saying that "it is."

b. *Reason's Observation of Organic Nature:* In view of the fact that we are coming at this point to an examination of "living" beings, it might be well to recall the unique and all-encompassing meaning which Hegel attaches to the term, "Life."

As was mentioned earlier (Part II, A), "Life" is primarily used by Hegel to connote the process in which otherness is continually becoming selfhood, and subjectivity is continually becoming objective.

We are now situated in the aftermath of the stage where self-consciousness became "Reason," i.e., a subjectivity implicitly aware of its union with all of objectivity. Reason in its "Observations" is now trying to find an echo in the world to reflect its "Life" (which consists in this union of subjectivity and otherness). By this means, it hopes to corroborate this basic awareness which it has.

When it turned to the inorganic world, however, it did not find a union of subjectivity and otherness; but rather, the subjective aspect—universal laws governing inorganic phenomena—sundered itself sharply from the "otherness" of corporeal existence.

Reason now turns to organic nature, hoping there to find objects which will faithfully reflect the union or fusion of subjectivity and objectivity in Reason.

In an elaborate and detailed investigation, Reason finally will come to concentrate passionately on finding a linkage between an "inner" and an "outer" in organic beings—even making fine distinctions about the "inner of the outer" and the "outer" of the "outer"—but all to no avail.

Finally, Reason in desperation will turn its attention to man, to examine various aspects of the empirical ego—but even there will be unable to find an adequate reflection of the certainty it had.

But then, by a kind of negative rebound, Reason also will come to understand the unique way in which "inner" and "outer" are conjoined in itself.[13]

In organic nature, there seems to be an incorporation or incarnation of "universal law" in the material world. For organisms rise so far above the elements from which they are constituted, that they cannot be explained even in terms of the determinate "matters" which the mind distinguishes and draws into the unity of its own universal laws. In other words, we cannot so easily say, with regard to organisms, that they are regulated by extrinsic *all-pervasive* laws not ascribable to any particular body, or sets of bodies, or properties of bodies. But rather, each organism seems to embody its law, and to be a law to itself, i.e., to draw all of its particular constituents into a universal unity which the organism itself gives, has, and *is.*[14]

How can this be so? Do organisms have the universalizing negative unity of existence-for-self, like consciousness? Do they create concepts? What is the nature of this inner mechanism which gives unmistakable evidence of some sort of existence-for-self? And how is this inner reality related to the outer expressions of organic life?

Reason hopes that by striving to answer such questions it will find a reflection of, and thus a clue to the understanding of, its own certitude of being in unity with the otherness of the world. Being unable as yet to turn into itself as an object to be observed, it must continue to examine nature in order to make its own immediate certitude of the unity of thought and being more explicit, and thus also more "true."

Reason at this point in its examination of nature is entranced by its discovery of a life analogous to its own life, in observable objects. It does not realize that the only life it can ever "find" is its own:

> Self-consciousness. . .finds itself as a thing, as a "life," but hastens to make a distinction between what it is and what it has "found." The distinction, however, doesn't exist. For just as the instinct of a brute animal, when it seeks out food and consumes it, brings forth in this activity naught but itself—so also instinctive Reason, in this phase of observation is finding nothing but its own life.[15]

Having made this first artificial distinction, Reason begins to make others. As if to counterbalance the *in*distinct unity of its apprehension of its own subject-object relationship, it begins to discern "distinctions" of inner and outer in organic beings, distinctions which are not easily unified.

Thus Reason comes at the outset to "observe" a dichotomy between the self-preserving tendency (existence-for-self) of organisms, and their teleology. The former is construed as something phenomenally observable, while the latter is relegated to the noumenal order (i.e., it is apprehended as "inner purpose," attributable perhaps to some divine intelligence, but certainly not attributable to the organic things themselves). Reason at this point is being quite arbitrary. For "purposiveness" is nothing but a subsumption of immediate existence into, and according to, the intentions of the self: thus it is an existence-for-self. And thus, if organisms really *expressed* an inherent existence-for-self, they would *ipso facto* be also expressing an immanent teleology.

But Reason, carried away by what seems to it to be a clear insight into the essential factors in organic existence, turns all of its attention now to this distinction of "inner" purpose and "outer" self-preservation. It conceives them as if they were two separate realities, each having certain definite determinations and limits. And on the basis of this prejudiced view, it proceeds now to try to determine the precise relationship between these two independent factors. It hypothesizes that the inner is related to the outer as the concept is related to reality; and from this it comes to formulate the law that *"the outer is the expression of the inner."* And it seeks now to find out just *how* the outer expresses the inner.

In formulating the above law, Reason does not fully understand the relationship between the "outer" and the "inner" (and in the strict sense there can be no relationship, since there is really no distinction), but only sees them as two formal aspects of the organic being, which each seem to have their own proper, peculiar content. The "inner," of course, is contrived to be the hidden aspect, outside the grasp of Observation, but needing to be presupposed to give rationality to that which is observed.[16]

The "inner" aspect is then further analyzed in terms of its own constituent moments; and the result of this analysis is that we come to classify the intrinsic teleology of organic nature in terms of the three essential life-orientations—*sensibility, reactivity,* and *reproduction.*[17] For the organic being is conceived as having an inner correlate to the existence-for-self which it manifests; and this inner correlate we call "sensibility." Again, in the very act of explicating its existence for-self, it becomes therewith being-for-another; and this we call the aspect of "reactivity." And finally, the aspect of "reproduction" expresses the fact that, for the *genus* to become for-itself, the individual must necessarily separate itself from itself, either producing a part of itself in separation or a whole individual.

As these inner orientations become explicated in their "outer" moments, however, they do not appear as determinate, isolatable universals, but coincide mutually with one another. And thus it comes about that sensibility, which is primarily located in the nervous system, coincides in certain ways with reproduction, which is primarily in the visceral areas. And the same "coinciding" character is to be found in the relationship of these two aspects to reactivity, which is primarily located in the muscular system. For example, sensibility considered in itself, in its *active* aspect of existing-for-itself, becomes re-active irritability.

Thus we must conclude on this basis that the distinctions of sensibility, reactivity, and reproduction are only logical distinctions, distinctions in the *concept* of the "organic"; and do not carry over *qua* distinct into the externalities of organic activities.

As a corollary, we must likewise conclude—with reference to the sphere of *measurable externalities*—that it is a mistake to think that the quantity of reactivity is really inversely proportional to the quantity of sensibility, etc.[18] For we could with just as much logic say that the quantity of re-activity (as a kind of negative expression of sensibility) is directly proportional to that of sensibility. Thus indeed we find that it is meaningless to affirm that the inner distinctions must manifest themselves in *any* measurable way as distinctive externalities. Rather, we find that when we come to this sphere of the external and the quantitative, we are overwhelmed on every side by the arbitrariness and unpredictability of nature—at least as regards the way it must subjectively appear to us. We cannot categorize things in this sphere with "necessity," as we can do in the logical sphere. And so we must be careful to restrict our observations of biological externalities to that which is actually given, and not to read logical laws into these appearances.

It also becomes immediately obvious that, as regards the outer *corporeal structures* of the organs—as well as with the functional externalities mentioned above—we must be careful of interpreting these as something exactly corresponding to inner distinctions of the concept of living organisms. For *in themselves* they are "dead"; and the classifications which anatomy makes of them are just classifications of static structures considered in precision from their organic actualities. For the true expression of the concrete organism, its essential, necessary "outer," would have to consist in movement and process, unless we wish to immerse the concrete significance or organic life in the constrictive abstract[19] confines of mere quantitative corporeal existence.

But *this* essential and necessary "outer" is only hypothesized, it does not appear to us directly. And since the appearances that we have *de facto* to deal with are the externalities of life-manifestations, and the static determinations of life-organs—we seem to come to an impasse, as regards the question of the validity of the original hypothesis we formulated, that "the outer is the expression of the inner." For all distinctive life-actualities are confused with one another at any external level (i.e., they are cancelled through the power of the universal). In order to arrive at a "law" of the relation of the inner (conceptual) to the outer (existent) aspect of life, we would have to turn our attention away from the process by which merely passive and static existence is endlessly superseded and negated by the life processes of an organism; and focus on that other moment, the moment at which these life processes turn back to themselves, i.e., life returns to itself. Par excellence, this would be the moment of thought, the self-contained "genus" which does not need to express itself through corporeal species, but is completely free.[20] This is the moment in which life really comes to exist as a concrete entity. It is also in this moment that the understanding rises above the state in which it merely makes distinctions of essence and existence, universal and individual—and comes to perceive the dynamic transitional relation between such reciprocals, to perceive the process itself in its concrete (individual) universality[21]—in other words, to perceive the true organism. But consciousness finds it difficult to come to an accurate formulation of any such concrete concept from its observations of organic life, for

> this Concept, which is pure freedom, is one and the same life in *all*
> its manifestations, even though its contingent expressions (Life as being-
> for-another) may trail out in ever so many directions. It makes no differ-
> ence to this onrushing flood what sort of mills it drives.[22]

Whether consciousness observes the life of a tree, or a bird, or a horse, it does not see any distinct expressions of life itself, but only distinct living things. Life remains in its freedom, and does not give us any clear idea of its really intrinsic properties from the manifold individuals and species which it parcels out over the earth. So Reason "lowers its aspiration-level" at this point, and ceases to try to formulate any definite laws pertaining to the intrinsic nature of life.

But Reason does not cease to try to make some sense out of its original intimation that "the outer is the expression of the inner." On the contrary, it now re-examines the "outer." It sees that the organism's outer aspect is that which is constituted from, and set up against, and interacting with, the inorganic "other," and tends to merge with that "other." Then on further examination it sees that *this outer aspect is precisely the organism itself,* at its moment of existence-for-another. Finally, amidst the incessant transitions of cancellations taking place between the inorganic and the organic in this sphere where the organism departs from its existence-for-self—it discerns in this exteriority as a whole a new "inner" and a new "outer"; in other words, *it finds an inner-outer relationship in the "outer" itself.*

This *"outer," in its "inner" aspect,* is the passive or "dead" universal of organic form, which reaches its terminus at the zone of the "other" and is set up against this "other" as against a region of the essentially *manifold* expression of life. The "middle term" which brings the organic to the borders of the inorganic manifold (in this inner moment of its outer formulation) is *number.* For number is simple, like the organic form; and is also determinate, like the expression of this form in the sphere of inorganic otherness.[23] Number is thus an inseparable characteristic of the inner aspect of phenomenal life taking on outer determinations.

Besides number, we also find *specific gravity* in this inner aspect of outer life. For this inner is tantamount to a static intrinsic intensity *(Insichsein)* through which the organic being is enabled to manifest itself as if it were inorganic in a stable individual form over against a context of the inorganic "other." And our term, "specific gravity," expresses precisely such prerequisite intensity.

Considered in its concept, the property of specific gravity in an organism does not contain in itself any of those non-essential distinctions which become enmeshed with it as its intensity comes just to the border of the manifold "other." But rather—considered here in abstraction—it has not yet begun to ramify itself extensively in such a way as to finally make it an objective particularized reality in the world of the "other."

The outer phenomenal organism in its "outer" aspect, i.e., at that moment in which the outer form takes on an extension of relations, manifests a differentiation which is not essentially attributable to the purely intensive moment of specific gravity. And this "differentiation" is *quantity.* Quantity itself, since it is not an *essential* distinction canceled in the universality of simple life, cannot be *recognized* as distinct except in the milieu of a plurality of all kinds of other non-essential properties—all of which have no intrinsic purpose in themselves.

Then if we take this outer aspect of the "outer" as a *whole,* construe it in abstraction as "self-existence *in* otherness," or "cohesion"—we would finally have, with *cohesion,* an "outer" outer offering a diametrical correlate to the "inner" outer of specific gravity.

But *our attempt to formulate a law governing the relationship* of this "inner outer" to that "outer outer," is bound to end up again in a deadlock. For there is not extant any direct or inverse proportion between the specific gravity of an organism and any properties taken from the side of the organism's extensive cohesion.

What is more, in concentrating upon the inner and outer aspect of the outer organism, we have abandoned the organism *qua* living, and concentrated on the organism *qua* inorganic, i.e., *qua* taking on characteristics of a stable, quantitatively analyzable "thing." Thus also we have lost sight of the freedom of the true organic inner, which is the freedom of the universal genus, indifferent to its particular embodied form. We have contented ourselves with examining the more manifest freedom of the "inner of the outer" (the "inorganic" inner of the organism)—a freedom which appears as an *existent,* when the organism considered inorganically takes its stand as determinate, and thus free in a special way from the manifold otherness outside itself. In other words, we have abandoned the true universal negativity of life for the particular negativity of number:

> Determinateness in the inorganic is the simple negative which counterbalances the moment of being-there-for-another; and this simple negative is, in its ultimate particular determinacy, a *number.* But the organic exemplifies a special kind of particularity which is *pure negativity,* and *ipso facto* cancels that static determinateness of number which obtains in the more homogeneous types of being.[24]

How, then, are we to conduct an examination of that *pure negativity* which is truly and completely reflection-upon-self? This pure negativity, if it realized itself in terms of its own abstract, universal moment, would be nothing else but *thought.* But in *nature,* it cannot express itself as determinate thought, but rather as the determinate *species* which become embodied in individuals through the agency of the inner and outer "outer" (the inner and outer quantitative aspects). But it does not unfold its intrinsic *universality* in organisms.[25] And this very fact gives us indication that its proper outer expression in "nature" could only be a *universal individual* [26] falling outside the various particular organic embodiments.

If we wanted to understand organic life in its universality, then, we should turn to an examination of this universal individual. But what "middle term" do we have for conducting this examination?

In this *Phenomenology,* in order to examine the nature of the "spirit" which appears in empirical consciousness, we have chosen as our "middle terms" the Forms of Consciousness, in which we find a concrete development of the self-reflection of spirit in terms of dialectic necessity. Is there any comparable "middle term" which would allow us to examine the universal life appearing in the universal individual? Such a middle term would have to combine the *definiteness* of the genus (in the species) and the *singleness* of the universal individual, and be open to the perceptual observation of Reason.

Obviously such a middle term does not exist. But rather, the two "extremes" in organic nature—the genus and the universal individual—"fall apart." And, as the appearances would have it, they are at odds with each other:

> The genus. . .suffers. . .violence from the side of the universal individual. . .in which universality does not in any way fall short of congruous actual expression. . .namely, the Earth, which as a universal negativity, supersedes

the systematization of determinate genera by imposing the distinctions germane to itself.[27]

Thus in organic nature we do not *see* life unfolded in its universal inner determinations, but only as life-in-general, which, instead of expressing its distinctions distinctively, unfolds them indifferently as number and a manifold of sense properties; and which, in doing this, is continually challenged by the universal individual (the earth), which is congenitally oriented to mercilessly establishing its own distinctions to the detriment of the orderly unfolding of life.

At least, this is the way universal life appears to us in nature. Thus if we are looking for phenomenal evidence of the merger of universal thought with particular being, and universal Being with the particular self—we would be well advised to turn elsewhere.[28] The most we can get out of a study of organic nature is vague meanings, hazy intimations of a universal life expressing itself rather meekly under the shadow of the wilful capriciousness of Mother Earth.

c. *Reason's Observation of the Human Psyche:* Self-conscious Reason, in seeking to find out in what sense the world is at one with its own spirit, must, if its investigation is to be complete, pass through three phases.[29] Observation of the world of nature; observation of its own spirit; and observation of the relationship of nature to spirit in the individual human being. Having completed the observation of the inorganic and organic world of nature, Reason now turns inward to see whether it can find by an examination of the human psyche any illumination as to the relationship of union between thought and being, inner and outer, subjective form and objective content.

Since we are taking the attitude of *Observation* towards the psyche, however, we must focus precisely on those aspects which have sufficient stability and objectivity to offer themselves as quasi-passive material for classification and critical evaluation. We find only two such aspects: 1) the concepts of the mind, which seem to be mutually interrelated in certain fixed ways, thus giving rise to logical laws; and 2) the acquired attitudes and capacities of the individual personality, which seem to be related in certain fixed ways to the "universals" of a) environmental influence, and b) hereditary endowments.

1) *Logical laws* are the result of man's endeavor to explicate the sole phenomenon which exhibits in itself the opposition of universal-and-individual Life—namely the phenomenon of the concept, or of consciousness *qua* Concept. The Concept, as the unity of the primal oppositions (universal and particular, subjective and objective, singleness and multiplicity, infinite negativity and finite determinations) has a rich content which is only potentially explicit to consciousness. It remains for consciousness, then, to bring the essential conceptual determinations into the negative unity of universality, i.e., to formulate laws relating the various aspects of the concept among themselves. And these laws we commonly refer to as "Logic."

It is commonly objected that such laws are empty, formal abstractions without content; but the main objection against them is just the opposite:

Logical form takes on the aspect of a stable formulation of relationships. . .or indubitable (formal) truth supplying a framework for multiple laws. . . . But when the logicians rip them from their native habitat of mental processes and reestablish them in abstract particularity—it is not content that they lack, for there is a definite content there; but rather form. For they are essentially disappearing moments receiving unity and form from thought itself.[30]

The constructs of logic are thus staticized thought-content, *without* the subjective form that only conscious individuality can and should infuse into them. Thus also they are an "outer" not effectively joined with its "inner," and can give us no worthwhile insights even as to the borderlines or bridges between consciousness and the world.

2) *Psychological laws* result from the inability of consciousness to see intuitively the intrinsic connection of the universal in its self-existence and in its moment of individuality. Thus it is led to formulate a multiplicity of rather tentative laws governing the relationship of the universal moments (habit, customs, passions, faculties, modes of thinking, environment) to the individual modality of reacting spontaneously to, or assimilating, these universals. In emphasizing the universal, it takes up a negative attitude towards singularity and individuality. In emphasizing the individual on the other hand, it takes up a negative attitude towards universal being (which is, nevertheless, also *its* universal being).

It is, however, rather presumptuous to formulate laws governing the influence of universal reality on the individual. The individual man as a spiritual being is himself a universal assimilating the "given" universals of habit, customs, etc., *on his own terms,* and in such a way that that which he does *not* accept through assimilation or consciousness remains *inorganic* (i.e., neither universal nor individual). By no means does everything which comprises the "spherical surface" of the centered individual's "universal influences" find its reflection automatically at that center.

The influence of reality on the individual connotes, if we attend to the power of the individual, the opposite to what it seems to mean: namely, that the individual himself either permits the reality impinging on him to have effect, or else checks and diverts its influence. In the light of this, "psychological necessity" becomes. . .an empty word.[31]

Thus the effect of external circumstances on the individual is determined solely by that individual. And the internal faculties, etc. which seem to affect the way a man thinks, are in reality completely determined by the restless, negative universal thought-activity of the individual, which gives rise to them in the first place.

Upon this realization, the psychological laws about the relationship of universal being to individual consciousness dissolve and lose the stable, "necessary" sense that they had before. And consciousness turns elsewhere now to determine in what sense it is united to objectivity.

d. *Reason's Observation of the Embodied Psyche.* Reason, having failed to observe any necessary relationship between individual consciousness and "universal" influences, makes now a final attempt to determine a thought-being relationship in terms of a new inner-outer relationship—the relationship of the inner determinate activity of the individual *personality* to its outer phenomenal appearance in the human *body*.

The "expression" of the inner by means of the body may be distinguished into 1) the passive, existential expression given to the determinate character of the personality by the general natural shape of the body; and 2) the active organic expression of personality through the "body" of the deeds and thoughts of the individual.

The passive, existential expression given to the inner man by his bodily shape, would seem to be comparable to the arbitrary conventional signs of *language*. For in playing the role of a subsistent natural embodiment, it is like a symbol, giving contingent external expression to some inner meaning.

The active, organic expression through action, on the other hand, would be comparable to the *use* which is made of a language. The individuality accepts its bodily form as the symbolic instrument by which it must express itself, and proceeds to utilize this instrument with greater or lesser facility. But in language itself, one continually finds himself either expressing too much (exposing himself and his meanings maladroitly or superfluously in the words he uses) or expressing too little (in that he is using as his medium conventional words which have a very different nature from the thoughts they are calculated to express). And so also, as regards the expression of a man through his bodily nature, it often happens that the inner man may not find expression, in the case of one who is awkward in expressing himself; or the outer may not truly express the inner, in the case of an intentional deceiver; and so forth. And in general there seems to be an inevitable disproportion between the individual man and the expression he gives to himself by his actions through and in his body.

Palmistry, physiognomy, and *phrenology*—which immediately come to our mind as purporting to give scientific formulation to an inner-outer relationship in man—would seem to have in mind an "outer expression" of the former type, i.e., the passive, existential expression of inner personality.

Palmistry would seem at first glance to differ from pseudo-sciences like astrology, in that it does not seem to be relating two arbitrary things merely externally related to each other, but two aspects intimately connected as "inner" and "outer." For, in a way, the focal point of a man's deeds is in his hands—which seem to give an immediate or primary phenomenal expression of his individual fate (in contrast to the purely external expression of nature and fate which is to be found in his environment). But on further examination it will be seen that the true outer expression of a man's fate and fated character would not be found concentrated in the hands; for fate is itself

> only a phenomenal appearance of some inner unconditioned distinctness which constitutes distinct individuality as something existing in-itself.[32]

Thus the individual's fate could best be described as some unseen inner terminal point at which his personality reflects into itself. But *this* terminal point is an essential in-itself which can *never* become for-consciousness. By definition, it must always remain behind the scenes, as a mystery. If it works itself out in the actions and development of an individual man, we can never point to those actions and that development and say, "that is his *fate.*" For we can never know what other potentialities and dispositions *might* have worked themselves out. And individual fate, by definition, is the sum-total of human potentialities, considered as having an effect on the actual state of a person, but never to be completely identified with any particular actual state.

And so, if we consider such unseen potentialities as reflected in certain bodily features, or even as reflected in a more diffuse way at any arbitrary "arrested" moment of bodily activities—we are still dealing with an existent, determinate "outer," and the indeterminate "inner" still escapes us, and seems to be only contingently connected with the "outer." We can never attain to this in-itself *in itself.*

Physiognomy, which refers the individualization of mind to its physical expression in countenance, and which judges the actuality of mind on the basis of bare, immediate sensuous appearance—must end up in the realm of opinions comparable, in validity, to opinions about what the weather is going to be like tomorrow, etc. For the true actuality of inner mind, and mind's transition into individuality from the non-being of abstract essentiality—consists precisely in the determinate *acts* which cancel this state of abstraction and bring it into reality. "Before" the mind passes into act, there are only vague, abstract possibilities for theft, bravery, murder, beneficience, etc. And thus physiognomy is a pseudo-science for the simple reason that, while it pretends to give necessary connections with actual states of character, it can really go no further than offering simple opinions about bare possibilities on the basis of contingent sense impressions.

Having failed, in palmistry and physiognomy, to find any necessary relationship between the "inner" and an externally articulated corporeal "outer," we turn our attention at last to the *internal* organs. Perhaps these will show themselves to be an "outer" giving adequate expression to the "inner" of man.

The operation of the mind upon the externally articulated organs of man, and upon the outer world, may be attributed in various ways to many non-objectified internal organs, including the spinal cord. But if, relying on the universal assent about the intimate connection of mind with the *brain,* we avoid getting into discussions about the spinal cord, etc.—we may suppose that it is the brain that is the "mediating organ" by which mind, in its moment of purely internal self-distinction, comes to be able to act upon the outer objective articulations, through which immediate sensuous indifference is being continually negated by the present actuality of the individual person. Thus the brain would, under these terms, be mind itself in its *corporeal existence-for-itself.* It would be the primal organ, by which the actions and feeling finding expression in the body are able to be transmitted in as yet *unarticulated* corporeal form to the outer body. Then, if the brain is a bodily for-itself, the *skull* correspondingly takes on the aspect of a bare existent, an *in-itself,* set up over against the brain as something purely indifferent in its static form to the activity of the latter. But now the *connection* between the skull and the brain will be *causal* only if there is involved, in the implicit nature of each, a *necessary* relation to the other.

Phrenology sees in the skull—the *caput mortuum*, as opposed to the brain, or *caput vivum*—the true "outer" of the human mind, the immediate external evidence in stable form of the predominant feelings, moral character, intelligence, etc., of a man. However, in taking this standpoint it gets involved in pure conjectures. For who can relegate the general diffuse feelings which seem to be at the bottom of specific pleasures and pains to a certain part of the skull? Or who can tell me with impunity that by the shape of my head he knows I am a murderer, or should be one if I haven't actually become one? Or who can say with certitude that the skull will expand in such and such parts under impetus from such and such a quantity of intelligence? Indeed all such conjectures, by relying on possibilities, give equal force and validity to the very opposite possibilities. The error of all such thinking lies precisely in this, that it is to give undue attention to the bare possibilities of the implicit mental *dispositions* of a *free* self-consciousness—dispositions whose being is most truly a non-being.

> The primordial being of the mind consists in natural pre-dispositions, over which it exerts free control, or which at least require certain favorable circumstances if they are to attain to actuality. In other words, the "primordial being" of mind is for all practical purposes tantamount to non-being.[33]

We cannot determine the *actualities* of mind on the basis of some arbitrary "necessary relation" to its dead, static form of existence separately in-self and objectively for-consciousness, such as we find in the human skull.[34] For the true actuality of mind could only be found in that formal activity of manifestation of consciousness itself which is neither static (like the skull) nor established in corporeal otherness (like the brain)—but is itself the immediate manifestation of the true *inner* reality of mind.[35]

Paradoxically, rational Observation, having now refuted phrenology, where it found the *worst* possible formulation of the law of the "inner" and the "outer" (i.e., the formulation in which the "inner" is related to an abstract, static existent)—arrives as if by a rebound at its highest point. From viewing *this* "outer" as the expression of the "inner," Reason receives an immediate and necessary impetus into the directly opposite viewpoint—that Reason will never *find* itself existing as "outer," but must *become* its own object through its own activity.

If we recall that Reason started out in the stage of Observation trying to find empirical evidence of the union of thought with being, evidence that "the Mind is (in some way) a Thing,"—we can now attain to a unified overview of the stages Reason has recently passed through, in the following chart:[36]

As we can see from this chart, Reason in its observations makes a complete circle, returning, at the conclusion of its examination of the embodied consciousness, to the identical position that it had begun with—namely, the position that Reason is to be found in the dead, i.e., merely "existent," world; and it therewith rejects that position for the second time.

THE OBSERVATIONS OF REASON

REMOTE SUBJECT OF OBSERVATION	PROXIMATE SUBJECT OF OBSERVATION	RESULT OF OBSERVATIONS IN TERMS OF THE QUESTION "WHAT EVIDENCE IS THERE, THAT 'THE MIND IS A THING'?"
1. the *merely "existent" world*	inorganic nature	the laws of nature revert to the locus of the mind; while their content reverts to the things themselves.
2. the "living" world	organic nature	inner teleology reverts to the locus of a superhuman transcendent Intelligence; while outer existence reverts to the organisms
3. consciousness	logical and psychological laws	form and universality revert to the transcending Mind; while content and particularity revert to the "laws"
4. embodied consciousness	laws about the relation of inner potentialities to outer actualities in man	inner potentialities revert to the locus of Mind-in-itself; while outer actualities revert to the *merely "existent" world*

Observation at the conclusion of all these endeavors comes to the point where

it explicitly realizes what was present to us all along implicitly in its concept—that Reason, after becoming certain of itself, seeks *itself* as objective reality.[37]

Thus Reason is properly its own object; and mind, in a very real sense, *is* a thing. But it is important to understand just in *what* sense the mind is a thing:

The proposition that "the mind is a thing" has a true and a false connotation:

1) *Its true connotation* is that mind has passed from the stage of the "unhappy Consciousness," in which it gradually rose to an immediate, incipient, implicit union *with* objectivity; through the moment of Reason, in which it *was* objectivity (i.e., in which the coincidence of the processes of consciousness and self-consciousness first became apparent); and through the stage of Observation, where it concentrated on the aspect of consciousness, as opposed to self-consciousness (i.e., tried to apprehend in what sense "the mind is a *thing*"); and now is prepared to examine the other aspect, the aspect of self-consciousness (to find out in what sense "the *mind* is a thing").

It must be remembered throughout that Reason has gotten well beyond those initial stages of understanding where consciousness could only formulate finite laws, and finite combinations of subject plus predicate. When it realizes that "the mind is a thing," it realizes this as an "infinite" judgement, in which subject and predicate mutually engender and cancel each other (see Ch. III.C). But it still remains for it to inspect both the subject and the predicate, from their own proper sides, to come to a full knowledge of the significance of this infinite judgement. Having concentrated on the predicate, it now proceeds to the subject, to "mind:" not to find mind in things, after the manner of conscious objectivity; but to produce thinghood from mind, after the manner of a self-conscious subjectivity.

2) *Its false connotation* is that which is implied by a literal interpretation of the words, and in the context of a "finite" judgement—namely, that mind somehow finds its objective expression as a thing of sense, in the skull, the brain fibres, etc. This is to do violence to Reason by combining the opposites of thing and mind in an arbitrary way. The process of Observation has shown in a negative way that such a procedure is futile, as being a departure from the pristine purity of the infinite judgement. Indeed, when such a vulgar understanding of the statement that "mind is a thing," finds itself alongside its pristine and profound significance—we have something comparable to nature's paradox of combining the sublimest function of procreation and the low, or vulgar, function of urination in the same bodily organ.

2. "THE MIND IS A THING:" CONSCIOUSNESS COMES TO "FIND" THE MIND AS A THING BY CREATING THINGHOOD OUT OF THE MIND

By way of introduction to the following sections, it would be well to recall for the moment the processes that Consciousness underwent during its stage of Understanding. The "Infinite Concept," which came to the fore as the *result* of the developments of Understanding, was implicit in the beginning, in the notion of Force. But consciousness did not confront it directly in the beginning, but had to work gradually towards the terminal moment at which the Infinite Concept itself became the in-itself which engaged the attention of consciousness, and thus became an object for-consciousness. And then, finally, since the Infinite Concept brought *subjectivity* into focus in objectivity, Consciousness through consideration of the Infinite Concept became transformed into Self-Consciousness; and thus we passed into the stages of Self-Consciousness proper.

A parallel process has taken place during the stages of Observation. Reason in the beginning was the generic Category of the union of consciousness and self-consciousness. This generic category was not explicitly perceived in the beginning, but was only implicit in all the objective appearances that consciousness still had to deal with. But Reason *qua* consciousness (Observing Reason) turns its attention to these objective appearances one after the other, and at the end confronts—objectively, as an in-itself—the categorical union of subject and object, consciousness and self-consciousness. In doing this, it therewith confronts *its own* union with objectivity; and from this fact we receive impetus into the subsequent stages, in which we are no longer concerned with the specifically conscious aspects of Reason, but with the self-conscious aspects of Reason (which, it should be remembered, is itself an implicit fusion of both consciousness and self-consciousness).

This development now of self-conscious Reason (Reason becoming individualized) will prove to be in large part parallel to the developments in the stage of Self-Consciousness proper: We will start from an immediate union of self-consciousness with its own otherness, and lead up to a union with this otherness in its universality. As we accomplish this, the union of self and "other" will cease to be something just in-itself, and will become a realized actuality, a for-itself.

But the processes will not be exactly parallel to the processes in Self-Consciousness proper. There are some differences: For a) the "other" here is no longer an alien "other," but one with which self-conscious Reason is in immediate union. And so the development here does not begin with a bifurcation into "Master" and "Slave" (self-consciousness and its alienated alter-ego) but with a duplication of individuals, each of which is considered to be a self-consciousness-made-objective, and each of which is in union with the other (and thus considers the other as an extension of his own self-consciousness). And b) as this "other" becomes universalized here, we do not reach towards an absolute transcendent "Beyond," but rather towards the *spiritual substance* which both contains and permeates all particular self-consciousnesses as its "moments," and at the same time transcends all these individual moments.

From our point of view,[1] we could say that this latter—the spiritual substance—is the realm of the Ethical World, a world which is composed out of "things" of a special type—namely, self-consciousnesses who are individually aware of their implicit union with the universality of all spirits, and whose awareness of this fact derives a) from the immediacy of the customs and mores prevalent in society, and b) from the thought-constituted abstractions of law obtaining in society.

Thus—again from "our" point of view—Reason here has become the fluent universal substance which breaks up into, and apportions itself among, the various particular self-conscious spirits extant in it—much in the same way that the infinite energy of light becomes focused in, and epitomized in, the innumerable star-formations in the stratosphere.

This ethical substance is at once the *universal form* which endows all individual actions with any significance they might have; and a *content* as well—namely, the content that all the various individuals are continually producing. Because of this fact a) we must not conceive individuals any longer as merely accomplishing individual tasks, but must rise to the apprehension that each individual is accomplishing the universal task of the spiritual substance; and b) we must not conceive the unchangeable universal here as being merely immediately united with the particular self-consciousness, but rather as the *expression* of self-consciousnesses, i.e., as a universal world containing all individual self-conscious "things" in itself.

From the point of view of Reason-becoming-individualized,[2] the individual at this stage is only implicitly united with his spiritual substance. That is, he cannot yet say, "this is my substantiality." But rather, since from the point of view of

Reason the spiritual substance has not yet appeared as a fluid universal in transparent reciprocity with its individuals—but rather appears *de facto* as a particular determinate "free nation" existing in mere immediacy—the relationship between the individual and his spiritual substance appears as an unmediated opposition. This opposition has two aspects: a) On the one hand, the individual appears to have become *uprooted from* the universal spiritual substance, to have fallen (at some stage of history) from the felicitous state where he was immersed in his own spiritual bedrock, and not alienated from it; on the other hand, b) the individual seems to be progressing *towards* this spiritual substance (as something to be *produced*). (These two aspects are not incompatible with each other, since the spiritual substance is *not*—as it may seem to be—some specific nation confined to some determinate period of history, but is implicitly a fluid universal both creating, and being created by, individuals through a mutual reciprocity obtaining throughout all eras in history.)[3]

Insofar as Reason is "producing" its spiritual substance, we find ourselves at the vantage point of self-conscious Reason, which, in the aftermath of the stages of Observation, has come to an explicit awareness of its implicit unity with objectivity. It now remains for Reason to *make* this implicit unity into something explicit—i.e., to go beyond awareness to being. Thus Reason now hopes to "find" itself precisely by actively *producing* its implicit self (which is the union of consciousness and self-consciousness). When Reason does produce this implicit self, and is effectively *united* with this its "product," the union that ensues will constitute its "happiness."[4]

Insofar as Reason has been "uprooted" from its spiritual substance, it is an isolated "moment" of the essential spiritual reality, subsisting, as it were, on its own. But every moment of an essential reality must, as it becomes unfolded, manifest itself in its *essentiality.* Thus also the self-conscious individuals who have fallen away from their spiritual substance, come to think of their own individuality as "essential," i.e., they come to think of themselves as subsisting in singleness and isolation from others and from the spiritual substance which vivifies all individuals. As a result of this attitude, they also begin to look upon the laws and customs of the spiritual substance—not as concrete facets pervading the whole—but as thought-determinations existing in abstraction from reality.

Reason now begins to manifest attributes congruent with either of these latter aspects:

Reason as *producing* the ethical substance *precedes* the ethical substance and is oriented to it as a goal. It approximates to this goal by making its implicit nature *explicit.* But this implicit nature appears phenomenally in the form of raw impulses, needs and inclinations, which are cancelled in their immediacy, and "get lost" in their sublated forms.

Reason as *having been uprooted* from the ethical substance is *subsequent to* the ethical substance, which takes on the aspect of a distant *origin,* of a selfless floating adjective, all of whose universality has devolved to the various individual subjects who give it life. Or again, we could say that the ethical substance appears as a remote symbol of the implicit destiny or nature of self-consciousness. Self-consciousness, which tends to characterize its determinate nature in terms of its impulses and inclinations, hesitates and is taken aback when it considers this remote symbol of its "true" nature. Why must its true nature, its true destiny, appear as something extrinsic to itself? How can self-consciousness become reconciled intrinsically with its inner destiny? In order to answer such questions, self-conscious Reason orients itself to a special goal: it wants to make explicit the fact that the ethical substance is the essential being of *its own* implicit nature.

"*Morality*" in the strict sense—i.e., in the special signification which accrues to that word in our (post-Kantian) milieu—refers to the process we have just described, i.e., the process in which the individual self-consciousness makes explicit the fact that its own Reason, working itself out practically, is fundamentally united with the universal spirit of society as a whole. Thus morality, in this sense, connotes the rise of the individual to a higher state, i.e., to a state which supersedes his immersion in *Sittlichkeit,* or the ethical substance in its state of immediacy. This subjective sense of morality would have as its "objective" correlate, the process in which morality arises out of the ethical substance itself. But since we are confining ourselves here to a consideration of Reason from the vantage point of the individual self-consciousness, this latter correlate will not be brought out explicitly.[5]

Self-conscious Reason, then, in its twofold dialectic reciprocity with the ethical substance, starts out as an individual self-consciousness in immediate union with other individuals. It is not threatened by any *substantial* otherness, i.e., any otherness which stands on its own account, as something alien and unassimilable. But rather, the otherness here is an otherness expressly offering itself to Reason to be sublated. From this starting point, Reason takes on the aspect of a positive determinate focal point of desires and impulses (positive purposes). But then, as Reason goes on to make explicit its self-existence, it gives actuality to its own unsubstantial otherness (the universal "negative" purpose which cancels these positive purposes and sublates them). Thus consciousness, already in union with otherness, comes continually to intuit its true self in this unsubstantial otherness which comes into actuality, and in other self-consciousnesses to whom this universal negative purpose is extended.

When Reason elevates this continual process to the status of a law, it expresses its individuality as the "Law of the Heart."

When it incorporates the notion that sacrifice of individuality is essential to individuality—it arrives at "Virtue."

Then finally, when it comes to find happiness in activity (work), it will have made explicit its original concept—that the proper object of Reason is its own self-expression as a real *objective/self-conscious* individuality.

a. *The Moment of Hedonism.* Self-conscious Reason, existing in seeming isolation from its spiritual substance, is not the divine spirit of universality in knowledge and action which becomes explicit in the spiritual substance. Rather, it is the "spirit of the earth," wherein there is an emphasis on individual inclination, the lust for life and the enjoyment of life; and wherein there is incorporated the narrowly circumscribed view that

> the only being which is actual and real is the being which becomes the
> actuality of an individual consciousness.[6]

Reason in this stage of immediacy is a simple union of subjectivity (existence-for-self) and objectivity (existence-in-self). The objectivity in this case is not something alien and extrinsic to consciousness, but the inner nature or destiny of Reason itself, which is apprehended as being responsible for all "objectivity" in the ordinary sense. This inner destiny is for-consciousness, since consciousness is explicitly *aware* of it. But this awareness (the for-consciousness) is only an "existent" in the same sense that consciousness "exists:" it is not yet a mediated determinate existence (a for-itself) appearing phenomenally in the objective world. Thus Reason now instinctively grasps about to make this for-consciousness into a for-itself.[7]

Since Reason is fundamentally a unity-in-difference with its "other," and since "Observing" Reason has now transcended inferior types of otherness, the process of arriving at the explicit for-itself will involve coming into a unity-in-difference with an *other self-consciousness*. And this unity-in-difference will constitute what may be called "the enjoyment of pleasure," in the paramount sense of that term:

> The enjoyment of pleasure. . .is the consciousness of self-consciousness'
> own actualization in another consciousness which also has the aspect of
> self-subsistence; or we could say that it is an intuitive experience of the
> oneness of two self-subsistent self-consciousnesses.[8]

Thus with pleasure in this sense we come to a special kind of unity which preserves the differences between two self-consciousnesses, and thus also preserves and promotes the relationship between them.

It should be noted that there is a marked contrast between pleasure in this sense and the simple "desire" which came on the scene in the stage of immediate Self-certainty, and which was calculated to *destroy* its "other."[9]

Pleasure in the aforementioned sense should lead to an existential "expansion" of self-consciousness.[10] But in order to do this for a *Rational* self-consciousness it is essential that it should make explicit the necessary elements in categorical Reason—namely, the categories of Unity, Difference, and Relation (which are the "content" of Reason's relationship of unity-in-difference). But this "content," if we consider it judiciously, proves to be not really an existential content. It does not, in any way, add being-in-the-world to the being-for-consciousness. And what is more, we could say that this "content" exemplifies the lifeless actuality of thought and the bare *necessity* of Reason's inner destiny: For necessity

> is precisely that about which it is impossible to say *what* it is actually
> doing, or what laws regulate it, or what positive content it has. For it is the
> pure concept of the absolute, intuited as *Being*. And thus it is purely and
> simply an empty *relationship,* maintaining itself irresistibly and imperturb-

ably–but accomplishing nothing but the annihilation of individuality.[11]

And so, where Reason sought to obtain for itself an existential content, it finds that it implicitly only wanted to attain to a thought-content (the necessary relationship obtaining among the categories of Unity, Difference, and Relation); and where Reason sought to lay hold on "life," it finds itself in continual confrontation with unmediated necessity, its own inclination, which is irresistibly and immovably dealing out death to individuality, which was looking for an explicitly rational mode of self-fulfilment.[12]

But finally, self-consciousness comes to abandon its immersion in immediate feeling-states, and to recognize explicitly that this "necessity" which appears so alien to the spontaneous expansiveness of pleasure, is its own inner nature, and *ipso facto* an otherness with which it is basically in union.

This assimilation of self-conscious Reason of the notion of necessity brings it to a new mode of categorical union with otherness–namely, the promulgation of the "Law of the Heart."

b) *The Moment of Moral Sentimentalism.* The consciousness which has emerged from the immediacy of hedonism formulates the "Law of the Heart." This law states that, since necessity is inherent in all of the desires of the individual, it behoves man to realize that his true and basic law lies in this inner necessity itself (in the "heart"). Those who, in delight at their new insight, champion this law, come naturally to view all objective human and divine ordinances as alien to the true universality and law which must spring from the heart itself.[13] But what such people fail to realize is that

> the essential actuality and effectuality of consciousness is such that consciousness can only become truly existent when it becomes the unadulterated (completely objective) universal. That is, it must become the universal in which the particularity of consciousness (which entrusts itself to this universal *precisely* to become "this definite immediate particularity") is *submerged* and transformed.[14]

These, of course, would be hard words to the apostle of the Law of the Heart. He fails to heed this truly objective universal, because he is so completely enamoured of *his* universal. And, consistent with his predilection, he strives to adhere to his universal, and to get others to adhere to their *own* individual universals.

Nevertheless, all those who strive to conform to the Law of the Heart are bound to end up in frustration, because in formulating this law and bringing it to reality, they are constituting it in the form of universality which self-consciousness gives to it–so that it is no longer something belonging to the "heart," but in truth becomes just as objective and external to the heart as those other human and divine ordinances which they were impugning. In addition, they find that *other* men do not recognize the validity of their own enunciated laws, but rather seem to be opposed to them: and they thus come face to face with the uncomfortable awareness that it is only the formerly detested human and divine ordinances which *could* effectively express, in an objective way, the truly inherent universal in the individual consciousness. That is, it is only that vast system of ordinances which could truly present a "law for *all* hearts." Consciousness thus, in the throes of such frustrating contradictions, sees itself as *mad*—as holding onto unreality as reality, and vice versa.

Self-conscious Reason thus becomes a *"Mad Consciousness,"* which continues to take its own implicit intentions to be truth, its own purposes to be universal, and its own particular existence to be inconsequential (since it wills to raise this particular existence to universal reality)—but which also comprehends the fact that its own universality *seems to be* at odds with an external universality. This consciousness is finally caught in the "frenzy of self-deceit"—in which consciousness, though still in possession of itself, becomes utterly distraught at the presence of its ambiguous object; namely, the universal human and divine ordinance which, as an "alien formulation of individual intentions," is a "nothing" for consciousness *qua* individual, but is true reality for consciousness *qua* consciousness-in-general.

The "mad" consciousness thus passes now from the stage where it wished to establish the Law of the Heart out of a sincere concern for mankind; and takes on bellicose behavior patterns, revolting in the most extreme ways against the ordinances of "priests," "despots," etc.

The universal human and divine ordinance, on its side, is not by any means free from blemish, but is just as "perverted" as the "mad" consciousness. For it presents the two-faced aspect of being a) on the one hand, a stable passive inner universality guaranteeing some life and reality to the "Law of the Heart," by providing some semblance of order (through a cancellation, to some degree, of the aspirations of individuals); but b) on the other hand, the sphere of the collective independent self-existence of particular consciousnesses, *the* perverted sphere where there is a continual tug-of-war to establish one's own individual existence and the law of one's own heart at the expense of others.

Insofar as the universal human and divine ordinance presents the prior aspect (of being a stable passive inner universality), we have the presupposition conditioning the possibility of *virtue,* which consists essentially in

> becoming a self not *qua* individual but *qua* essence established in law (in that, namely, which is intrinsically true and good); in realizing that individuality is deceived and deceiving; and consequently in feeling duty-bound to sacrifice the individuality of consciousness.[15]

But insofar as the universal human and divine ordinance presents the subsequent aspect (of being a collection of individuals each striving to establish *his* universal law)—we have the conditions constituting the "Course of the World" *(Weltlauf).*

In order to arrive at true universal individuality, self-consciousness must now weather the inevitable conflicts between the self-sacrificing advocate of Virtue, and the extreme individualists who contribute to the erratic "Course of the World."

c. *The Moment of Abstract Moral Idealism.* Self-conscious Reason, in its progress towards true individuality, has passed through two stages: In the first stage (hedonism), self-conscious *individuality* was simply opposed to the empty *universality* of necessity. In the second stage (moral sentimentalism) individuality and universality existed in *unity* in the Law of the Heart; while they existed in *opposition* in the universal ordinance (because of the conflict between the moments of abstract passive universality and independent subsistent individuality).

Now we are coming to a sphere where individuality and universality *each* exist in *alternate unity and opposition* in *both* the individual and the general World Order:

In this third stage,

1) *Virtue,* as a sacrifice of the individual to the universal, is extolled as an antidote to the inconsistency of the moral sentimentalist, who wishes to "have his universal and individualize it, too."

Virtue is in itself the *opposition* of the individual consciousness to itself, the sacrifice of individuality, for the sake of emphasizing and making explicit the implicit reality of the universality which it "believes" to be present a) in itself, and b) in the various divine and human ordinances. It is an *opposition also* to those ordinances which do not manifest this implicit universality, or at least do not seem to manifest it.

But in carrying through these oppositions, Virtue unexpectedly comes to appreciate the importance of individuality. It comes to see, namely, that

> (Individuality) . . . is a single moment common both to Virtue and to World Order. . . . It is that type of consciousness through which existence-in-self becomes directly for-another. . . . It is indeed the very *actualization* of that which exists in-itself.[16]

In other words, Virtue comes to the realization a) that if its own implicit universality is going to become actual, it must somehow become manifest in or through its own individuality; b) that the "true" inner universality that it points out in the World Order could only become realized in or through individuals; and c) that if its opposition to the World Order is to be meaningful at all, it must be conducted on the battlefield of actualized, i.e., individualized, universality or "goodness." Thus—albeit reluctantly—it finds its self at every turn needing to give deference to individuality, and coming into *unity* with individuality.

2) The *Weltlauf,* on the other hand, is in itself a unity of the universal and the individual, insofar as it is a *World* Order of *individuals* seeking pleasure or seeking to formulate their own universal nostrums. But as individuality strives to assert itself, it—and consequently the World Order also—runs up against the *opposition* of the implicit universal. And this state is "madness," insofar as it is conscious; and a perversion of individuality, insofar as it produces the universality of objectivity.

The struggle between the "Knight of Virtue" and the World Order thus begins, as we have seen, at the springboard of individuality which is shared in common by both; and the battle between the two camps is fought with an identical weapon—namely, the weapon of real existence over against each other.

The *course of the battle* proceeds as follows:

1) *The Knight of Virtue,* motivated by a belief in the essential unity of his own purpose (the attainment of the universal good) with the inherent principle of the historically progressing world, looks forward to the ideal moment when this principle (and therefore also his self-less purpose) will become something in-and-for-itself, a potentiality fully actualized in mankind. He hopes that this achievement can be brought about by an "attack from the rear," i.e., by the very necessity that implicit goodness and universality should come into existence, in spite of "selfish purposes." Thus he is forced—if he is consistent with his own expectations—to reverently stand by, unwilling to destroy the reality of the world processes (since his purpose is to foster the universality in its reality); and unwilling also to destroy the weapons of his enemy (the good which the enemy has brought into real existence), seeing that he has dedicated himself to the good. (Hegel has in mind here, not the moral or religious reformer who would be more specifically envisioned in the Law of the Heart but rather the moral philosopher who makes it his habit to formulate unreal ideologies, or impracticable moral principles—"universals" which "ought to be," but—because they are *too* universal, i.e., utterly abstract—never *are*.)

And thus the result is that the Knight of Virtue—unless he wishes to merely repose and stagnate in the implicit universal with which he (like his enemy) is endowed (i.e., the total complexus of capacities and natural powers)—is faced with continual frustration: He is willing to sacrifice individuality in order to fulfill his aspiration to bring to reality the *truly* implicit universal. But the only way he can bring his latent powers into actuality is through individuality. And the only implicit good that can be made explicit is that universal good which *is* brought about and *will be* brought about in and through the world order. For a universal good can only become an explicit good *for the Knight of Virtue himself* by being explicated and individualized *in the World Order itself.*

2) *The Weltlauf,* on the other hand, is a most formidable opponent. For it has the singularly fortunate advantage of having and making everything objective,[17] i.e., for-consciousness (since it is by definition individuality-made-explicit). And thus it cannot be "taken from the rear," so to speak, by an implicit universal good forcing itself to realization (as the Knight of Virtue had hoped would happen). For nothing can happen in the conscious world outside the will and control of the *Weltlauf.*

The *Weltlauf* even sees the universal purposes which the Knight of Virtue has, as something which is "for itself," i.e., for its own benefit. And all in all, it had this opponent at its mercy from the start; since it is only the good that becomes explicit *in* the *Weltlauf* that could possibly become explicit for, and in, the Knight of Virtue. In other words, the Knight of Virtue is in the singularly weak position of having to borrow weapons from his enemy.

Thus the *Weltlauf* must conquer. But nevertheless, while conquering, it is also conquered in a sense. For while the conflict with the Knight of Virtue ensued, it came to realize that the individuality permeating its laws and ordinances (which individuality it had originally flouted, and which had proved so unsatisfactory to the Knight of Virtue) has proven not to be so individual as it had seemed. Rather, after it was challenged, it began to show itself to be a self-existence at the service of the same implicit universal purposes that the Knight of Virtue devoted himself to. In short, it would be impossible to produce something purely individual in the world even if one desired to. If an individual self-existence is to be separated from its universal roots, this separation can take place only by a purely *mental* distinction.[18]

B. Explicit Reason, as the Simultaneous Manifestation of the "Outer" of Mind and the "Inner" of Thinghood

In the stage of Abstract Moral Idealism, the Knight of Virtue took abstract universal purposes for *objective truth,* and was continually dissatisfied by his subjective certainty of an individual existence which did not conform to such purposes. The *Weltlauf,* on the other hand, started out from the *subjective certainty* of individual purposes (the particular self-existence of the hedonist, or the quasi-universal "laws" of the moral sentimentalist), and took the realization of these purposes as "objective truth"; but found that this objective truth was always in conflict with the original purposes (because of the unfolding of Destiny, or because of the multiplicity of "Laws of the Heart").

The resolution of the opposition between the Knight of Virtue and the *Weltlauf* comes about when consciousness *becomes* the Category (of Reason) pure and simple; that is, when it is no longer searching for the union of the self and other, or trying to produce a union of the self and other, but *is* the union of the self with an other which it both finds and produces. *In terms of the dialectic movement,* the categorical union of self-and-other became a for-consciousness (an awareness) during Observation; this awareness of inner-outer union became for-itself (an objective fact in the world) through Individualization; and now it ceases to be an objective-which-negates-the-subjective (the existence for-itself of Reason), and becomes an objective fact which makes transparent its subjective roots (Reason existing in-and-for-itself, i.e., Reason both knowing the category explicitly, and being the category explicitly).

The individual consciousness at this point no longer has inner purposes which are in some way at odds with outer reality. For now no inner purpose has significance which is not immediately adapted to outer reality. And it no longer looks upon universality as something opposed to individual realization; but has come to the insight that there is no true individuality which is not universal, no true universality which is not implemented in the activity of individuals. Thus the individual consciousness arrives at a very special kind of "action:" an action, namely, which

is not concerned with changing anything or fighting against anything; but presents the form of the pure transition from covert to overt existence; and the content which is now expressed in and through deeds is not considered to be something other than the deed itself, but is known to be the in-itself existence of the deed.[1]

Explicit Reason thus might be best described as a self-contained "circle," which starts from itself, produces only itself, and returns continually to itself. It takes pleasure in its Destiny, makes a Law of the Heart which is a law for action, and advocates a morality which furthers objective existence in the world (and thus is no longer "morality," in the old sense).[2]

1. INDIVIDUALITY AS SUBJECTIVE/OBJECTIVE REALITY IN ITS IMMEDIATE "ANIMAL" STATE

In order to appreciate the type of expression at which individuality has just arrived, we should advert first to the fact that a different kind of "universal" has just come on the scene. Here we are not primarily concerned with an "objective" universality, a generic being comprising many types of subordinate beings and properties of being in its compass. Neither do we have to do mostly with a "subjective" universality drawing multiple thought-determinations into this negative unity. Rather, we are dealing with one of the most fundamental "universals"—the universal relationship which pervades the unity-in-distinction of subject and object. Reason, having come now to express this new type of universality, is no longer caught in the dichotomy of inner and outer, intent and existence; but is itself *Subjective/Objective Individuality (die Sache Selbst)*[3]—the fundamental or pivotal negative universal unity of selfhood and thinghood, which was a pre-condition for all the Forms of Consciousness we have considered thus far.

The Subjective/Objective Individuality, as a manifestation of universality in a more fundamental sense, also incorporates actuality or activity in its most fundamental sense—i.e., as the pure spiritual transition from implicit purpose to outer expression—a transition, however, which does not require *leaving* one pole or state to pass onto or into another, but is "circular" (maintaining itself at one pole while passing to the other), and thus is not "transitory," as are other transitions.[4]

The universal transitional activity of the Subjective/Objective Individuality is not meant, however, to be a universal in abstraction. When it is realized in abstraction in individuals, the result is a certain type of practical Idealism which could be called the "Honest Consciousness." The Honest Consciousness, enthralled by the notion of its union with, and consequent control over, otherness, proceeds to apply the abstract unity of Subjective/Objective Individuality in an indiscriminate way to its accomplished and unaccomplished intents, and to the intents and accomplishments of others. Thus it strives to gain an "honest" satisfaction of its abstract categorical awareness, by subsuming all possible intents and accomplishments into negative unity with *die Sache Selbst*.

From one point of view, this idealistic attempt gives us an important insight into the nature of Subjective/Objective Individuality: namely, that it cannot be appropriated by any particular individual, but (implicitly) is the activity of a universal spirit vivifying all individuals in society. And this fact becomes apparent empirically by the way that individuals will "pitch in" to help others attain some common intention, and will strive to bring their own intentions into the "light of day" of public approval, where they are the very antithesis of private property.

But aside from this insight, we have to aver that the "Honest Consciousness" is a bit too zealous in its aspiration to attribute every possible determinate facet of human realization to the abstract *Sache Selbst.* For *de facto* this *Sache Selbst* is not an indeterminate and generally applicable predicate, but is unintelligible apart from a certain specific content. And at this point, where individual consciousness has not yet elevated itself to become universal spirit, the *real* Subjective/Objective Individuality is one characteristically colored by the intents, talents, and dispositions of this or that particular individual. This fact is well illustrated empirically if we advert to the fact that, even if a person has become fully "individualized" (cf. the previous sections on Individualization), he will ordinarily have a connatural orientation to willing his *own activity,* and not somebody else's, and also not some essential activity *in abstracto.*

And so, while we grant that Subjective/Objective Individuality is the activity of universal Spirit, we must emphasize the fact that it is also essentially the activity of this or that determinate individual:

> Of its nature, the Subjective/Objective Individuality is. . . an [essential mode of consciousness] whose reality is the activity of the particular individual and of all individuals, *and* whose activity is immediately for-another (i.e., it is a public *fact,* but a special kind of fact which is the "activity of one and all.")[5]

And since we have not yet arrived at the vantage point of spirit as the activity of all individuals, but are situated still at the perspective of the individual progressing in consciousness, this individual aspect—the aspect of being particular and determinate—is the only one explicit to us at this time, and thus merits a proportional emphasis.

The Subjective/Objective Individuality, therefore, is emphatically a *determinate Sache Selbst,* a *determinate* subject-object reciprocity, a fluid categorical unity of determinate subjective and objective "moments." [6]

We can describe the development of the Subjective/Objective Individuality as follows:

1) *The moment of implicit purpose:* This had its origin in the determinateness of individuality that

> is not just a limitation or restriction that self-conscious individuality has to supersede; but is also (considered as an existent quality) a simple elemental "coloring," from which and in which it conducts its operations.[7]

Thus insofar as the determinate individuality has a native endowment of talents, dispositions, character, etc. (its natural "coloring"), the subjective element does not start from "zero" in conceiving purposes and intents, but is conditioned to be oriented to certain purposes rather than others, by this very "coloring" which it has.

2) *The moment of actualization of purpose:* This can be subdivided into three constituent moments: a) the beginning; b) the means; c) the end.

a) *The beginning* of the actualization of purpose consists in the various circumstances which impinge on the individual, and which (at this stage of consciousness) are permeated with subjective significance, and thus take on the aspect of the "interesting."[8]

b) *The means for the actualization of purpose* consist (i) internally in *talent,* which is nothing but individuality itself taken in the sense of implicit means; (ii) actually and extrinsically in the *unity* of this internal talent for action with the content which was presented as of "interest" to individuality. (N.B. the connection of the aspect of interest with the given circumstances here must take place in such a way that the transition is not a mere antithesis, but an "outer" corresponding to the original intents.)[9]

c) *The end of the actualization,* i.e., the "finished work." The finished work in context here is essentially some object external to the individuality, the external phenomenal expression of the deeds of the individuality *in* his own environmental situation. This work, as an existent object falling off from the individual who accomplishes it, is a transitory fact, in which the union of purpose with being, and of original essential nature with purpose itself is constituted in a purely accidental relationship; it is not objective truth itself, but its transitoriness disappears in the universality of true objective reality.

The finished work expresses the determinateness of individuality in the determinateness of an existent form limited and negated by other forms (the forms of the work of other individuals). In itself this "work," in its static determination and limitation, is an exact and true expression in a "quantitative" way of the greater or less ontological limitation of the inherent nature of the individual. In this sense, it is an expression which is intrinsically good and satisfying, and cannot be designated as "bad" except by virtue of some further reflection extrinsic and unessential to its nature as "work." But this work is also something public, "for-another." And in this sense it stands over against other determinate works, in comparison with which it is judged by individuals, on the basis of their universal power (and their innate interest in subject-object reciprocities). And in society as a whole, the work of each individual stands over against the work of similar individuals in an "alien" way—since only an individual's *own* work can contribute to *his* union with reality.

(There seems to be a contradiction in saying that a person can only *know* his individual purposes in the finished work, and yet saying also that he must bring to completion his (*already* conscious) intents. But this is only an apparent contradiction. For actually there is no starting point here, but only circular processes: The interest is a kind of self-knowledge, which gives rise to self-knowledge, which gives rise to new interest, etc.)

3) *The moment of the fact or deed,* i.e., the objective expression of Subjective/Objective Individuality. This is the expression of man's essential work. It is not any individual existent object that may have been produced, not any phenomenal movements of his activity; nor is it any all-pervading intention. Rather, it is the individual himself, as both a subject and an object; or, more precisely, it is that essential activity by which he relates himself to himself as both subject and object. Thus that which is "produced" is individuality itself; and the "producer" is also simultaneously a task to be accomplished.[10]

The Subjective/Objective Individuality thus reveals itself explicitly in this third moment, showing definitively that it is neither merely objectively existing work nor intent universalized as genus; but is rather the succession of the moments of individuality actualized by the simple form of universal subjective/objective activity—the activity of a consciousness immediately present to itself as a categorical synthesis of form and content.

2. SUBJECTIVE/OBJECTIVE INDIVIDUALITY RISES TO THE NOTION OF A SOCIETY GOVERNED BY LAWS

The Subjective/Objective Individuality, as we have seen, always makes manifest a *determinate* relationship of purpose to existence, inner to outer. But in the very act of explicating this relationship, in the very act of becoming for-itself, it is revealing its implicit nature. And the implicit nature, the in-itself, in the case of Subjective/Objective Individuality, is no longer the implicit desires or purposes or dispositions of the individual *subject,* but rather the universality of the category which binds the determinate moments of subjectivity and objectivity together, while at the same time keeping them apart. Thus the implicit nature is this *preeminent universal.*[11] And as Subjective/Objective Individuality proceeds to make its determinations more and more explicit, it *ipso facto* must reveal this universality more and more.

The universality which becomes revealed is not something peculiar to any particular individual. Of its very nature, it transcends the moments of individuality, while at the same time giving them definition and meaning. As rational Individuality becomes aware of this fact, it begins to feel unmistakably that it is acting under the impetus of this universal transcendent in-itself (or, perhaps more precisely, that it is giving rise to this universal in-itself *by acting* as a Subjective/Objective Individuality). And as this universal in-itself is seen to transcend one individual, so it is seen to transcend him *qua* individual, i.e., it transcends any individual.[12] Thus the rational individual rises to the notion of a transcendent universal in-itself, an ethical substance pervading all true individual activity while at the same time becoming expressed in and through such activity.

In all the previous stages of consciousness, it was necessary to constantly shuffle about, comparing apparent truth with equally apparent certitude, reconciling the particular with its congruent universal, tracing the relationship between inner purpose and outer reality. But now, when consciousness makes the categorical unity of subject-and-object explicit in and through and *to* itself, it finally possesses an object which it will not have to abandon because of its one-sidedness. For consciousness now sees and possesses and *is* the *categorical union of the fundamental oppositions.* Thus, as far as the individual conscious-ness is concerned, it stands at the vantage point of the *absolute* (completely mediated, no longer one-sided) truth.[13] It *cannot* go beyond this Absolute, because its own substantial power now is nothing but the power of the universal transcendent in-itself; it *will not* go beyond it, because it individually, sponta-neously, willingly, is giving reality to its *self* through this universal. We have thus arrived at the final "Form of Consciousness."

But insofar as consciousness is specifically the union of *universality* and *partic-ularity,* i.e., of the ethical substance and determinate self-consciousness, its pre-vious seemingly independent existence (as a consciousness, taking on various "Forms") is reversed—without being subverted. For the individual self-conscious-ness is now seen to be but a "moment" (albeit a free and independent moment) of an ethical substance which exists as the universal reality.[14]

This "ethical substance," the transcendent societal union of discrete individu-als, insofar as it appears as an object in and through and for and *to* conscious-ness, takes on a certain definite, delimited form. It appears as a universal sub-stance distinguished from, and also becoming distinguished in, individual self-consciousnesses. It remains for consciousness to describe the determinate *ways* in which this substance transcends and unites the various distinct self-conscious individuals. Thus consciousness is led to enunciate the various ethical *laws,* which describe the manner in which the individual's actions should accord with the universal action of all. Examples of such laws are: "Everyone should speak the truth," and "Love thy neighbor as thyself."

As consciousness formulates such laws, it thinks that it is describing the vari-ous aspects of necessity which obtain in the *content* of the ethical substance. But when it subjects these laws to analysis, it finds that this is not exactly the case.

For example, it is "necessary," in general, that individuals in the ethical sub-stance should speak the truth. But what is the truth? The basic truth they are aware of, is their union with the ethical substance. But there is no need to formulate a law about *that* truth. It is already a necessary, thought-constituted existence. Aside from that basic truth, what other truths can we require to be revealed? Obviously, in most circumstances an individual will have a limited knowledge of contingent affairs, and will have to make judgements about how much of this knowledge is worth revealing. Or again, because of contingent circumstances, it might be foolhardy (detrimental to the ethical substance) to reveal all, or even any part, of what one knows. And in general, we must realize that the perfection and excellence of the Subjective/Objective Individuality con-sists essentially in its immediate *particular* transcendence of, and assessment of, and reaction to, contingent details. This is what constitutes it a determinate *individuality.* So it would be superfluous to formulate a "law" which would imply a prior knowledge of all these contingencies which—by definition—appear only at the instance of (and *through* the application of) determinate activity.

And again, it would be superfluous to make the *law* that we should "love our neighbor." If we are going to love him intelligently, the prime requisite is that we should do for him what the ethical substance is doing for him, i.e., we should do the universal for him. But this we are already doing, if we have come to unity with the ethical substance. The judgements about contingent ways of loving our neighbor will be *ipso facto* optimal judgements in contingent situations, if only we maintain our unity with the ethical substance.

And in brief, it is *impossible* to make meaningful laws governing the content of activities of individuals in the ethical substance. If any laws are made, they are merely tautological re-formulations of the *formal* relationship of the ethical substance to the individual self-consciousness.

As applied to the *content* of human activity, these "laws" are nothing more than *hypothetical* "commands," which take on the logical form of "Do this, if you *can* do this," or "Do this, if you *want* to do this." But by definition, one who affirms the universality of the ethical substance has both the power and the will to act truly humanly (i.e., fully consciously) in all the various contingencies that present themselves. So these "commands," like the universal laws they are based on, have no efficacy, no necessity, in human life.[15]

But they can, of course, be subjected to a purely speculative analysis to determine their formal interrelationships. And this is what rational consciousness now sets about doing.

3. SUBJECTIVE/OBJECTIVE INDIVIDUALITY ESTABLISHES ITSELF WITHIN THE SPIRITUAL SUBSTANCE

Self-conscious Reason, turning its attention to the purely formal universal laws which it discerns in the universal spiritual substance, and realizing that they are purely formal, elects to adjudicate them by utilizing a purely formal methodology. That is, it applies the "principle of tautology" to them. By the principle of tautology is meant the Law of Contradiction: "A thing cannot be and not-be at the same time and with reference to the same aspects." Reason, by means of this principle, analyzes the various universal laws to see whether there is anything self-contradictory in them. It presumes that if a law proves to be non-self-contradictory, this will prove its validity.[16] And thus consciousness, by checking all the various universal laws in this way, intends to end up with a certain repertoire of valid universal laws which will be congruent intellectual representations making explicit the true nature of the ethical substance.

As long as consciousness considers the law in a relatively simple formulation, without going into too many of its implications and consequences, almost any law will prove to be non-self-contradictory.[17] But if it goes on to sufficiently elaborate the implications of any law, it inevitably finds, to its chagrin, some self-contradictions:

For example, if *communism* is the universal law for all individuals, the distribution according to need which is essential to communism contradicts the equality of individuals, which is a principle fundamental to ethical society; and a strictly homogeneous division of goods would contradict the notion of a "fair share (a share proportioned to the needs of the individual). Again, if *private property* be the universal law for all individuals, the perpetuity of property under such a system would contradict the essentially transient nature of property; the exclusiveness of the "mine" would be contradicted by the identity which the "mine" gives with all other egos; and the simple "for another" of the thinghood of property would be contradicted by its "for me."

When consciousness, pondering over such examples, wonders how it can happen that both a law and its opposite can lead to self-contradiction, it needs to consider two very pointed questions: a) *Whose* laws is consciousness testing? and b) *Who* is doing the testing?

a) Do we have a case here where one individual is trying to legislate universally for all men? No matter to what distant horizons of universality a particular individual extends his vision, he is still a particular individual, and it would be presumptuous to try to make *his* law efficacious for all men (no matter how abstract and innocuous its formulation may be). Or do we have a case where consciousness is actually confronting laws *of* the ethical substance, and testing them? In this case, it would not be encountering laws which "ought" to be, but laws that simply *are.* If the laws *are,* why do we need to test them for validity and truth? Their existence in the state of preeminent universality *ipso facto* constitutes them as true. These are not laws to be tested, but to be lived by (if the individual wishes to come to fully conscious ethical existence—which existence is also a prerequisite for making laws).

b) What sort of person is the individual who is doing the testing? Does he harbor a vague *belief* in the law, and hope to confirm that belief by the "testing" process? But "belief" here would no doubt be a euphemism. For the laws of the ethical substance are the blood and sinews of individual ethical life. One embraces them, and lives by them, not because they are his own laws, but because he (the Subjective/Objective Individuality) is not just a particular individual, but a universal individual, i.e., one who lives and breathes the ethical existence of the conscious world of spirit. If one "believes" in certain of the laws of the ethical substance, this simply implies that he doubts them or wants them to conform more to his own whims. And if one starts out from such a negative premise, there can be little wonder that he ends up finding "self-contradictions" where it suits him. [18]

And thus Hegel says,

> True ethical sentiment consists just in holding fast and unshaken by what is right, and abstaining altogether from what would move or shake it or derive it. . . . I . . . am, by my beginning to test laws, thereby already on an immoral track. [19]

Through a consideration of the questions concerning the motives of the individual "law-tester" and the extent of his legislative capacity, consciousness comes to the realization that both the moments of law-testing and law-making are unstable, contingent moments, basically peripheral to existence in the spiritual substance. If these moments are allowed to have their sway, they give rise to infinite capriciousness and disintegration in society, or to a tyranny, bolstered by force, of the particular whims of an individual.

Thus self-conscious Reason, as it sees these unstable moments cancel themselves out, transcends its detached attention to abstract law as an object, and comes to the following two mutually complementary insights:

a) *The ethical substance* is not *just* a bare formal universality pervading human social existence. For during the processes of law-testing it offered its formal determinations as a content to be tested. It became simultaneously both form and content, i.e., became self-reflected thought. Thus it accommodated itself to the exigencies of a self-consciousness. And as self-conscious Reason became aware of its own capriciousness and arbitrariness in testing the laws of the ethical substance, this substance itself became victorious—not by proving itself to be or have any determinate thoughts, but by proving itself to be the self-identical substance of self-consciousness proper. Thus it no longer seems to stand over against self-consciousness, as a bare genus of societal unity; but (since the individual has removed the arbitrary barriers to an appreciation of the ethical substance) has attained *self-consciousness* itself, in and through the individuals who become reconciled to it in truth.

b) *Self-conscious Reason,* on its side, having cancelled the accidental particularity of the moments of law-making and law-testing, comes to see the essential relationship of particular to universal in its case, i.e., comes to see that the one lacks significance without the other. Thus it comes to view the ethical substance as the *universal self-consciousness* of all, containing each self-conscious individuality as an essential moment; and (because of its universality) incorporating all the essential laws for human society—not those laws which "ought" to be "believed" (the ideologies of the "honest consciousness," etc.), but those laws which *are* and are operative in, and constitutive of, actual concrete ethical existence. Thus, without any more questioning or objection, it opens its gaze to that summary and paramount "rightness" which

> ". . . is not for now or yesterday, but is always there, living on, emanating from—no one knows where."[20]

Thus also individual consciousness disappears now as an isolated individual with many abstract Forms of Consciousness. And in its stead we find a *world* of consciousness, in which individual rational beings

> are the integral parts of an organic unity filled to overflowing with life—spirits transparently clear to themselves—guileless heavenly shapes which, in the midst of their differences, hold fast to the untarnished innocence and single-mindedness of their spiritual origins.[21]

Individuality has given itself over wholeheartedly to universality; and, in compensation for its generosity, has received a new type of existence, which preserves the differences of individual consciousness, but at the same time sublates them once and for all beyond the limitations of mere individuality.[22]

COMMENTARY

Hegel's Preface

1. Hegel's preface to the *Phenomenology* was written after the completion of the *Phenomenology,* and was intended not only to bridge the gap between the *Phenomenology* and the *Logic*, but also to set the *Phenomenology* in its cultural and historical context.

The analysis of the first half of the *Phenomenology,* which begins here, will be conducted largely in paraphrase form where the exposition of the text is concerned. References to German texts, cross-references, and commentary relating to historical antecedents or consequents, or parallels, will be relegated to footnotes coordinated with the straightforward analysis.

2. Towards the beginning of the Preface, Hegel speaks of the possibility of presenting the "external necessity" for a philosophical system, and comments, "Really the sole justification for an enterprise with this goal [the goal of making philosophy into a scientifically respectable system] would be a demonstration that *the time has arrived* for the elevation of philosophy to the status of a science; this demonstration would be [self-] justified, since it would show the necessity of its aim even while accomplishing it." (Dass die Erhebung der Philosophie zur Wissenschaft an der Zeit ist, dies aufzuzeigen würde daher die einzig wahre Rechtfertigung der Versuche sein, die diesen Zweck haben, weil sie dessen Notwendigkeit dartun, ja sie ihn zugleich ausfuhren würde).

In the context, this could mean either

a) that the *Phenomenology* as a whole shows the internal necessity of this goal, in the act of accomplishing it. If this is what is meant, then the implication would be that the Preface to the *Phenomenology* could not show the "necessity" of the *Phenomenology,* and would, in a certain sense be superfluous. In this case, Hegel's elaboration of a rather long Preface, after emphasizing the superfluity of such a preface, would seem to be an inconsistency.

or b) that the preface to the *Phenomenology* would show the external necessity of this goal (of making philosophy into a scientific system) at the same time as the main body of the *Phenomenology* accomplished this goal according to its internal necessity. This interpretation seems preferable, since it avoids the inconsistency mentioned above, without doing violence to the text.

3. The idea that quantitative progressions can give rise to a qualitative "leap" is enunciated also by Kierkegaard, e.g. in his *Concept of Dread*, p. 34, where he states that quantitative guilt increases in the human race to a point where it can condition the individual's "leap" into sinfulness. The same principle is also of importance in the dialectical materialism of Karl Marx.

4. By "science," Hegel means the systematic organization and exposition of speculative truth. What *we* generally refer to as "science"—i.e. the various empirical sciences—are only approximations to Science in the full and paramount sense, in Hegel's estimation.

5. Cf. Plato, *Theaetetus* 173 D: "The Philosopher 'flies all abroad' . . . measuring earth and heaven and the things which are under and on the earth and above the heaven . . . but not condescending to anything which is within reach."

6. *Immediacy* vs. *mediacy,* substance vs. subject, essence vs. form, intuition vs. mediation: These are terms much-used by Hegel throughout the *Phenomenology,* and are best understood as complementary reciprocals:

"Immediacy" is an object of consciousness in a state of relatively passive givenness, potential to further active development into a mediated stage. E.g.,

"2" accepted as a starting point and as relative to "2^2" would be immediate; and the mediated "2^2" would be immediate with reference to "2^3."

"Substance" is that which confronts consciousness as something fully existing in-itself, and potential to becoming fully assimilated, i.e. to existing completely for-consciousness, the subject. A substance becomes subject if, while having reality in-itself, it has also the potential to be for-itself. For example, an infant is explicitly a substance, but also implicitly a subject, since it has the potential for self-knowledge. Substance-in-general, as universal being, is implicitly also subject, since being exists only in and through thought; but not explicitly, as long as being seems to be something outside of thought and opposed to it.

"*Essence*" is a unified determinate being in its aspect of existing-in-itself, and as containing implicitly the multiple determinations of its fully developed *form.* For example, spirit, which properly is existence in-and-for oneself, is present in sense-certainty according to its essence (i.e. implicitly), but not according to its full and proper form, to attain which it must go beyond sense-certainty to pass through multiple determinate ways of existing for-oneself.

"*Intuition*" is direct perceptual awareness, or any state of cognition analogous to direct perceptual awareness. Such states of "immediacy" must be abandoned, however, if they are to be presented in the context of organized, systematized, conceptual knowledge, each of whose components receives significance not directly, but indirectly, by being related to, i.e. mediated by, the other components. Thus, for example, when on the basis of multiple perceptions one comes to formulate some determinate law, the concept of "the law" is mediated knowledge, with reference to the immediate perceptions upon which it is founded.

7. For example, Spinoza, who in his *Ethics* deduces all finite "modes" in the world from God, the absolute all-encompassing substance consisting of infinite attributes.

Hegel in his *Geschichte der Philosophie* (Frommanns, Stuttgart, 1959, Vol. 19), Part III, p. 409, states that the deficiency of this abstract divine substance is that it simply drew all individual and subjective particularities into a massive thought-unity which effectively destroyed their former state of existence: "Spinoza's God is conceived only as substance, not as spirit, not as concrete. In the wake of this abstractenss, the self-subsistence of the human soul is dissipated—in contrast to the Christian religion, where each individual appears as destined for salvation. But with Spinoza, on the contrary, the individual subject is just a mode, an accident, an unessential nothing." (Gott nur als Substanz, und nicht als Geist, nicht als konkret gefasst wird. Somit wird auch die Selbstständigkeit der menschlichen Seele geläugnet, während in der christlichen Religion jedes Individuum als zur Seligkeit bestimmt erscheint. Hier dagegen ist das geistig Individuelle nur ein Modus, ein Accidenz, nicht aber ein Substantielles.)

8. This implies that one must depart from the immediacy even of Schellings' "Intellectual intuition" (an active production of the mind)—to attain to true conceptual knowledge.

This seems to be the major issue—at least in the Preface—on which Hegel breaks away from Schelling: and Schelling, after reading just the Preface to the *Phenomenology,* commented in a letter to Hegel: "Of course everything can be reconciled, with one exception. I confess that so far I do not comprehend the sense in which you oppose the Concept to intuition. Surely, you could not mean anything else by it than what you and I used to call Idea, whose nature is to have one side from which it is Concept, and one from which it is intuition." (Quoted and translated by Kaufman, *op. cit.* p. 321).

9. The Preface to the *Phenomenology* might be an example of such an external

"proof." See n. 2, *supra.*

10. *P.,* p. 23: Ein sogenannter Grundsatz oder Princip der Philosophie, wenn es wahr ist, schon darum auch falsch ist, weil er Grundsatz oder Princip ist.

11. The idea seems to be that spirit, which understands and masters the inorganic otherness of the world through science, will not be fully the master until it understands and controls knowledge itself.

12. When this process of assimilation has been completed, the particular individual becomes a "universal individual." ("Inorganic" here means "alien.")

13. The mediaeval schoolmen, for example, spoke of the universal as the common essence separated from sensuous particulars by the mind. As separate, it then became potentially reapplicable to corresponding concrete existents.

14. This is found in Hegel's *Logic*; and in his *Philosophy of Nature* and *Philosophy of Spirit* through which the "mediations" of the *Logic* eventually lead to the unmediated mediation of Absolute Spirit.

These three sections together form Hegel's "System," or the *Encyclopedia of Philosophy,* which was published in three successive editions, in 1817 (the first edition), in 1827 (the second edition, revised and amplified), and in 1830 (again revised). The *Logic* in the *Encyclopedia* is an abbreviated and re-ordered presentation of the two volume *Science of Logic* (the Major Logic) which was published in 1812-1816. The *Philosophy of Law* from the latter parts of the System were later expanded and published in 1821 (Hegel's *Philosophie des Rechts*). Some of Hegel's university lectures on various sub-sections of the System were also published posthumously on the basis of lecture drafts and student notes. The most notable of these posthumous publications is Hegel's *Philosophy of History,* one of the final sub-sections of his System.

15. This reconciliation will take place in "Absolute Knowledge," at the end of the *Phenomenology of Spirit.*

16. "Triplicity" took its inception from the syllogistic triads of Aristotelian logic. Kant's "restoration" of triplicity refers 1) to the triplicity of understanding-judgement-practical reason (where the apparent gulf between understanding, whose laws are conditioned by sensible phenomena, and practical reason, which produces natural effects according to a priori concepts of freedom—is bridged by judgement, whose own autonomous a priori concepts (natural beauty and teleology) supply the transition from sensibility to human and moral feeling, and from nature to supra-nature or freedom); 2) to the four classes of Kantian "categories"—quantity, quality, relation, and modality—in which the third category in each class arises by a synthesis of the first two categories in that class: Thus in the class of "quantity," the category of "totality" is unity-in-plurality (a synthesis of unity and plurality); in the category of "quality," "limitation" is reality in negative form (a synthesis of reality and negation); etc. See Hegel's *Lectures on the History of Philosophy,* III, p. 477.

Cf. also Kant, *Critique of Judgement* (N.Y.: Haffner, 1951), pp. 32-34, and *Critique of Pure Reason,* B 110 f.

Fichte, a critical disciple of Kant, then developed the triplicity of thesis-antithesis-synthesis:

The *thesis* is the simple identity of ego with itself; in which relationship matter and form are both unconditioned, and the real is identical with the logical.

The *antithesis* is the simple non-identity of ego and non-ego. In this relationship, the matter (ego) is conditioned by its negation, which itself is the unconditioned "form."

The *synthesis* is the "stance" in which the ego takes up the vantage point of absolute ego, and effectively distinguishes ego and non-ego, setting their boundaries from below, as it were. Here the form (the reciprocal determinations of ego and non-ego) is conditioned (mutually conditioned), but inheres in a "matter" (the totum of opposition) which is unconditioned.

This latter "triplicity" had become a dull formalism in Hegel's time, a mechanical procedure applied without insight into content.

17. *P.* p. 32: Die Erfahrung wird ... diese Bewegung genannt, worin das Unmittelbare, das Unerfahrene, d.h. das Abstracte, es sei des sinnlichen Seins oder des nur gedachten Einfachen, sich entfremdet, und dann aus dieser Entfremdung zu sich zurückgeht, und hiemit jetzt erst in seiner Wirklichkeit und Wahrheit dargestellt, wie auch Eigentum des Bewusstseins ist.

18. The Hegelian dialectic, which proceeds more or less in triadic fashion, is a "method" only in the wide sense of the word, since it does not involve the application of conscious constructs or procedures to an external content, but the patient explication of formal determinations and relationships that are "already" implicit in the content. (Thus, since the distinction between form and content is tenuous and artificial, the distinction between method and content, or subject-matter, is equally tenuous and artificial.)

Hegel's disclaimer of a method is reminiscent of Socrates' disclaimer of teaching anything to anybody: Socrates only assisted implicit ideas in his hearers to become explicit; as the speculative philosopher, in Hegel's estimation, only assists in the explicitation of implicit content, through a process of "mediation."

19. Schelling held that philosophy must begin with the "Unconditioned Absolute," a synthesizing premise which contained three aspects—the *Ur-grund,* the *Grund von Existenz,* and *das Existierende.*

This unconditioned Absolute is hailed by Schelling as "... that which is not, but which is the ground of existence, the primeval night, the mother of all things" (quoted by Kaufman, *op. cit.,* p. 387). In obvious reference to this statement, Hegel says in the Preface to the *Phänomenologie* (p. 19) "to pass off one's Absolute as the night wherein (you could say) 'all cows are black'—that epitomizes the Naïveté of an empty brand of knowledge." (Sein *Absolutes* für die Nacht anzugeben, worin, wie man zu sagen pflegt, alle Kühe schwarz sind, ist die Naivität der Leere an Erkenntnis.)

Thus Schelling, like Fichte before him, gets involved in a formalism oriented towards subsuming all the facts in the world into the ambit of a few pivotal principles. This would make philosophical knowledge very easy, even semi-automatic, if it were possible. But unfortunately it is not possible. And attempts to achieve the impossible result in numerous philosophical absurdities; witness, for instance, the theory of Schelling that, since electricity represents a relative bipolarity, the Understanding (which dichotomizes things) is electricity; and that, since magnetism represents a relative unity, it corresponds to Reason (which unifies things). Or one could cite the following line of reasoning from Schelling's *Allgemeine Deduction...,* paragraph 1:

"The plant represents the carbon pole, the animal the nitrogen pole. Thus the animal is the south pole, while the plant is the north." (Cf. Hyppolite translation, *Phenomenologie,* p. 43n., p. 44n.)

In making such "deductions," however, Schelling is hardly worse than Fichte, who in his *Grundlage des Naturrechts,* deduces the existence of organic bodies from man's need to have a body to give his ego determinate relationships with other egos, and deduces plants and animals from man's need to have food.

Hegel admits, of course, his indebtedness to both Fichte and Schelling for their groundwork in developing the principle of "triplicity." But he objects strenuously to their formalistic and strange applications of absolute principles or triadic schemata to the factual world.

20. This seems to be primarily a reference to the $\hat{\epsilon}\hat{\iota}\delta o\varsigma$ of Plato, but, as is often the case with observations made in the *Phenomenology,* is capable of multiple

interpretations or applications. For example, Thomas Aquinas in *De ente et essentia,* Ch. I, defines "form" as the definiteness *(certitudo)* of a being; and this characterization is similar to Hegel's characterization of concrete form *(die konkrete Gestalt)* as a "simple determinateness" *(die einfache Bestimmtheit).*

21. "Determinate being" would not be able to exist as determinate unless it were taken up into the mediations of thought, which separates or abstracts determinate natures and assigns them their place in the conscious world of spiritual "being."

22. *P.,* p. 55: Was, auch dem Inhalte nach, in irgendeiner Kenntniss und Wissenschafft Wahrheit ist, diesen Namen allein dann verdienen kann, wenn es von der Philosophie erzeugt worden; . . . die andern Wissenschafften, sie mögen es mit Räsonnieren, ohne die Philosophie, versuchen, . . . ohne sie nicht Leben, Geist, Wahrheit in ihnen zu haben vermögen.

Hegel's Introduction

1. Kant, in his *Critique of Pure Reason,* purports precisely to draw such limits—the limits of "understanding"—beyond which there are only unassimilable things-in-themselves, concerning which our faculty of "reason" has a tendency to speculate, invalidly. Kant clarifies this in his *Critique of Judgement,* p. 11.

Kant's intention, as Hegel puts it, is to examine the nature of our instrument—knowledge—before we venture to use (or misuse) that instrument. But to *examine* knowledge is itself an act of knowledge. And if we seek to examine knowledge in the abstract, so to speak, before going on to concrete knowledge about things—we find ourselves in the foolish position of the man who would like to learn to swim before jumping in the water (Cf. *The Logic of Hegel,* Wallace tr.; London, Oxford, 1931, p. 17). In other words, any examination of knowledge must be conducted on concrete acts of knowing related to definite types of objects.

2. For the general meaning of *ansichsein,* existence-in-self, see the Glossary, p. 193.

An object has the aspect of *ansichsein* when it is in immediate opposition to consciousness, i.e., other-than consciousness, and is thus also for-consciousness as implicit content which has not been revealed to, and assimilated by, consciousness.

3. The distinctive operation of consciousness is to come to possess itself, i.e., to become *für sich,* for-itself. The world is instrumental to this self-possession, i.e., it is something "for consciousness." But in order for the world to be "for consciousness," it must in the first instance be outside of consciousness, i.e., a mere *ansich* (an in-itself). But then when its implicit significance becomes explicit to consciousness, the world becomes also explicit to itself; that is, it lays hold upon its own notion, and thus becomes something "for-itself."

4. Scholasticism uses a similar terminology. A concept of the mind as *intentio prima* (first intention) expresses something in reality (e.g., Being), but as *intentio secunda* expresses our formulations of reality (e.g., logical being, which is an *ens rationis*).

5. It should be reemphasized here that "experience" for Hegel is not synonymous with sense impressions or perceptions. See Ch. VII *supra.* See also Murray Greene, *Hegel on the Soul,* p. 31.

6. Hegel here is echoing Descartes' *Cogito.* Descartes, after showing that it would be possible to entertain doubts about sense data, the data of the imagination, and all the ratiocinative products of the sleeping or wakeful mind, hits upon two "facts" that are indubitable—the fact of the existence of some reference point, or *ego,* and the fact of the activity of *doubting.* For we do not

merely find, but *produce* these facts by the very activity of doubting. (Cf.
Descartes' *Discourse on the Method of Rightly Conducting the Reason and
Seeking for Truth in the Sciences,* Holdane & Ross tr.; N.Y.: Dover, 1955, Vol.
I, Pt. 4.)

In Hegel's terminology, the activity of the thinking mind is a unique "fact"
which *becomes* an in-itself by *being* for-itself, and does not cease being objective
by being assimilated to the subjectivity.

7. The idea that the end and the epitome of all knowledge is full *self-knowledge* was first made explicit by Aristotle, who in XII *Metaph.*, 9, describes the
perfect knowledge of God as a "thinking upon thinking." Thomas Aquinas
expressed the same metaphysical concept in his doctrine on angels who, in the
very act of ideating their own natures, would produce in this ideation a reflection of all things (cf. e.g., *S. Theol.,* I-II, Q. 50, a. 6).

8. Hegel, like Plato in the *Sophist* (230B), proposed by means of a methodology of "dialectic" to sound the death knell for all the "conceits" which freeze
the human mind into a status quo. And Hegel's dialectic, like Plato's, comes into
play precisely under the impetus of oppositions or contradictions which need to
be mediated or synthesized. (Cf. *Republic,* VII, 524D.)

9. *P., p.* 68: Der sich auf den ganzen Umfang des erscheinenden Bewusstseins
richtende Skeptizismus macht dagegen den Geist erst geschickt zu prüfen, was
Wahrheit ist, indem er ein Verzweiflung an den sogenannten naturlichen Vorstel-
lungen, Gedanken, und Meinungen zustande bringt.

10. *P., p.* 69: Das Ziel . . . dem Wissen . . . notwendig . . . ist da, wo es nicht
mehr über sich selbst hinauszugehen nötig hat, wo es sich selbst findet und der
Begriff dem Gegenstande, der Gegenstand dem Begriffe entspricht.

11. *P., p.* 75: Das Besusstseyn . . . wird . . . einen Punkt erreichen . . . wo die
Erscheinung dem Wessen gleich wird, seine Darstellung hiemit mit eben diesem
Punkte der eigentlichen Wissenschafft des Geistes zusammenfällt; und endlich,
indem es selbst dies sein Wesen erfasst, wird es die Nature des absoluten Wissens
selbst bezeichnen.

12. This "absolute standpoint" is generally taken to be "absolute knowledge,"
expounded at the end of the *Phenomenology.* But the conditions for this standpoint would also be fulfilled by the *Sache Selbst* as a negation of all limited
aspects of individual consciousness (see section III B, *Explicit Reason,* below).
And there are also grounds for supposing that this standpoint is reached in its
most complete form only in "Objective Spirit" towards the end of Hegel's
Encyclopedia (see Otto Pöggeler, *op. cit.,* p. 283).

13. This "phenomenal exposition" is a description of science itself, as a phenomenon in its totality. If certain phenomenal appearances of science are
"mere" appearances, i.e., appearances which do not quite do justice to the true
reality of science, this will best be demonstrated by consideration of the appearances in comparison with one another. It is hoped that by the sum-total of such
considerations, science will finally come to know itself—which will amount to a
"knowledge of knowledge."

PART ONE: A

1. For a very concise description of these Forms of Consciousness, see Hegel's
"Philosophie des Geistes," in the *Enzyklopädie,* 3rd edition, paragraphs
418-421.

2. The attitude described here would seem to be a presupposition of that
Realism which says that "all our knowledge derives from the senses" or that
"truth is the conformity of our mind to given sense data"—as long as no system
of transcendental autonomous *a priori* constructs is introduced to counterbal-

ance the "authoritativeness" of sensation. (In the latter event, one would seem to have definitely left the sphere of sense-certainty.)

An exemplification of this attitude might be found in the position of Robinet and other 18th century French philosophers, concerning whom Hegel states in his *History of Philosophy* that "They accept sensation and matter as the only truth, to which must be reduced all thought, all morality, as a mere modification of sensation." This is a type of extreme reductionism which adopts an idea of Locke, and erects it into a one-sided exclusive principle. Cf. *Hegel's Lectures on the History of Philosophy* (London: Routledge and Kegan Paul, 1968), Vol. III, p. 398f.

3. "Truth" in the strict sense, and in the context of the *Phenomenology*, is subjective/objective reality, in-itself, a reality which is ordinarily determined and limited in its appearance for-consciousness. "Certainty" is in general any attitude which seems to be in positive possession of the truth. For example, if a group of artists were positioned around a single stable model, and depicting that model from their several vantage points—each of them, in his depiction, would express the certitude which he has of the truth, i.e., of the objective state of the model precisely as subjectively modified by consciousness. But obviously, in order for full certainty to obtain, all determinate depictions would have to be synthesized to give a complete concept of this model as appearing to subjectivities-in-general—which would constitute the full "truth" of the model-as-depicted. Likewise, in the *Phenomenology*, the full truth will arrive only at the end, with "absolute knowledge," in which all finite viewpoints are synthesized to produce the most accurate possible representation of the world and self-consciousness in their interrelationship and fusion.

4. Kierkegaard makes a striking adaptation of the notion that the only true "now" is the universal "now," to an essentially Christian point of view. The Christian, says Kierkegaard, is one who, in dealing with an "instant," does not get immersed in its isolated particularity, but finds in it the revelation of the eternal "now" towards which he is advancing through faith. Cf. *The Concept of Dread,* p. 78 (Lowrie tr.; New Jersey: Princeton University Press, 1957).

5. At this point we should note that Hegel's use of the term "universal" envisages a much wider and more flexible applicability than its traditional use in Aristotelian logic.

In a syllogism of the form A is B, B is C, therefore A is C—the term "C" is said to be a "universal," in so far as it had a much wider extension, relative to "A"; that is, "C" includes "A" within the scope of its signification, while the converse (that "A" includes 'C') would not be true. But there is also a "syllogism" in life processes which results in another type of "universal:" The bud disappears with the advent of the blossom (to use an example which Hegel gives in his Preface, with reference to the succession of philosophical systems); and the blossom, in its turn, gives rise to the fruit, which takes its place. Speaking in terms of the dynamics involved, we could say that the fruit results from the fact that the plant refused to stop at blossoming, but negated the static existence of this moment, and went beyond it. Thus the fruit is more "universal" in relation to the blossom and bud, in the sense that, by successive negations, it arrives at a result which includes the negated moments while at the same time going beyond them.

In the manifold contexts in which Hegel uses the term "universal," he ordinarily means a stage or an aspect in the flux of existence, which is a relative negation of the particularities in that context, while at the same time incorporating these particularities and bringing them to a unity. For example, the state is a universal, relative to its members, whose individuality it checks and negates, and at the same time sublimates.

6. *P.*, p. 86: Das Hier, das gemeint wird, wäre der Punkt; er *ist* aber nicht, sondern, indem er als sei end aufgezeigt wird, zeigt sich das Aufzeigen, nicht unmittelbares Wissen, sondern eine Bewegung, von dem gemeinten Hier aus durch viele Hier, in das allgemeine Hier zu sein, welches . . . eine einfache Vielheit der Hier ist. . . .

7. The thesis that we cannot give intelligible expression to sensuous particularities, but only to universals, is intimated also by Thomas Aquinas in *De substantiis separatis,* Cap. 81 (*Tractatus de substantiis separatis,* Lescoe ed.; Ohio: Messenger Press, 1962): "The human *mind* can know nothing except in terms of its universal nature. . . . Man has cognition of singulars through sensation, but he can think only about universals." (intellectus humanus cognoscere non potest res nisi secundum universalem naturam. . . . Homo singularia quidem cognoscit per sensum, universalia vero per intellectum).

PART ONE: B.

1. What "falls to itself" could turn out to be many things. It could be the a-priori forms and concepts of Kant, the imagination's "law of association" which Hume spoke of, or the "blank tablet" of the mind, which Plato speaks of in his *Theaetetus.* No determination is made at this point as to what this "element of subjectivity" might consist in.

2. Consciousness, by withdrawing from the objects from which it gleaned its perceptions, in a certain sense "restores" these objects to themselves (after having "drawn out" the objects from their existence in-self, by the preliminary processes of perception). Thus in this sense the ego-transmuted objects "return" to themselves, or become "for-themselves."

3. Cp. Hegel's discussion of the *fürsichsein* of Leibniz' monads, in the *Lectures on the History of Philosophy,* Vol. III, pp. 346-347; German ed., p. 470-471.

4. In other words, the intrinsic reason why a perceptual object can be for-itself only by being for-another, is that to be for-self is to be for self-as-other. The prime analogue here is consciousness, which can only know itself, and thus be for-self, by separating itself from itself in making itself objective—which amounts to becoming "other than" itself. As we shall see later, in the section on "self-consciousness," consciousness, in becoming for self-as-other, becomes immediately for-other-selves. And in like manner here, the perceptual object, in appearing to be for itself-as-*other*, appears also to become immediately for-other-objects.

PART ONE: C

1. Baillie in his translation of the *Phenomenology* very often renders *Begriff* as "notion" rather than "concept." Kaufmann remarks—rightly, it seems—that this is not a felicitous rendering, since the English word, "notion," generally connotes a vague or hazy idea. In view of this, we will render *Begriff* as "concept" generally, but especially in this section where the concept of "Concept" is treated at length.

2. Accordingly to Hyppolite (*op. cit.,* p. 119), the notion of Force which Hegel presents here is related to the Leibnizian notion of force as the "sole real unity" of the discrete world of matter.

For a parallel treatment of Force in Hegel's *Logic,* see the *Encyclopedia of Philosophy,* 3rd. ed. §136 ff.

3. An alternative way of explaining the transition that takes place here might be as follows: The prime analogue for this whole development is the relationship between perceptual consciousness (the for-itself) and the sensuous manifold (the for-another). As the perceptual consciousness becomes aware of *its* distinction

from the manifold, it begins to see in the perceptual *world* a reflection of this primal distinction. But as consciousness becomes aware of the fact that its distinction from the manifold presupposes some *unity* of conceptual form and sensuous content, it also becomes correspondingly aware of the unity of form and content—and of the other tentative "distinctions"—in the perceptual world. At this point it has definitely gone beyond perceptual consciousness.

4. Cf. Kant, *Critique of Pure Reason,* pp. 265ff, A 249ff. Appearance for Kant becomes the "middle term" between the "noumena" which the appearances represent, and the concepts of the understanding, which are empty constructs unless supplied with empirical content through intuition of sensible appearances. These appearances, insofar as they serve as this "middle term," are called "phenomena" by Kant: "Appearances, so far as they are thought of as objects according to the unity of the categories, are called phenomena." *(Ibid.,* A 248.)

5. *P.,* p. 111: In diesem *innern Wahren,* als dem *absolut Allgemeinen,* welches vom *Gegensatze* des Allgemeinen und Einzelnen gereinigt und *für den Verstand* geworden ist, schliesst sich erst über der *sinnlichen* als der *erscheinenden Welt* nunmehr eine übersinnliche als die *wahr* Welt auf.

6. *P.,* p. 111: (Dieses) Ansich. . .ist . . . die erste und . . . selbst unvollkommene Erscheinung der Vernunft.

7. For Kant also the awareness of the noumenon as the negative boundary of the phenomenon leads ultimately to "Reason." But for Kant Reason involves an unsuccessful attempt to reconcile the noumenal and phenomenal worlds, while for Hegel Reason is construed in a positive sense, as the successful transcendence of what Kant would call the "dialectic" or antinomy between noumenon and phenomenon, inner and outer.

8. *P.,* p. 113: *Die Erscheinung ist sein Wesen* und in der Tat seine Erfüllung.

9. Hegel here begins to describe the transformation of the phenomenon into law. This process is also a topic for analysis in Schelling's philosophy. According to Schelling, "The Phenomenal (the material element) must entirely disappear, and laws (the formal element) alone remain. Hence it comes to pass that the more that which is in conformity with law breaks forth in nature itself, the more the outward covering disappears; the phenomena themselves become more spiritual, and finally cease altogether." (Hegel, *Lectures on the History of Philosophy,* Vol. III, p. 517; German ed., p. 651.)

As we shall see in what follows, the phenomena in a certain sense "cease altogether" when Understanding formulates the ultimate abstraction of "general law."

10. See p. 194, Baillie.

11. As an example of the sense in which law is the stable universal expression of change and difference, Hyppolite makes the following observation: "In the free fall of a body there is continual variation in space and time, but the relation between these variables maintains a certain constant reciprocity, such that the well-known mathematical formula, $d = 1/2gt^2$, is the "stable" expression of the perpetual instability of these two variables." *(Op. cit.,* p. 124.)

12. P. 196, Baillie.

13. Compare the line of reasoning in Hegel's dissertation *De Orbitis Planetarum* (Jena, 1801) with regard to "centrifugal" and "centripetal" force: "The distinction between centrifugal and centripetal force is meaningless; since the laws which are formulated about these two forces are in reality only mathematical laws of motion, hiding behind the physical name and disguise of "forces.' " (Ex quibus omnibus primum efficitur, inanem esse vis centrifugae et centripetae distinctionem, sed leges quas virium centripetae et centrifugae esse perhibent, revera esse leges motus mathematicas, physica virium specie et nomine contaminatas.—Glockner ed., Vol. I, p. 17.)

14. This is a reiteration of the position of Hume, denying that any intrinsic necessity obtains among elements represented in specific laws applied to natural phenomena.

15. *P., p.* 118-119: Der Verstand *hat* aber den Begriff *dieses Unterschiedes an sich,* eben darin, dass das Gesetz einesteils das Innre, *Ansichseiende,* aber *an ihm* zugleich *Unterschiedne* ist.

16. *P., p.* 120: Unser Bewusstsein ist aber aus dem Innern als Gegenstande auf die andere Seite in den *Verstand* herübergegangen und hat in ihm den Wechsel.

17. According to Harris (*op. cit.,* p. 25, p. 142), Hegel's idea of a *verkehrte welt* seems to have had its genealogical beginnings in his youthful conception of Heaven as an inverted, possibly illusory, image of the world. In the philosophical sphere it recalls the Kantian notion of a "supra-sensible world" which is a "necessary illusion" encountered by the Understanding.

18. *P., p.* 121: Wird das erste Übersinnliche, das ruhige Reich der Gesetze, das unmittelbare Abbild der wahrgenommenen Welt in sein Gegenteil umgekehrt; das Gesetz war überhaupt das sich Gleichbleibende, wie seine Unterschiede; jetzt aber ist gesetzt dass . . . das sich Gleich stösst sich vielmehr von sich ab, und das sich Ungleiche setzt sich vielmehr als das sich Gleiche . . . . *Diese zweite übersinnliche Welt* ist auf diese Weise die *verkehrte* Welt.

19. Hyppolite in his translation of the *Phenomenology* adds the following explanatory note on this statement (p. 132): "In the external part of the circuit of a galvanic pile, the current runs from the copper to the zinc; but in the internal part it runs from the zinc to the copper."

20. Cf. Hegel's *Philosophy of Right,* paragraphs 99-103, and 220.

Through all these examples our attention is drawn to the "dialectical" method and/or subject-matter which goes beyond the method and subject-matter of Descartes, and Hume, and Kant, and other "philosphers of the Understanding." Dialectical philosophy does not seem to be primarily concerned with drawing together sense data into the stable unity of laws. Rather, it seems to deal with those "bread and butter" concepts which are presuppositions, and which everyone takes for granted, and "understands"—e.g., the concepts of being, time, space, motion, magnitude, knowledge, love, sensation, personality, etc. These concepts, whether they are enunciated by laymen or specialists, are already unities created out of some manifold. But just as Aristotle proposes, after uncovering the forms of things in his *Physics,* to develop a science which will investigate the principles of form itself (a *Metaphysics),* so also the philosopher, in Hegel's estimation, will not just accept the conventional conceptual unifications made of sense data but will try to probe deeper to find essential distinctions lurking even in the unities which have been formulated. As a result of his investigation of this inner realm, he will inevitably discover paradoxes. He will find, as Hegel puts it, that "everything turns into its opposite," pleasure into pain, being into negation, thought into objectivity, unity into multiplicity, etc.

The appreciation of dialectic antinomies, such as the Kantian cosmological antinomies, is not the highest stage of philosophy. Philosophy must go beyond mere dialectic to the "infinite Concept," i.e. true speculative philosophy in the Hegelian sense, which reestablishes unity amidst dialectical oppositions.

21. *P.,* p. 123: Allein solche Gegensätze von Innerem and Äusserem, von Erscheinung und Übersinnlichem, als von zweierlei Wirklichkeiten, sind hier nicht mehr vorhanden. Die abgestossenen Unterschiede verteilen sich nicht von neuem an zwei solche Substanzen, welche sie trügen und ihnen ein getrenntes Bestehen verliehen. . . .

22. Here we have a phenomenological account of the way that Fichte's principles came to supersede Kant's. Fichte realized that Kant's unity of apperception,

which drew the manifold of sense experience into the unity of space and of time and of the categories, could be neither merely a subjective nor merely an objective unity. The unities which the transcendental ego formulated were basically manifestations of the primal unity of ego *and* non-ego, subject *and* object. So Fichte strove to make explicit this principle which was implicit in Kant, i.e. to show that the finite determinations which the ego made were more fundamentally manifestations of the unconditioned (infinite) self-determination of ego in the form of self-distinction (i.e., taking place only through a relation to the non-ego). In other words, when consciousness makes any determinate law of nature, it is limiting and determining the non-ego, and at the same time being limited and determined by the non-ego (which gives definite boundaries to the ego); and this mutual determination of ego and non-ego, in theoretical knowledge, is simply a result of the inner necessity of consciousness to make itself into non-ego to have any knowledge whatsoever. If, by averting to this process, we come to apprehend a determinate concept of the Understanding not solely as determination of ego by non-ego, but also as determination of non-ego by ego—we then see this concept in terms of the "infinite" motion giving rise to all knowledge. That is, we see it as an infinite concept.

This also brings us out of the sphere of theoretical knowledge (where the determination of ego by non-ego is emphasized) to practical knowledge and self-consciousness (where the determination of non-ego by ego is emphasized). Thus, after spending some time in explaining the "subjective" distinctions and properties inherent in "objective" concepts, we will arrive eventually and naturally at focusing on the subjectivity itself, in the sections to follow.

23. *P.*, p. 125: Diese einfache Unendlichkeit, oder der absolute Begriff ist das einfache Wesen des Lebens, die Seele der Welt, das allgemeine Blut zu nennen, welches allgegenwärtig durch keinen Unterschied getrübt noch unterbrochen wird, das vielmehr selbst alle Unterschiede ist, so wie ihr Aufgehobensein, also in sich pulsiert, ohne sich zu bewegen, in sich erzittert, ohne unruhig zu sein.

For an analysis of Hegel's usage of the term "Life," see the following chapter.

24. This amounts to the dissolution of the Kantian thing-in-itself. As Fichte puts it, "The ego as intelligence (understanding) remains dependent on an undetermined non-ego; it is only through this that it is intelligence. In order to attain independence and true *infinitude,* we must pass from the ego as Understanding to the ego as Self-Consciousness." Cf. Hegel's chapter on Fichte in his *Lectures on the History of Philosophy,* Vol. III, p. 495; German ed., p. 631.

25. *P.*, p. 128: Indem ihm dieser Begriff der Unendlichkeit Gegenstand ist, ist es also Bewusstein des Unterschieds als eines *unmittelbar* ebenso sehr Aufgehobenen; es ist *für sich selbst,* es ist Unterscheiden des Ununterschiedenen, oder Selbstbewusstsein.

PART TWO: A

1. For example, after the Understanding formulates the laws of positive and negative electricity, and also understands the internal logical preconditions which necessitated its formulation of some such law, it gets to the point where at one and the same time it is giving valid objective existence to its law, and also appreciating the fact that the law is *its* law. Thus Understanding when it becomes complete breaks up into two moments: the creation of universal constructs, and the constant return to the subjective roots of these constructs. When the *latter* moment becomes emphasized, Understanding proper gives way to the attitude of Self-Consciousness proper.

2. *P.*, p. 136: Das *Wesen* ist die Unendlichkeit als das *Aufgehobensein* aller Unterschiede, die reine achsendrehende Bewegung, die Ruhe ihrer selbst als abso-

lut unruhiger Unendlichkeit; die *Selbständigkeit* selbst, in welcher die Unterschiede der Bewegung aufgelöst sind; das einfache Wesen der Zeit, das in dieser Sichselbstgleichheit die gediegene Gestalt des Raumes hat.

3. Hegel sums up this one total process by saying that *substance is subject*, and *subjectivity is substantial*. What he means by this is that—in the world as a whole—Absolute Being is offering itself to consciousness, and becoming consciousness; and the Absolute Self (cf. Kant's transcendental ego) is continually finding itself in being, and changing into being. These two Absolutes constitute a unity-in-duality, insofar as they are two complementary processes. And if we choose to emphasize their *unity*, we speak of them as one Absolute—as Life.

But when we speak of Life as the "unity" of the processes of Being's subjectification and the Self's objectification—we must be careful to note in what sense we are using the word "unity," here. For, as Hegel says (*On Christianity*, Knox tr.; N.Y.: Harper, Cloister, 1961, p. 254), the "unity" of Life "is not a negative simplicity, a unity produced by abstraction. . . Pure life is being." In other words, it is not just a universal concept drawing multiple discrete elements into a thought-unity, but the existential pre-condition which makes thought possible and which makes concepts possible.

But to say that Life is "being" is misleading, since there is the danger that we might equate "being" with substance or the "other." And to say that Life is a non-abstract unity is misleading, since it is hard to conceptualize a unity which is not abstract—at least from multiplicity.

In order, then, to understand the precise meaning of Life in the *Phenomenology*, let us recall a point that we made in the Introduction to this study (sec. IX); that the vantage point of Hegel is at the *unity* of the transcendental (unifying) ego and the empirical ego, which enters into the manifold of sense data. Thus Hegel in this sense is situated at the *unity* of a unity and a manifold.

Corresponding to Hegel's specific vantage point at the writing of the *Phenomenology*, the Life that he describes there is a unity of a unity and a diversity. The "unity" which it unifies is the Absolute Self, which tends to draw everything into unity by the operations of consciousness. The "diversity" which it unifies is the "otherness" of Absolute Being, which contains diversity *primarily* because *it* is diverse from the Absolute Self. Life itself then, is that which has to do with unifying the one thing that the Absolute Self does *not* unify—namely, the Absolute Self and Absolute Being.

Life as the unity of unifying consciousness and diversifying otherness is a *non-abstract* unity. That is, it is not within that sphere of thought-determinations by means of which the transcendental ego comes to unify the manifold of sense data. But it is the background which must be presupposed for any of the operations of the transcendental ego to take place (the transcendental ego must be in union with otherness before it can proceed to create determinate unities out of otherness).

Life as the unity of consciousness and being, is also "being" in a special, "absolute" sense. It is not that being which is set in opposition to the self, and created by the objectification-operations of the self. But rather, it is that being which must be presupposed as the background to the creation of any determinate beings—namely, the "existential" union of Absolute Being and the Absolute Self (without which there could be no determinate thought-designated "beings," nor could there be being-in-general as the sum-total of such determinate thought-designated "beings").

4. The attitude of Self-Consciousness in the beginning possesses only a bare minimal knowledge of the subjective roots of "objectivity." These roots must be elaborated fully; their connection with objectivity must be accurately elucidated.

5. *P.,* p. 137: Das allgemeine Leben . . . indem es das *Andre* in sich setzt, (hebt) diese seine *Einfachheit* oder sein Wesen auf, d. h. es entzweit sie, und dies Entzweien der unterschiedslosen Flüssigkeit ist eben das Setzen der Individualität.

6. *P.,* p. 140: "Der Geist. . . in der vollkommenen Freiheit und Selbständigkeit ihres Gegensatzes, nämlich verschiedener-für-sich-seiender-Selbstbewusstsein(e), die Einheit derselben ist: *Ich, das Wir, und Wir, das Ich* ist.

PART TWO: B

1. *P.,* p. 143-144: Seine Wahrheit wäre nur, dass sein eignes Fürsichsein sich ihm als selbständiger Gegenstand, oder, was dasselbe ist, der Gegenstand sich als diese reine Gewissheit seiner selbst dargestellt hätte.

2. *P.,* p. 144: Es ist allein das Daransetzen des Lebens, wodurch die Frieheit, wodurch es bewährt wird, dass dem Selbstbewusstsein nicht das *Sein,* nicht die *unmittelbare* Weise, wie es auftritt, nicht sein Versenktsein in die Ausbreitung des Lebens das Wesen,—sondern dass an ihm nichts vorhanden, was für es nicht verschwindendes Moment wäre, dass es nur reines *Fürsichsein* ist.

3. The bodily existence of consciousness is its particularity *(Einzelheit),* its contingent existence here or there *(Dasein).* (Cf. *Phän.,* p. 144.) Consciousness must negate its sensuous immersion in particularity and contingency if it is to show itself as free.

Compare Sartre's description in *Being and Nothingness* (N.Y.: Philosophical Library, 1956, p. 82, p. 308) of the emergence of the "for-itself" from the evanescent contingency of man's bodily "facticity."

4. The situation envisaged here might be clarified negatively by the example of "shame:" If I notice that another is gazing at me indifferently or amusedly as an object, I may feel shame, because of his lack of recognition of my self-concept. He in his turn, noticing my shame, may feel shame at not having extended to me that recognition. In order for my shame to be dispelled, he by *his own activity* would have to give some echo or reflection of my own free determinations—such that I would be enabled to "recognize" a free response to my own freedom.

5. According to Harris (*op. cit.,* p. 304) the dialectic of Master and Slave which begins here is reminiscent of certain descriptions of the German Feudal Lord, found in Hegel's early writings.

6. The drama of the Master-Slave conflict has been renarrated rather frequently by philosophers after Hegel—but with a somewhat different cast and a somewhat different plot:

In *Kierkegaard's* version (cf. the *Concept of Dread,* Ch. V, *passim*), the creature, the bondsman struggling with sin, is confronted by the demands of the Creator, or Lord, who is exempt from all sin. As a result of this confrontation, and the indefinite nature of these demands, he is overtaken by an *absolute,* indeterminate, and internal *dread of guilt*—a dread which can be negated only by abandoning his external attachments, and "working towards" inwardness, i.e., towards the purity and certitude of Faith.

In *Marx's* version, the "master-slave" dichotomy takes place in the socioeconomic sphere. Man is basically trying to realize his productive capacities. Certain men—the capitalists, who have money and the means of production at their disposal—manage to get other men to do their work for them, while they reserve to themselves almost exclusively the enjoyment of the products of that work. Thus the capitalists hope to be productive by means of their slaves, but to enjoy the fruits of this productivity by themselves. But as it turns out, the capitalists estrange themselves so far from the sphere of work-upon-objects that they become bereft of any true productivity; and rather than enjoying the fruits of their productivity, they end up habitually plundering the fields of production which their slaves have bought and plowed by the sweat of their brow. The slave-workers, on their side, driven on by the fear of the awesome economic and political power which the capitalist wields, gradually come to concretize the abstract ideals of self-productivity that originally spurred on the capitalist, and thus become the personification of the creative powers of man, of man's capability of finding himself and producing himself by his labor in and on the world. In *Nietzsche's* version, the drama takes place in the moral sphere. All men are spurred on by the basic life-drive, the "will-to-power." The masters are those who personify this basic drive to the fullest; and without any cowering before conventional morality, proceed to develop their own spontaneous, independent moral code, and to dictate this code to those who are less endowed with the genius of humanity. The slaves, or the masses, are those who do not have the ability to develop the will-to-power, and thus must rest content in a slave-morality, which extolls weakness, obedience, suffering, pity, charity, etc.—and which allows others to legislate for them. But the slaves, because of their tendency to incorporate their values in *objective,* external institutions, cultural concomitants and legal sanctions, seemingly get the upper hand, because of the connatural distaste of the Masters for external and conventional determinants. Thus the slaves bring about a reversal of sorts. But (Nietzsche hopes) this reversal will be itself reversed, and the Masters will soon be restored to their rightful preeminence. Cf. *The Genealogy of Morals,* First Essay, 16; Second Essay, 24.

In *Sartre's* version, finally, we have a special type of reciprocal conflict, in which every consciousness is continually a Master in one sense (insofar as it sees others as objects *pour-soi*) and a Slave in another sense (insofar as it becomes an object *pour-autrui*). There are tentative solutions to this dichotomy (e.g. love), but ultimately no way out of the opposition—no way, that is, to attain to true "inter-subjectivity" as an existential fact. Even Heidegger's "being-with-others" (*Mitsein*) (according to Sartre) does not provide a way out—because it is an a-priori construction which does nothing to corroborate the existence of subjects in concrete mutuality. See *Being and Nothingness,* Part Three, Ch. 1, III; and Ch. 3, I and III.

Various attempts have been made to apply Hegel's Master-Slave dialectic to the contemporary world. For a neo-Marxist approach, see Alexandre Kojeve, *Introduction to the Reading of Hegel* (N.Y.: Basic Books, 1969). See also my article, "A Non-Marxian Application of Hegel's Master-Slave Dialectic to Some Contemporary Politico-Social Problems," in *Idealistic Studies,* III, 3, Sept., 1973; and Darrell Christensen, "Hegel and the Contemporary Crisis of Authority," in *Idealistic Studies* III, 2, May, 1973.

PART TWO: C

1. Here begins the merger of the Master and Slave consciousness. The "stoic" can be either a master, like Marcus Aurelius, or a slave, like Epictetus.

2. *P.* p. 153: Diesem Selbstbewusstsein weder ein anderes als es, noch die reine Abstraktion des Ich das Wesen ist, sondern Ich, welches das Anderssein, aber als gedachten Unterschied, an ihm hat.

3. *P.,* p. 156: Das Bestimmte. . .hat nichts Bleibendes an ihm und *muss* dem Denken verschwinden, weil das Unterschieden eben dies ist, nicht *an ihm selbst* zu sein, sondern seine Wesenheit nur in einem Andern zu haben.

4. In Kierkegaard's ethics, the first step towards the freedom of self-transcendence is "stoicism," which is imperfect and deficient insofar as it is "abstract" freedom: "The first form which the choice (of oneself) takes is complete isolation. . . . (The individual's) action has no relation to any surrounding world,

for he has reduced this to naught and exists only for himself. The life view here revealed. . .found expression in Greece in the effort of the single individual to develop himself into a paragon of virtue. . . . He withdrew from the activities of life. . .to act . . . in himself. . . . The fault lay in the fact that this individual had chosen himself altogether abstractly." (*Either/Or*, II, Swenson tr.; N.Y., Anchor-Doubleday, 1959, pp. 244-245).

5. Cf. the following characteristic statement of Epictetus, which illustrates the stoical attitude of waiting for objectivity (otherness) to "negate itself:" "Make it your study," he admonishes, "to confront every harsh impression with the words, 'You are but an impression, and not at all what you seem to be.' Then test it by those rules that you possess." Cf. "The Manual of Epictetus," in *Greek and Roman Philosophy after Aristotle*, Saunders ed. (N.Y.: Free Press, 1966), p. 133.

6. Thus Sextus Empiricus, denying that there can be stable determinations of truth or falsity, goodness or badness, either in conceptual reality (the non-evident) or in sensible reality (the evident) advocates a complete "suspension of judgement" in their regard: "If reason is such a trickster as to all but snatch away the appearances from under our very eyes, surely we should view it with suspicion in the case of things non-evident so as not to display rashness by following it. . . . Since the Dogmatists suppose they apprehend (the non-evident) from the things evident, if we are forced to suspend judgement about the evident, how shall we dare make pronouncements about the non-evident? " Cf. *Greek and Roman Philosophy After Aristotle*, p. 156, p. 182.

The difference between Epictetus and Sextus Empiricus is the difference between saying that any truth will show itself to be relatively false, and saying there is no truth or falsity.

7. *P.*, p. 156: Als *Skeptizismus* . . . ist sie Moment des Selbstbewusstseins, welchem es nicht *geschieht,* dass ihm, ohne zu wissen wie, sein Wahres and Reelles verschwindet, sondern welches in der Gewissheit seiner Freiheit dies andere für reell sich Gebende selbst verschwinden lässt.

8. *P.* p. 158: Wird ihm die *Gleichheit* aufgezeigt, so zeigt es die *Ungleichheit auf*; und indem ihm diese, die es eben ausgesprochen hat, jetzt vorgehalten wird, so geht es zum Aufzeigen der *Gleichheit* über.

9. When Hegel speaks of self-consciousness in its self-identical *subsistence* and *unchangeableness,* he seems to have in mind the transcendental ego of Kant and Fichte—the absolute subjectivity which draws all the particular determinations of the empirical ego into a negative universality, and finally discovers that the otherness of its fully universalized formulations seems identical at base with the essential otherness of the objects which appeared as "other to" (transcendent to) the empirical ego. But this abstract philosophical insight continually seems to contradicted by the facts of everyday life.

10. *P.*, p. 159: Dieses *unglückliche, in sich entzweite* Bewusstsein . . . selbst *ist* das Schauen eines Selbstbewusstseins in ein anderes, und es selbst *ist* beide, und die Einheit beider ist ihm auch das Wesen; aber es *für sich* ist sich noch nicht dieses Wesen selbst, noch nicht die Einheit beider.

11. Kierkegaard, in his essay, "The Unhappiest Man" (*Either/Or,* Vol. I, p. 217 ff.), interprets Hegel's "unhappy consciousness" as a situation in which the essence of a self-conscious individual is no longer present to him, but in some manner outside him, such that the individual manifests a dichotomy of temporal alienation.

He then goes on to show how such a situation develops when a person lives in the past, or in the future, without being reconciled to their present self, their present essence.

In *Sickness unto Death,* he examines many other senses in which the individual may fail to be reconciled to his own eternal essence, and thus enter into the various states of "despair."

12. *P.*, p. 161: Sie verläuft sich durch diese Momente, einmal unwandelbares dem einzelnen überhaupt, dann selbst einzelnes dem andern einzelnen entgegengesetzt, und endlich mit ihm Eins zu sein.

13. In the elaboration of the three moments of the development of the Unhappy Consciousness, it is helpful, when speaking of the "Unchangeable," to take the transcendental ego as the primary analogate, primordially exemplifying all types of changelessness, transcendence, and "eternal" universality; and, when speaking of "self-consciousness," or simply "consciousness," to understand the empirical ego, dimly aware of the presence of its own transcendental ego, but far from being reconciled with the latter.

14. Hegel's description of the efforts of self-consciousness to find its stable essence is, as Loewenberg points out, *Hegel's Phenomenology: Dialogues on the Life of Mind* (Illinois: Open Court, 1965), p. 104f., redolent of the efforts of an adolescent to "find himself." At this particular stage in the "search," one is also reminded of the pubescent's search for love. The pubescent begins to feel physical attraction and infatuation, but is incapable of relating to any love-object in the context of true romantic love. The cause for this can be traced to a fundamental lack of spiritual depth in the pubescent himself. So also, self-consciousness' failure to come to a definite encounter with the Unchangeable at this point, can be traced to the fact that it needs to work to acquire the requisite spiritual interiority as a pre-condition for this encounter.

15. As was mentioned in the introduction to this study (Sect. VI (e), 4), Hegel very often draws on experiences in social and individual history. So also, the three "moments of the second stage" in the process of unification of the Unhappy Consciousness could refer, for example: a) to the expectation of a savior or Messiah in the ancient religions of the world; b) to the desire—from time immemorial—to experience self-transcendence through mysticism (a desire which became especially vocal in the Mediaeval and late Mediaeval eras in the Western world); c) to the consolidation of "faith, hope, and charity" as the three "theological virtues" in early Christianity; d) to the development of the dogma of the Holy Trinity in the Patristic ages of Christendom; and e) to the theoretical synthesis of subjectivity and objectivity in German Idealism in Hegel's era.

The present "moment," 2(b), correspondingly, would take on disparate connotations as applied to such particular contexts. As applied to (a), it would connote the moment of the appearance of God in an "incarnate" form definitely apprehensible to the empirical ego. This incarnate God would be at one and the same time the revelation of God (the "Son of God") and the result of the efforts of the human race (the "Son of Man"). As applied to (b), it would connote the moment when the mystic gets beyond sensuous devotion, to strive for inner, spiritual, personal union with the divinity. As applied to (c), it would connote the moment of "hope," when the Christian begins to actively strive for the Salvation he has believed in, by making a responsible use of the "graces" offered to him. As applied to (d), it would connote the moment when consciousness realizes that the Unchangeable Father, to truly know or possess Himself, would have to separate Himself from Himself, thus producing his own likeness—the Son, the distinct image of God, and also the "Word" which God communicates to men. And as applied to (e), it would possibly connote the moment when Fichte got beyond the subjectivism of Kant's transcendental deductions to realize that the transcendental ego reveals itself in that which appears to the empirical ego as transcendent objectivity.

Kierkegaard, very likely influenced by Hegel, makes an application of this same second "moment" to the moral sphere. As Kierkegaard interprets it, this moment would be the time when an individual comes to a distinct awareness of an "external, ideal self" emerging in his personality. (*E./O.*, II, pp. 265-274.)

Carl Jung, very likely not influenced by Hegel, speaks of psychological transcendence in terms remarkably redolent of Hegel's analysis of the second "moment": In psychiatric practice, he found that in cases where people were no longer able to project the image of the divinity, and were in danger of dispersion of psychic energy, the ambiguous situation was often alleviated by the dream or vision of a "mandala symbol"—the symbol of deiform completeness (usually a circle containing sets of quaternities). This symbol was found to coincide in major characteristics with "mandalas" in ancient and modern religions, myth, etc. In the case of the individual patient, this "particular revelation" of the divinity and of one's own potential self is usually accompanied by a feeling of profound inner peace. Cf. Jung, *Archetypes of the Unconscious* (Hall tr.; N.Y.: Pantheon, 1959) p. 10, pp. 360-361, pp. 383-384, pp. 38ff.

16. Spirit, in its movement away from existential immediacy, gives new determinate significance to the latter.

Kierkegaard enunciates the same general notion, in regard to the emergence of Christianity in the natural and aesthetic Greco-Roman culture:

"Sensuousness was first posited by Christianity. This is quite natural, for Christianity is spirit, and spirit is the positive principle which Christianity has brought into the world. But when sensuousness is understood in its relationship to spirit, it is clearly known as a thing that must be excluded; but precisely because it should be excluded, it is determined as a principle, as a power; for that which spirit—itself a principle—would exclude must be somthing which is also a principle, although it first reveals itself as a principle in the moment of its exclusion" (*Either/Or*, Vol. I, p. 60).

17. As was mentioned above (footnote 15), the experience generalized here could connote many and varied experiences in history and in individual development.

For example, this third "moment" of the second stage could connote a) the subordination of people to their religious leaders (sages, priests, and prophets); b) the subordination of the mystic to inspirations from God (given in the form of visions, "internal words," unexplainable feelings or impulses, etc.); c) the emphasis in early Christianity on the virtue of charity as essential union with the will of God; d) the emphasis on the doctrine of the Holy Spirit, as the "spiration" of the divine will, which both the Father and the Son have in common; and e) the attempt of Schelling to synthesize the "necessity" of history with the "freedom" of the human will in his absolute (in which "intellective intuition" recognized the unity of free will and necessity).

18. (Das in sich Zurückgekehrte. . .eben das Selbst, und das Selbst die sich auf sich beziehende Gleichheit und Einfachheit ist. *P.*, p. 22.)

If the self is that which "returns upon itself," and if that *"which returns"* and that *"upon which it returns"* are not to be considered as two passive, static poles; then the self *most properly* is its relat*ing* to itself, or its mediation of itself.

Kierkegaard explains selfhood in much the same manner in *Sickness unto Death* (N.Y.: Anchor, 1954), p. 146.

"The self is a relation which relates itself to its own self, or it is that in the relation (which accounts for it) that the relation relates itself to its own self. . . . If the relation relates itself to its own self, the relation is then the positive third term, and this is the self."

19. The Terms that Hegel uses in describing the emergence of the "mediating consciousness" do not expressly refer to the creation of any new type of individual consciousness in the social context. Its primary signification seems to be that

consciousness, or some power in consciousness, becomes the mediator for consciousness. But the mediating consciousness could also, perhaps, refer to some certain individual role in society. And thus Baillie interprets it as referring to the "priesthood." We might also extend the term "priesthood" to the kind of speculative philosophy which Hegel extolls—insofar as this philosophy amounts to a mediation of the perennial conflict of opposites.

20. The development of the "mediator" might be clarified by averting to Freud's description of the evolution of the super-ego, as an "inner mediator:"

The male child in the throes of the Oedipus complex, unable to vie with the father as a rival for the mother's love, ordinarily resolves his dilemma by "identification" with the father. This identification results in an inner ego-ideal (super-ego) which amounts to an "incorporated father," or a "fatherly conscience," and which appears to the ego now as an inner, but not fully conscious, standard or guideline.

Thus the child's ego, by allowing its behavior to be "mediated" by the father, comes to set up in itself a father-image which serves thereafter as an intrinsic "mediator" of behavior within consciousness. Cf. Freud, *The Ego and the Id* (Riviere tr.; N.Y.: Norton, 1960), pp. 24ff.

21. The affirmation of the universal will on the part of the particular individual brings man, according to Kierkegaard, into the "ethical sphere of existence:"

"Only when the individual himself is the universal, is it possible to realize the ethical. . . . He who regards life ethically sees the universal, and he who lives ethically expresses the universal in his life, he makes himself the universal man, not by divesting himself of his concretion, for then he becomes nothing, but by clothing himself with it and permeating it with the universal." (*Either/Or*, Vol. II, p. 260.)

PART THREE: A-1

1. "Consciousness" in the strict sense is referred by Hegel to a relationship of awareness in which the ego seems to be encountering an "other" as separate from itself. "Self-consciousness" in the strict sense refers to an awareness in which the ego seems to be encountering itself, after the manner of an "other." But often Hegel uses the word "consciousness" as a general term comprising within its extension also self-consciousness proper. The context will indicate the usage.

2. *P.*, p. 177: Was *ist,* oder das *Ansich* nur ist, insofern es *für* das Bewusstsein, und was *für es* ist, auch *an sich* ist.

3. *P.*, p. 176: Die Vernunft ist die Gewissheit des Bewusstseins alle Realität zu sein; so spricht der Idealismus ihren Begriff aus. "Reason is consciousness' certitude of being all reality: thus does Idealism give expression to its fundamental concept."

4. It should be noted here that Hegel is using the term, "Reason," in a sense which is very different and much more positive than the sense in which Kant uses it.

According to Kant, practical reason is something we deduce to as producing phenomenal determinations from the vantage point of "freedom" (*Critique of Judgement,* p. 32f., fn.): while pure (speculative) reason is a faculty which contributes to illusion in the theoretical sphere, by producing certain all-encompassing pseudo-determinate concepts, like "God" and "Freedom," and then pretending that these concepts are not *purely* speculative, but also empirically verifiable (*Prolegomena,* p. 76ff.).

In his *Lectures on the History of Philosophy,* Vol. III, p. 529 (German ed., p. 666), Hegel points to Fichte's and Schelling's usage of the term "Reason" as a usage which superseded Kant's: "Schelling, like Fichte, begins with I = I, or with the absolute intuition, expressed as proposition or definition of the Absolute, that 'Reason is the absolute indifference of subject and object.' "

5. *P.*, p. 178: . . . ohne sie (die Einheit des Selbstbewusstseins) absolut negatives Wesen,—nur dieses hat die Negation, die Bestimmtheit oder den Unterschied an ihm selbst,—begriffen zu haben. . . .

6. Cf. *Enzyklopädie*, 1st ed., p. 130, paragraph 162.

7. *P.*, p. 179: Denn die vielen Kategorien sind *Arten* der reinen Kategorie, heisst, *sie* ist noch ihre *Gattung* oder *Wesen,* nicht ihnen entgegengesetzt. Aber sie sind schon das Zweideutige, welches zugleich das Anderssein *gegen* die reine Kategorie in seiner *Vielheit* an sich hat. Sie widersprechen ihr durch diese Vielheit in der Tat, und die reine Einheit muss sie an sich aufheben, wodurch sie sich als *negative* Einheit der Unterschiede konstituiert.

8. *P.*, p. 178: Die *Kategorie* . . . ist dies, dass Selbstbewusstsein und Sein *dasselbe* Wesen ist; *dasselbe,* nicht in der Vergleichung, sondern an und für sich. Nur der einseitige schlechte Idealismus lässt diese Einheit wieder als Bewusstsein auf die eine Seite, und ihr gegenüber ein *Ansich* treten.

9. As Baillie mentions, this could refer to the idealisms of Fichte or Berkeley. Fichte, for example, after assenting to the idealistic contention that "consciousness is all reality," still requires an alien *Anstoss,* or impact, from without, to contribute to the reality of consciousness—which contradicts his main insight.

10. Hegel in the few following sections gives an introductory phenomenological overview of what would later become his Philosophy of Nature (in the *Encyclopedia*)—the particular part of his "System" which is conspicuous for having been rejected by so many Hegelians. But not by all. As Findlay (*Hegel: A Re-examination*) says (p. 269), Hegel's Philosophy of Nature "is one part of the system. . .that many Hegelians have thought fit to ignore entirely mainly on account of the outmoded character of the science on which it reposes. Nothing can, however, be more unfit than this ignoring, and, in view of Hegel's undoubted greatness, more impertinent. . . . That the natural science appealed to by Hegel is outmoded is, moreover, irrelevant. The scientific views of Hegel's day are as deserving of respect as the transitory opinions of our own." M.J. Petry has recently published a 3-volume translation-with-commentary of Hegel's *Philosophy of Nature* (N.Y.: 1970).

11. "Matter," says Hegel, "is not a thing that exists, it is being in the sense of universal being, or being in the way the concept is being." (Baillie tr., p. 292). Thus Hegel is not concerned with the sensuous and particularized "secondary matter" (as the Scholastics called it), but with the "prime matter" that Aristotle spoke of. But while Aristotle saw this as an invisible substratum, Hegel (in accord with his Idealist persuasion) sees it as a non-empirical superstratum; and while Aristotle left it devoid of any determinations, Hegel points it out as a universal necessarily concretized into manifold thought-constituted determinations (determinate "matters").

12. Cf. *P.*, p. 189: Was allgemein gültig ist, ist auch allgemein geltend; was sein *soll, ist* in der Tat auch, und was nur sein *soll,* ohne zu *sein,* hat kein Wahrheit.

For an example of the viewpoint Hegel is criticizing here, cf. Johann Gottlieb Fichte's *The Vocation of Man* (Chisholm tr.; N.Y.: Library of Liberal Arts, 1956), pp. 93-99.

Hegel's criticism at this point does not refer directly to moral laws, but these same principles will be brought to bear on the subject-matter of morality later on in the *Phenomenology*: A moral law which only "ought" to be, does not even exist as a moral law. See pp. 443 and 451, Baillie.

13. The viewpoint we have just described is the viewpoint of the subjectivity trying to find itself in objectivity. The opposite viewpoint—that of the substance

of Nature becoming subject—is implied in the former viewpoint, according to the exigencies of the dialectic. If we assume this opposite standpoint, we find that the otherness of organic nature proves to be just the opposite of Reason—i.e., not a union of subjectivity and objectivity, but a falling-apart of the two poles—a discrete standing-apart of objective organisms from the (subjective) purposefulness which seems to direct their activities.

Thus while subjectivity and objectivity show their *unity* in an indistinct way in immediate Reason, they show their *distinction* in the world observed by Reason, without giving any hints as to their point of unification.

14. The same idea is presented in a somewhat different way by Kant, in his *Critique of Judgment*. According to Hegel's reading of Kant, "Internal adaptation to end signifies ... that a thing is in itself end and means, its end is not therefore beyond itself. In the contemplation of the living creature we do not remain at the point of having something sensuous before us ... for we regard it as cause of itself, as producing itself." Hegel then goes on to show how this conception of natural teleology derives historically from Aristotle. (Cf. *Lectures on the History of Philosophy*, Vol. III, pp. 470-471; German ed., p. 602-603.)

15. *P.*, p. 196: Das Selbstbewusstsein ... findet sich als ein Ding, *als ein Leben*, macht aber noch einen Unterschied, zwischen dem, was es selbst ist und was es gefunden, der aber keiner ist. Wie der Instinkt des Tieres das Futter sucht und versehrt, aber damit nichts anders herausbringt als sich, so findet auch der Instinkt der Vernunft in seinem Suchen nur sie selbst.

16. This would seem to be an oblique reference to the Kantian phenomenon-noumenon dichotomy.

17. This is a categorization propounded in the writings of Herder and Kielmeyer, and adopted also by Schelling. (Cf. Hegel, *Lectures on the History of Philosophy*, Vol. III, p. 514; German ed. p. 648.)

18. It is interesting to note that Sheldon, in his *Varieties of Temperament* (N.Y.: Harper, 1942), proposes theories which seem almost to be sophisticated reformulations of the theories Hegel is referring to. Sheldon says, for instance. that aggressivity (conditioned by a highly developed muscular system) has a negative correlationship with sensitivity (conditioned by a highly developed nervous system), and also with affectivity (manifested primarily by the "viscerotonic" temperament, which is based on a body type emphasizing visceral and reproductive powers).

19. Hegel uses the terms, "concrete" and "abstract," in a sense very different from their traditional signification in philosophy. Traditionally, "concrete" referred to the sensuous, only potentially intelligible existent; whereas "abstract" referred to universal elements discerned by the intelligence in concrete particulars, and separated from the latter. But Hegel's "concrete" is that which is thought-constituted, or approximates to thought; while his "abstract" is that which is alien from or resistant to thought, enjoying an isolated existential immediacy.

Kierkegaard uses these terms in Hegel's sense. For example. in *Either/Or* (I. p. 53), where he is discussing the abstract and the concrete in art, he states that "the more abstract the medium, the smaller the probability (of a numerous representation); the more concrete, the greater. But what does it mean to say that the medium is concrete, other than to say it is language, or is seen in approximation to language; for language is the most concrete of all media. The idea ... which comes to expression in sculpture (on the other hand) is wholly abstract."

20. Cf. *P.*, p. 217; Baillie, p. 322-323; *Ph. of History* (Dover), p. 77.

21. In the immediately following section, Reason will return to the *vicinity* of

the concrete universal, and make some approximation to an observation of the pure interiority of life, by considering certain questions about the human psyche, which by definition would be the closest phenomenal manifestation of life in its pure character as *thought*.

22. *P. p.* 211: Dieser Begriff oder reine Freiheit ist ein und dasselbe Leben, die Gestalt oder das Sein für anderes mag in noch so mannigfaltigem Spiele umherschweifen; es ist diesem Strome des Lebens gleichgültig welcher Art die Mühlen sind, die er treibt.

23. Plato similarly posited number *(mathematica)* as the middle-term joining pure universal thought with sensuous particularity. And the intermediate position which it occupies derives from two facts: a) number is unchangeable, like the universal Ideas, and b) number is also multiple and particular, like sensible objects. (Cf. Aristotle's critique of Plato's *mathematica in Metaph.*, I, 6, 987b, 11ff.) The "mathematica" do not, of course, show *how* sensuous objects are related to universal Ideas, but only supply us with a clearer intuition of the fact of their relationship. So also, "number" only gives us a clearer understanding of the relationship of this "outer" to its "inner"—but does not go into the "how" of this relationship.

24. *P.,* p. 217: Sie (die Bestimmtheit) daher schon an diesem (dem Unorganischen) . . . als das einfache Negative dem Dasein als dem Sein für anderes gegenübersteht; und dies einfache Negative ist in seiner letzten einzelnen Bestimmtheit eine Zahl. Das Organische aber ist eine Einzelheit, welche selbst reine Negativität (ist) und daher die fixe Bestimmtheit der Zahl, welche dem *gleichgültigen Sein* zukommt, in sich vertilgt.

25. Schelling held that the Absolute, as the unity of subjective freedom and objective nature, was not conceptually comprehensible; but appeared openly in an immediate, quasi-intuitive manner in organic nature. Here Hegel refutes the notion that we can observe in organic nature a presentation of the *synthesis* of free universal life and organic objectivity; for the two poles, far from being in synthesis, are sundered sharply from each other in organisms.

26. As we shall see, Hegel uses this term to describe the earth as the single totality of all particular genera.

27. *P.,* p. 219: Die Gattung . . . erleidet . . . Gewalt von der Seite des allgemeinen Individuums . . . [an dem die Allgemeinheit ebenso äussere Wirklichkeit (hat)]. . . *der Erde,* welches als die allgemeine Negativität die Unterschiede, wie sie dieselben an sich hat . . . gegen das Systematisieren der Gattung geltend macht.

28. As Hegel mentioned above (p. 109), *Phenomenology* would give us such phenomenal evidence, at least with reference to consciousness.

29. Cf. *P.,* p. 185 (Baillie, p. 283).

30. *P.,* p. 222: Dieser Form. . .wird *ruhiges Sein* von Beziehungen, . . . oder absolute Wahrheit. . .vieler verschiedener Gesetze. . . . Aus diesem Zusammenhange der Bewegung aber von der Betrachtung herausgerissen und einzeln hingestellt, fehlt ihnen nicht der Inhalt, denn sie haben einen bestimmten Inhalt, sondern sie entbehren vielmehr der Form, welche ihr Wesen ist. . .als in der Einheit des Denkens verschwindende Momente.

31. *P.,* p. 226: Der *Einfluss* der Wirklichkeit. . .auf das Individuum erhält durch dieses absolut den entgegengesetzten Sinn, dass es entweder den Strom der einfliessenden Wirklichkeit an ihm gewähren lässt, oder dass es ihn abbricht und verkehrt. Hiedurch aber wird die *psychologische Notwendigkeit* ein. . .leeres Wort.

32. *P.,* p. 231: Das Schicksal ist auch wieder nur die Erscheinung dessen, was die bestimmte Individualität *an sich* als innre ursprüngliche Bestimmtheit ist.

33. *P.,* p. 247: Das *ursprüngliche* Sein [des Geistes] nur *Anlagen* sind, über

welche er viel vermag, oder welche gunstiger Umstande bedürfen, um entwickelt
zu werden; d.h. ein *ursprüngliches* Sein des Geistes ist ebensowohl als ein solches
auszusprechen, das nicht als Sein existiert.

34. Cf. also *Enzyklopädie,* 1st ed., p. 243-244, paragraph 326.

35. This would be human activity, or mind freely manifesting itself. But the
problem still remains: how can we approach this latter, except as phenomenon,
or outer expression? Until this problem is solved, the inner-outer predicament
will still remain.

Kant, in the *Critique of Pure Reason,* B570-B586, comes to a similar
predicament with regard to the freedom-necessity relationship. He notes that the
empirical determinations of human activity are themselves pre-determined intel-
lectively by Practical Reason—which we must presuppose as the transcendental
subject of all such actions (just as we naturally suppose transcendent objects
underlying phenomena outside us). He then goes on to emphasize that we can
have no *science* of such purely intelligible and a-temporal determination. All we
can say is that it does enter into the realm of phenomena—no doubt by immediately determining certain key conditions in the series of conditioned human
actions. But we cannot express the *why* or *how* of this *entrance* into the natural
phenomenal world—this fusion of freedom and necessity.

36. Here follows an analysis of the summary which Hegel himself gives towards
the end of the long section on Observation.

37. *P.,* p. 252: Die Beobachtung ist damit dazu gekommen, es auszusprechen,
was unser Begriff von ihr war, dass nämlich die Gewissheit der Vernunft sich
selbst als gegenständliche Wirklichkeit sucht.

PART THREE: A-2

1. "Our point of view" refers to the viewpoint of the phenomenologist, or of
the *Phenomenology* as a whole. "The point of view of Reason" refers to the
particular viewpoint being considered in this section of the *Phenomenology.* For
a further discussion of the difference between these two viewpoints, see the
Introduction to this study, Sect. IX *supra.*

2. See comment 1, above.

3. Hegel's approach here should thus be distinguished from the point of view
of political philosophers such as Plato, Aristotle, Hobbes, and Rousseau, who
either represented society as a somewhat static integral reality constituted from
its "atomic" units (the individuals making it up), or else concentrated on the
historical genesis of society as something produced by individuals combining for
common ends from the time of antiquity.

4. It should be noted here that Hegel characterizes "happiness" in a way quite
different from the characterizations of Kant, who variously defines happiness as
"general well-being and contentment with one's condition" (*Fundamental Principles of the Metaphysic of Morals,* p. 11), and as "the entire satisfaction of
wants and inclinations" *(Ibid.,* p. 22). In fact, Hegel seems to reflect the position
of Aristotle, who characterizes happiness as *"activity* in accordance with virtue"
(Nicomachean Ethics, "The Basic Works of Aristotle," McKeon ed.,; New York:
Random House, 1941, X, 7, 1177a, 11).

5. The process in which morality emerges from the ethical substance *is* brought
out explicitly towards the end of the *Phenomenology,* in chapter VI C.

6. *P.,* p. 262: Der Erdgeist. . .dem das Sein nur, welches die Wirklichkeit des
einzelnen Bewusstseins ist, als die wahre Wirklichkeit gilt.

7. In Kantian terminology, this would amount to a transition from Pure Reason to Practical Reason.

8. *P.,* p. 263: (Der Genuss) der *Lust.* . .(ist das) Bewusstsein seiner Verwir-

klichung in einem als selbständig erscheinenden Bewusstsein oder (die) Anschauung der Einheit beider selbständigen Selbstbewusstsein.

9. As Hyppolite observes (*op. cit., p.* 272), Hegel is apparently making reference here to an erotic love-relationship. But—taking into account the wide application in ordinary parlance of the word, "pleasure"—it is hard to say just why Hegel would not make it a little more explicit that he is referring to such a love-relationship. Kaufmann (*op. cit.,* 28) argues against those who find a Faustian theme here.

10. Basically, the concept of pleasure seems to involve a certain expansion or growth of the individual's consciousness of his power of acting in and on the world. Thus Aristotle (in the *Nichomachean Ethics,* 1153a, 15), describes it as *unimpeded* operation of the natural faculties. And Spinoza describes "pleasurable joy" as the primitive passion which furthers the drive towards self-preservation and thus also increases the body's power of acting (cf. *Ethics,* III, 11).

11. *P.,* p. 264: Die Notwendigkeit. . .ist eben dieses, von dem man nicht zu sagen weiss, *was* es tue, welches seine bestimmten Gesetze und positiver Inhalt sei, weil es der absolute als *Sein* angeschaute reine Begriff selbst ist, die einfache und leere, aber unaufhaltsame und unstörbare *Beziehung,* deren Werk nur das Nichts der Einzelheit ist.

12. Cp. Freud, whose description of the "Id" (the pleasure-principle) is very similar to Hegel's description of the inner destiny. For the id is the inner instinctual nature of man, which contains the collective "harboured residues of the existences of countless egos" (*The Ego and the Id,* p. 28). The ego "tries to mediate between the world and the id, to make the id pliable to the world and, by means of its muscular activity, to make the world fall in with the wishes of the id. . . . (But) it is not only a helper to the id; it is also a submissive slave who courts his master's love." (*Ibid.,* p. 46). Thus, just as self-conscious Reason finds that its inner nature takes on the aspect of necessity or destiny, Freud's "ego" finds that the id takes on the aspect of a master which it must placate. And just as destiny tends to deal death to the determinate individuality of self-conscious Reason, so also the "death instinct" is an essential component of the id, and not infrequently focuses aggressively upon the ego itself.

13. This attitude is exemplified in Rousseau, who says (*The First and Second Discourses,* Masters tr.; N.Y.: St. Martin's Press, 1964, p. 64), "Let us leave to others the care of informing peoples of their duties, and limit ourselves to fulfilling well our own. We do not need to know more than this. O virtue! sublime science of simple souls, are so many difficulties and preparations needed to know you? Are not your principles engraved in all hearts, and is it not enough in order to learn your laws to commune with oneself and listen to the voice of one's conscience in the silence of the passions? That is true philosophy. . . ."

14. *P.,* p. 270: . . .ist ihm (dem Bewusstsein) die Natur der Verwirklichung und der Wirksamkeit unbekannt, dass sie als *Seiende* in ihrer Wahrheit vielmehr das *an sich Allgemeine* ist, worin die Einzelheit des Bewusstseins, die sich ihr anvertraut, um als *diese* unmittelbare *Einzelheit* zu *sein,* vielmehr untergeht. . . .

15. *P.,* p. 274: Diese Gestalt des Bewusstseins, sich in dem Gesetze, in dem *an sich* Wahren und Guten nicht als die Einzelheit, sondern nur als *Wesen* zu werden, die Individualität aber als das Verkehrte und Verkehrende zu wissen, und daher die Einzelheit des Bewusstseins aufopfern zu müssen, ist die *Tugend.*

16. *P.,* p. 275, 280, 281: (Die Individualität). . .ist . .(ein) einfaches, beiden (d.h., der Tugend und dem Weltlauf) gemeinschaftliches Moment. . . . (Sie) ist das Bewusstsein, wodurch das *Ansichseiende* ebensosehr *für ein anderes* ist. . . . (Sie) ist gerade die *Verwirklichung* des Ansichseienden.

17. Compare this to Nietzsche's doctrine on master/slave morality in his *Genealogy of Morals.* According to Nietzsche, the "slave morality" had an advantage from the beginning, insofar as the "slaves" have a natural tendency to objectify

all their values in laws, institutions, and cultural adjuncts. Thus—like Hegel's *Weltlauf*—they have attained victory. But Nietzsche, unlike Hegel, projects the possibility of their future defeat. Cf. *op. cit.*, First Essay, 10.

18. In this section, as in others, Hegel shows his unmistakable bias towards the preeminence of the *universal.*

Kierkegaard takes exception to this bias; and, to the Knight of Virtue (the harbinger of true universal individuality) opposes his "Knight of Faith" (Abraham, the symbol of the priority of the particular individual over the universal):

"Hegel is wrong," says Kierkegaard, "in not protesting loudly and clearly against the fact that Abraham enjoys honor and glory as the father of faith, whereas he ought to be prosecuted and convicted of murder.

"For faith is this paradox, that the particular is higher than the universal. . . .

"The story of Abraham contains. . .a teleological suspension of the ethical. As the individual he became higher than the universal [when, in obedience to God, he prepared to sacrifice Isaac to God, even though murder is universally forbidden]. This is the paradox which does not permit mediation.

"The tragic hero renounces himself in order to express the universal, the Knight of *Faith* renounces the universal to become the individual. . . .

"[Unless] the individual as the individual is higher than the universal, then Abraham's conduct is indefensible, for he paid no heed to the intermediate ethical determinants." (*Fear and Trembling*, Lowrie tr.; N.Y.: Anchor, 1954, pp. 65, 77, 86-87, 91.)

PART THREE: B

1. *P.*, S. 284: Das Tun verändert nichts und geht gegen nichts; es ist die reine Form des Übersetzens aus dem *Nichtgesehenwerden* in das *Gesehenwerden*, und der Inhalt, der zu Tage ausgebracht wird und sich darstellt, nichts anderes, als was dieses Tun schon an sich ist.

2. Hegel here is getting ready to present, in his own way, what he considers to be the salvageable essence of Schelling's "intellectual intuition." As Hegel says in his *Lectures on the History of Philosophy*, Vol. III, p. 519, "The ego, as pure act, as pure action, is not objective in knowledge itself, for the reason that it is the principle of all knowledge. If it is to be object of knowledge, this must come to pass through a very different kind of knowledge than the ordinary. The immediate consciousness of this identity according to Schelling is intuition, but inwardly it becomes "intellectual intuition"; it is a knowledge which is the production of its object." German ed., p. 654.

3. *"Die Sache Selbst,"* which is used by Hegel as a technical term in this section, cannot be satisfactorily translated, since *Sache*, like *res* in Latin, can mean "thing" or "fact" or "cause" or "affair" or "significance" or "deed," etc. Baillie translates it variously as "the fact of the matter," "the real intent," "the main concern," "the objectified intent." But this leads to confusion, precisely because it is a technical term, intended to convey the concept on which the whole section turns. For this reason, in lieu of an English term which could satisfactorily translate *Sache*, we will substitute for *"die Sache Selbst"* "Subjective/Objective Individuality," which is not a translation of that term, but a verbal description of the concept Hegel is expounding in the context here.

For a discussion of some of the difficulties connected with the translation of *Sache Selbst*, see *The Legacy of Hegel*, edited by O'Malley, Algozin *et al* (The Hague: Martinus Nijhoff, 1973), pp. 258-260.

4. If we take into account a great difference of contexts, the non-transitory transition of the Subjective/Objective Individuality is quite analogous to the

non-transient "becoming" of Substantial being which we find in Aristotle (*Physics* V, 1, 225a, 34). For according to Aristotle, the transience of motion or change only obtains, strictly speaking, in a passage from one contrary to another. But in substantial becoming there is a passage between contradictories (i.e., from being to non-being). Therefore the passage is non-temporal, and is not truly a "motion." Here also the "transition" is between ultimate polarities—subjectivity and objectivity—and is thus not a transition in the strict sense of the word.

5. *P.*, p. 300: Die Natur der Sache selbst ist...ein Wesen, dessen *Sein* das *Tun* des *einzelnen* Individuums und aller Individuen, und dessen Tun unmittelbar *für andre* oder eine *Sache* ist und nur Sache ist als *Tun Aller* und Jeder. . . .

6. In order to grasp the nature of the type of consciousness described here, we might do well to consider certain expressions we are all familiar with, such as "self-expression," "self-assertion" (in the positive sense), "being yourself," etc. What could such expressions mean? They seem to point to a consciousness which has gotten beyond pleasure-seeking and selfishness, not by rigidly trying to adhere to abstract ideals, but by striving constantly and consistently to react conscientiously (with regard to what is deeper, and *ipso facto* better, in it) in whatever type of situation it is presented with, or in whatever type of task it is trying to accomplish.

7. *P.*, p. 286: ...Ist einesteils jene Bestimmtheit darum nicht Beschränkung, über welche es hinauswollte, weil sie als seiende Qualität betrachtet die einfache Farbe des Elements ist, worin es sich bewegt.

8. Hegel follows Kant in referring "interest" not to any particular intrinsic fascination on the part of the object, but to some internal principle in consciousness. Cf. Kant's *Critique of Practical Reason* (Beck tr.; N.Y.: L.L. Arts, 1956), p. 124: "To every faculty of the mind an interest can be ascribed, i.e., a principle which contains the condition under which alone its exercise is advanced. Reason, as the faculty of principles, determines the interest of all the powers of the mind and its own."

9. Objective "works" result from the conjunction of internal talent with externally presented content. Thus also does Aristotle describe works of skill as the result of the conjunction of the internal virtue of "art" with some external content. (Cf. *Nichomachean Ethics*, VI, 4; and the *Physics*, II, 1, 13.)

10. Cp. Kierkegaard's description of the "ethical" commitment which supersedes aesthetical (hedonistic and egotistical) existence: "At the instant of choice [the individual] is in the most complete isolation, for he withdraws from the surroundings; and yet at the same moment he is in absolute continuity, for he chooses himself as product. . . . When he chooses himself as product he can just as well be said to produce himself. Thus at the instant of choice he is at the conclusion, for he concludes himself in a unity, and yet the same instant he is at the beginning, for he chooses himself freely. As product he is pressed into the forms of reality; in the choice he makes himself elastic, transforming all the outwardness into inwardness. This concretion is the reality of the individual, ...his task. (*Either/Or*, II, pp. 255-256.)

11. See section B-1.

12. It is important to emphasize here that the Subjective/Objective Individuality is concerned with expressing a *special kind* of universality. Unlike the "Knight of Virtue," who champions an abstract universal, the Subjective/Objective Individuality brings about a concrete universal—the very union of consciousness and world, universal *and* particular.

13. It is important to realize that, for Hegel, an "absolute" is not the subsumption of some manifold of particulars into some universal unity, but rather a unity-in-distinction *of* universal unity *with* particular discreteness. This is similar to the sense in which Schelling uses the term, "Absolute." See Hegel's *Lectures*

on the History of Philosophy, Vol. III, p. 537; German ed., p. 675.
It is interesting to note that in a fragment of 1805 Hegel indicates that
"Absolute Knowledge" begins with this section, not at the end of the *Phen.* See
Pöggler, *loc. cit.,* p. 281.
   14. Although individual consciousness is in possession of its absolute now, and
can no longer progress to any higher vantage point, the ethical substance in itself
is in a state of abstract immediacy, and is capable of progressing to its own
absolute "truth." Part II of the *Phenomenology* is concerned with tracing this
development.
   15. An example of such universal laws might be the Kantian "categorical imperative" which, in one of its three formulations, reads, "Act only on that
maxim whereby thou canst at the same time will that it should become a
universal law" (*Fundamental Principles of the Metaphysics of Morals,* p. 38).
   Such a law, as Kant maintains, is definitely an "ought," something that
ought to obtain in society. But, Hegel observes, it is a pure "ought," an abstract
re-formulation which has no peculiar existential content of its own. It is an
ought that never "is."
   Hegel gives a brilliant criticism of this pure "ought" from another point of
view (the viewpoint of its emergence in the ethical substance itself) towards the
end of the *Phenomenology,* in his chapter on "Morality."
   16. Kant, in his *Fundamental Principles of the Metaphysic of Morals* (p. 39ff.)
tests duties in this way, by using the Law of Contradiction. A true "duty," in
general, is a law whose *opposite* would lead to self-contradiction.
   17. Even when (using the Kantian "test" mentioned in n. 16) we find a law
whose opposite would lead to self-contradiction, this does not imply that the
law itself is valid. It only implies that the implications of that positive law have
probably not been fully enough elaborated to show up their self-contradictions.
   18. The question naturally comes to mind: Would it not be possible that an
individual could be in doubt about what the laws of the ethical substance *are,* or
whether some particular law is a law of the ethical substance or not? In this
case, would it not be necessary to test the laws by some means, to solve these
problems? But if such problems existed, we would not have an "ethical society"
in Hegel's sense of the expression. For the ethical society of its very nature
precludes any kind of legalism, or any effort to define exactly what one "ought"
to do. For it is what we might call a massive interpersonal relationship.
   If two friends were continually examining what their duties were with
respect to each other (what the "laws" of the other person were)—we would
have reason to doubt that there is real friendship there. Likewise, with the
relationship of husband to wife, or the mutual relationship of family members—
any tendency to pinpoint laws would probably be a harbinger of a less-than-satis-
factory relationship.
   19. (Die sittliche Gesinnung besteht eben darin, unverrückt in dem fest zu
beharren, was das Rechte ist, und sich alles Bewegens, Rüttelns und Zurückfüh-
rens desselben zu enthalten. . . Ich. . .bin indem ich zu prufen anfange, schon auf
unsittlichem Wege.—*P.,* pp. 311, 312).
   Just as Hegel says that unwarranted reflection leads to immorality, so also
Kierkegaard says that it leads to sin (*Either/Or,* II, p. 56) or to a lack of
inwardness—which is equivalent to sin (*The Concept of Dread,* p. 126).
   20. *P.,* p. 311: "nicht etwa jetzt und gestern, sondern immerdar lebt es, und
keiner weiss, von wannen es erschien" (Sophocles, *Antigone,* v. 456, 457).
   21. *P.,* p. 311: Sind sie die Massen ihrer von ihrem Leben durchdrungenen
Gliederung, sich selbst klare unentzweite Geister, makellose himmlische Gestalten, die in ihren Unterschieden die unentweihte Unschuld und Einmütigkeit
ihres Wesens erhalten.

22. "Hegel's ethics rested on [*Sittlichkeit* (life according to the customs of one's country)], which was the most fundamental and ultimate basis of his whole way of thinking. . . . It rests on the contemplation of the ethical life of the classical peoples: its character is colored through and through by Greek antiquity. It is, to state the whole truth, according to its contents a description, and according to its philosophical form an absolutizing of the private and public, of the social, the artistic, and the religious life of the Greeks." (Kaufmann, *op. cit.*, p. 104, quoting from Haym, *Hegel und seine Zeit,* p. 160.)

For an analysis of the many-sided influence of Greek culture on Hegel's thought, see J. Glenn Gray, *Hegel and Greek Thought* (N.Y.: Harper Torchbooks, 1968).

CONCLUSION

In the Introduction to this book, we proposed to reserve to our Conclusion the final consideration of three questions concerning the *Phenomenology*: I. How is Part II of the *Phenomenology* related to Part I? II. Does Hegel's *Phenomenology* give us any new insight into the problem raised by Kant: "are synthetic a-priori judgments possible in philosophy?"? and III. How is the transition made from the *Phenomenology* to the *Encyclopedia?*

In considering the first question, we will be attempting not only to put our analysis and commentary on Part I into context but also to deal with a problem which not uncommonly faces even one who has read and comprehended the *Phenomenology* quite thoroughly: namely, the problem of *seeing* what he has read as a unified, organic totality. The second question relates to the penetrating and persuasive criticisms of metaphysics by Kant—criticisms which, because of the impact they have had in philosophy, should be taken into account by one who is attempting to evaluate what seems offhand to be a post-Kantian meta-physical system. The third question, finally, is an attempt to bridge the gap from the "Absolute Knowledge" of the *Phenomenology* to the "Absolute Idea" of the *Encyclopedia,* and thus to give a final summary view of the *Phenomenology* as the "introduction" which Hegel intended it to be to his "System."

I. How is Part II of the "Phenomenology" related to Part I?

If we went into great detail in describing the evolution of man from the lower species, we would inevitably run up against problems when it came to bridging the gap between *homo sapiens* and the hominoids. For although the qualitative difference between us and our ancestors is great, there are very minimal differences in essential biological structures—the size and constitution of the brain, etc. Therefore it seems almost a futile task to attempt to trace the psychic advances in terms of parallel advances in physical evolution. If an explanation is possible at all, we must turn to other variables, variables which show some progressive development throughout all of evolution, including human evolution. Otherwise we are left with a trajectory which suddenly takes an unexpected course, a course for which we can give no satisfactory explanation.

If we follow the trajectory of movement in Hegel's *Phenomenology* as a whole, there is an unmistakable shift of direction in Part II, as compared with Part I. All of a sudden, it seems, we enter a sphere of social and political and religious and ideological tensions, after an intense, prolonged, and elaborate concentration on the dynamics of individual consciousness. At the end of Part I we have passed from the simplest "Forms of Consciousness" *(Gestalten des Bewusstseins)*– sense-certainty, perception, self-certitude, etc.–to the most complex. But an analysis in terms of "simple vs. complex Forms of Consciousness" will not help us to bridge the gap between Part I and Part II. We must look for other variables.

The "variables" that seem most utilizable for this goal are the following: a) the concept of reminiscence, or *Erinnerung*; and b) the progressions of dialectical logic.

a) THE FUNCTION OF REMINISCENCE IN THE "PHENOMENOLOGY":

Hegel, in the final chapter of the *Phenomenology,* states that

> the goal of Absolute Knowledge is achieved along the pathway of the reminiscence [*Erinnerung*] of spiritual forms–as they exist in themselves, and also as they contribute to the development of their kingdom. Their preservation in this latter respect (i.e., according to the aspect of their conceptually concatenated development) . . . gives us the Science of the appearance of knowledge [*"Phenomenology"*].[1]

By this statement, Hegel makes a final differentiation between his *Phenomenology* and history, which is a remembrance of these spiritual forms, not in terms of their conceptual interrelationships, but "as they exist in themselves."

It is important to realize this difference. For we can easily be deceived, in following the text of the *Phenomenology,* into thinking that we are simply following the historical development, first of the individual, and then of society, to some sort of heightened consciousness or self-realization. This is not the case.

If we were to look for some precedent for what Hegel *does* in the *Phenomenology,* we might, as Hyppolite observes, find the closest relevant analogy in Plato's doctrine of the Reminiscence of Forms:

> The development [in the *Phenomenology*] from empirical consciousness to absolute knowledge is possible only if one can discover the "steps" requisite for such an elevation. These "steps" are already present in consciousness. In order to discover them, one must descend into the depths of his memory by a process comparable to Platonic "reminiscence."[2]

Plato, hypothesizing that the individual soul, before being conjoined with a body, had directly contemplated a complete and perfectly transparent world of pure Ideas, concluded that we progress in knowledge in this life by a continual, graduated reminiscence, or re-assimilation of these Ideas. We begin with the more readily apprehensible ideas of sensuous qualities (δοξαστά) and proceed step by step to the apprehension of abstract, universal ideas (νοετά).

So also, Hegel hypothesizes that every individual conscious *self* in this world has been created in the "womb" of many crisscrossing currents, both from within and from without. From within, this self has been fashioned from, and is the concrete, actual, present result of, the temporal, historical progressions of *experience*—beginning with the more peripheral, and tending inexorably towards the deeper, more complex, more "concrete" experiences. From without, it has been fashioned by all the varied monuments of culture constructed by, and out of, the human race. The fact that an individual has come to possess a self, and a self-consciousness, is a result of his gestation in this womb. In order for him to rise to a *knowledge* of his self and of his self-consciousness, he must retrace, by a process of reminiscence, the inner and outer developments which have brought him to the state of selfhood and consciousness of selfhood. The objective in view is that the individual should become fully lucid, fully intelligible, fully present to himself, as he comes to form this movent "X-ray" depiction of all the movements which *de facto* terminate in his present actuality. When he does this, his consciousness will become conscious to *itself*, i.e., actual and fully present; whereas formerly it was only potentially his possession, and was as distant from the grasp of his individuality as Plato's World of Forms.

We come at this point to the problem of the rationale behind the notable "break" from individual consciousness in Part I to social consciousness in Part II.

A solution may perhaps be best facilitated if we return to the example of Plato:

The process of recollection, in Plato, was not conducted by dint of pure, abstract introspective endeavors. The philosopher could not lift himself by his own bootstraps, so to speak, to the vision of the absolute categorical Forms. Rather, he stood in need of external stimuli. It was only upon being presented with a *content* of various mundane appearances, or the imaginative representation of these appearances, that the philosopher could come to remember the various *forms* of reality that corresponded to them, or that in some way were associated with or related to them.

So also, in the development of the Hegelian *Errinerung,* there are certain processes that take on the aspect of content, and certain that take on the aspect of form.

We should recall[3] that Hegel was not of that idealistic persuasion that strove to reduce being to thought, external reality to ideas. Rather, he recognized the autonomous existence of both objectivity and subjectivity; and one of his basic philosophical presuppositions seems to be that we can achieve a true synthesis of being and thought *only if* we recognize and preserve the autonomous reality of each.

The same observation holds for certain other reciprocities which we find expressed or implied in Hegel—in particular, the reciprocities of the individual spirit vs. Absolute Spirit, and of a-posteriori vs. a-priori knowledge. Although a superficial reading of Hegel might give one the impression that he simply submerges the individual in the Absolute, and mixes a-posteriori data willy-nilly with a-priori pre-conceptions—this is not the way Hegel wills to mix his opposites. The individual can come to complete synthetic union with the Absolute, *only if* he maintains his individuality as autonomous and differentiated from the Absolute. The a-posteriori and the a-priori [4] can become effectively fused only if they remain distinct.

With this in mind, let us return to the notion of the "inner" and "outer" currents giving rise to individuality. The inner currents, the history of experiences which the individual himself has gone through, are the a-posteriori *content* which the individual has acquired for himself. The outer currents, the cultural embodiments of Absolute Spirit, are pre-conditions, in the light of which all individual experiences take on meaning. Our individuality in its major outlines is a reflection of the cultural milieu. Thus the cultural environment takes on the aspect of pre-conditioning *form,* to which the content of individual experience must conform.

Thus, just as Plato required a content of external impressions for progression towards reminiscence of the Forms, so also Hegel in Part I of the *Phenomenology* requires a-posteriori reminiscence of (that is, philosophical reexamination of) the progressions of individual experience. It is an experience of experience. This supplies us with the *content* of individuality made conscious to itself. Then we come to the (philosophical) experience (i.e., reminiscence) of the a-priori *conditions* for individual experience, the "Forms of the World," (*Gestalten einer Welt*) impinging on the individuality from "without," i.e., from the side of Absolute Spirit.

The individual must first come to a conscious *possession* of his individual consciousness before he can retrace the various forms which it receives from without. And the individual who by means of "phenomenological" experience comes finally to make-present to himself both the content of his experience, and the form of its "a-priori" conditions, approximates to Absolute Knowledge (of self).

b) THE PROGRESSIONS OF DIALECTICAL LOGIC IN THE "PHENOMENOLOGY":

We can consider these progressions either 1) in the original Hegelian terminology;[5] or 2) in terms of a symbolic formalization of Hegel's dialectic.[6]

1) *In Hegel's terms,* we begin with an immediate, non-explicated in-and-for-itself (consciousness in the wide sense, the unique phenomenally apprehensible "thing" (in-itself) which is also a subject (a for-itself).

First we consider this in-and-for-itself as an in-itself, i.e., as the presentation of objectivity ("Consciousness" in the strict sense, i.e., as opposed to "Self-Consciousness"). Then this in-itself shows itself to give rise also to a for-itself aspect, i.e., the subjective modifications which are brought to bear on reality (the operations of Self-Consciousness Proper). Then, after the alienation of the "Unhappy Consciousness" has been transcended, the in- *and* the for-itself aspects of consciousness in the wide sense, become revealed simultaneously as a single in-and-for-itself. Thus we come to *Reason* (the in-and-for itself of consciousness apprehended *qua* in-and-for-itself).

In order to make the notion of Reason more explicit, we then re-consider the *in-and-for-itself* aspect of consciousness, (a) to determine how its outer projections (Reason in-itself, the rational world of scientific Observation) are related to the inner, hidden life of creative thought (Reason for-itself); (b) to determine how Reason for-itself (individuality confident of controlling its environment) is related to its "true" in-itself (the objectivity which Reason "finds" precisely by creating it); and (c) to come to a final all-embracing view of Reason as *Subjective/Objective Individuality*, i.e. individual self-consciousness as an "objective" moment of the consciousness of Absolute Spirit, and also as the medium through which the self-consciousness of Absolute Spirit is constructed into an objective "ethical substance."

At this point, the in-and-for-itself of consciousness is seen *explicitly* as an in-and-for-itself, i.e., as the Finite Spirit which results from the fusion of the in-itself in-itself (Absolute Being, Objectivity) and the for-itself for-itself (the Absolute, Transcendent Self).

In Part II we are immediately concerned only with the process which was "behind the scenes" in Part I, i.e., the process by which the Absolute Self and the Absolute Being are becoming fused in and through the determinations of finite spirit in the political, cultural, social, and ideological forms of the ethical substance which has become organically concatenated.

This process (the *development of* the in-and-for-itself *in-and-for-itself*) is first considered in-itself (i.e., after the manner of a universal social *consciousness*, in which spirit reveals itself progressively[7] as Absolute Being); then for-itself (spirit unfolding itself progressively as an Absolute, transcendent *Self-Consciousness*[8]); then finally as in-and-for-itself (i.e., as Absolute Spirit, the unity-in-distinction of Objectivity and Subjectivity, presenting itself at one and the same time under the aspects of consciousness and self-consciousness, and thus giving rise in the finite spirit to "Absolute Knowledge"). At this point we have the in-and-for-itself in-and-for-itself, *in-and-for-itself.*

2) *In symbolic formalization,* the total process may be outlined as follows:

Beginning with S (the subjectivity in the state of immediacy), we pass from concentration on the "immediate" objective aspects of consciousness, to the comprehension of "Sense-Certainty" as a subjective-objective reciprocity:

$$S \rightarrow O \rightarrow S{:}O$$

Mediated sensory awareness (SO) is then seen to be an experience conditioned by the fusion of disparate concepts in the perceptual *object*; which brings us to perceptual awareness (OS). But an examination of the concepts particularized in perception, leads us back to the conceptualizing subject (the Understanding, SO:OS), and to the process by which Understanding "vivifies" the perceptual world with its intelligible laws:

$$SO \rightarrow OS \rightarrow SO{:}OS$$

This insight of Understanding brings the focus of our attention on the power or "force" of self-consciousness, which confronts the "otherness" of objectivity as something which contributes to subjective awareness, but always remains adamantly extrinsic, or objective (OSSO). Self-consciousness finally becomes reconciled with essential otherness at the stage of Reason (SOOS:OSSO), which becomes explicit eventually as the unity-in-distinction of spirit in consciousness (i.e., the Subjective/Objective Individuality). The process from the Understanding's self-discovery through the appearance of alien otherness to the synthesis of selfhood and otherness, takes the general form,

$$SOOS \rightarrow OSSO \rightarrow SOOS:OSSO$$

At this point, we should pause to reflect that all the dialectical syntheses on odd-numbered levels are open-ended, presenting a subjectivity which is other-bounded, e.g., the first-level synthesis, S:O. On the other hand, all the dialectical syntheses on even-numbered levels are closed, presenting a subjectivity which is self-bounded, e.g., the second-level synthesis, SO:OS.

With this in mind, we come to the fact that Hegel declares the consciousness of the Subjective/Objective Individuality to be an "absolute" Form of consciousness,[9] beyond which we can go no further. Why, then, does he continue on to Part II, with the progressions to "Absolute Knowledge"?

The answer to this question, on the purely logical plane, seems to hinge on the fact that the Subjective-Objective Individuality is an other-bounded synthesis, and hence an other-bounded "Absolute." As other-bounded, it emphasizes the subjective/objective *distinction*[10]-in-unity of spirit, in consciousness. If we go one level higher in the logic of non-identity, we can attain to the *unity*-in-distinction of a *closed* Absolute, i.e., the notion of Absolute Spirit as an infinite subject-object interpenetrability, existing as a precondition for the state of absolute consciousness in the finite spirit.

Thus the synthesis which has been attained in the Subjective/Objective Individuality becomes a logical stepping-stone to a new process of mediation. When we see the Subjective/Objective Individuality as an objective moment of a universal ego animating a universal ethical substance—we begin to focus on that substance itself, which is the objectified or externalized aspect of the spiritualized world. This brings us to the treatment of "Spirit in-itself," the otherness which is a prerequisite for self-consciousness and at the same time is produced by self-consciousness—OSSOSOOS. Then, just as self-conscious individuality had led to this spiritual otherness, this otherness in its turn leads to heightened individual consciousness; and a final synthesis of these two movements (self-consciousness to spiritual substance, and spiritual substance to self-consciousness) is attained in the stage of Religion (SOOSOSSO:OSSOSOOS), becoming finally "absolutized," as Absolute Knowledge; which gives expression to the *unity*[11]-in-distinction of subject and object in its most explicit form; and in which the individual consciousness comes finally to realize that its finite distinctions are merely moments in the process of the unification of Absolute Spirit with Itself.

The essential movements which obtain in Part II are thus:

$$SOOSOSSO \rightarrow OSSOSOOS \rightarrow SOOSOSSO:OSSOSOOS$$

The entire dialectic of the *Phenomenology* can correspondingly be represented graphically and summarily as follows:

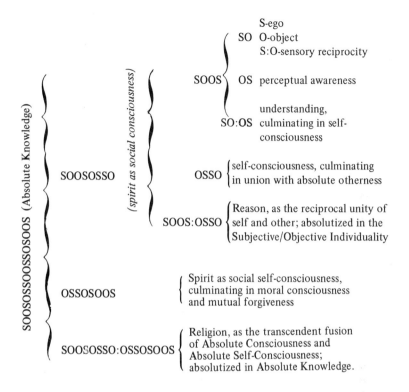

II. Does Hegel's "Phenomenology" give us any new insight into the problem raised by Kant: "Are synthetic a-priori judgements possible in philosophy?"

A. SOME PRELIMINARY REMARKS ON REALITY, JUDGEMENT, AND LOGIC

Before considering the specific problem raised above, it will be necessary to consider four related problems, in the context of which our discussion in this chapter will be conducted: 1. The relationship of judgement to "reality." 2. The notion of the operations of synthesis vs. analysis a) in general, and b) as applied to judgements in the Kantian sense. 3. The notion of the a-priori vs. the a-posteriori a) in experience in general, and b) as applied to judgements in the Kantian sense. 4. The Logic behind logic.

1. *The relationship of judgement to "reality."* Aristotle, towards the end of his *Physics,* comes to the notion of the existence of a "prime mover" by an analysis of motion: If *everything* in the world is moved by something else, the economy of motions in the totality of events would be impossible and unintelligible. So there must be some prime mover which gives the primary impetus to all motion

without itself being moved. Otherwise, we are faced with an actual infinity of movements in the world—something which our intellect simply cannot even conceptualize.

Granted that Aristotle's arguments do not have much relevance in themselves for us—because of their faulty presuppositions as to the nature of the physical universe, etc.—they do have relevance if we take them as symbolic representations of the nature of our thought processes: For we proceed in reasoning by attributing manifold predicates to manifold subjects in manifold ways. But not every attribute can be a predicate. There must be some attribute which is not a predicate of anything. And this "attribute" we call existence. We could also call it the "prime predicate," to distinguish it from other "finite" predicates. But the main point is: there cannot be an actual numerical infinity of steps in our progression to ultimate predicates.

And so, in all the true and meaningful predications which we can make, existence seems to be a presupposition. For instance, if I tried to put into logical form the proposition that "some non-existent object has the property F," I could not do this without symbolizing the "non-existence" as a *predicate,* such as G (or $\sim$ G). Then I would come up with the formula, $V \ x(\sim Gx \wedge Fx)$,[1] from which I could then infer $\sim Gy$ and Fy by means of existential instantiation. But by existential generalization from $\sim Gy$, I could subsequently arrive at $V \ z \sim Gz$, which would have to be translated as, "There exists an object z, such that it does not exist." This, of course, would cause no difficulty from a purely logical point of view, since logic is purely concerned with formal correctness. But to the mind which endeavors to delve beneath mere formal correctness to content (truth and meaningfulness), such a formulation would naturally elicit the question: do we not have to presuppose the *existence* of object z *in some sense,* if $V \ z \sim Gz$ is to be a meaningful proposition at all?

Of course, we can draw up propositions about Robinson Crusoe and gold mountains and square circles—subjects which admittedly do not have any physical existence. But Robinson Crusoe does exist in the area of discourse of "fictional characters," square circles do exist in the area of "self-contradictory ideas," and so forth. And this brings us to the problem of "areas of discourse."

The different senses in which things can "exist" can be conveniently distinguished as follows, in accord with three major spheres of discourse:[2]

a) *The sphere of physical existence.* If we are trying to determine the answer to the question, "does x exist?"—one of the best starting points would be to ask whether the name, "x," denotes a physical object. That is, does x purport to be something with tangible, sensible properties? If so, we can determine its existence or non-existence by observation and verification procedures, either in a scientific or the pre-scientific sense. For instance, if x is a unicorn, and the name, "unicorn," denotes the usual set of characteristics that are associated with that name in mythology, we can conclude that unicorns do not exist, on the basis of our inability to find any animal in the physical world with such a set of characteristics. If atoms and electrons are conceived of as having such-and-such physical properties, we can verify their existence by observing that the calculable effects that should accrue to such properties do, in fact, accrue.[3]

b) *The sphere of mental, or psychic, existence.* The mathematician is continually making judgements about, and by means of, the number 2. He could not do this if the number 2 were completely non-existent. And the world would not support professional mathematicians for long if it became apparent that, in truth, they were dealing seriously with non-realities. The number 2 does, then, exist in *some* sense. And if we say compromisingly, "well, yes, it exists, but *just* as an idea"—we are betraying a presupposition that would be very hard to prove: namely, that mental or psychic reality is in some sense less than physical reality. At least, it would be hard to prove this on the basis of any physical observations. And if we based our proof on any reflections in the purely psychic sphere, the proof might be self-defeating.[4]

At any rate, there seems to be a whole class of objects whose name does not essentially *imply* any physically observable or experiencable characteristics. In addition to the number 2, we might include concepts, love, unity, and relationship. If we are to make judgements judiciously about such "objects," it would seem to be necessary (since the two spheres of existence are often confused) to first determine in what *sense* they exist, and whether our processes of judgements about them must differ substantially because of the different nature of their sphere of existence.

The verification of the existence or non-existence of ideas will, of course, take a very different tack from the verification of physical existence. For example, I might show that a Bantu tribe in Africa has no idea of "ankle" or "knee," by examining their language, which has only one word, "leg," to cover all the subsidiary notions that we associate with "leg." Or I might show that the ancient Mayans had no idea of "hell," by examining archeological remnants. Or I might show that we do not have the idea of "virtue" that the ancient Greeks had, by means of etymology.

If, on the other hand, an individual wished to prove the existence of an idea which he *thought* he *himself* had, some different procedures would be involved. For example, if I wanted to prove to my own satisfaction that I indeed had a clear idea of what Kant meant by "a priori synthetic judgements," I might simply test this idea for non-contradiction against a background of other ideas of Kant; or check it for its clearness and distinctness in the Cartesian manner. Or better yet, I might try to *express* the idea to others conversant with Kant, in such a way as to gain public assent to my mode of expression. (This latter method would also seem to permit the verification of the existence of this idea of mine on the part of others, as well as of myself.)

c) *The sphere of transcendental existence.* There is a special class of objects which poses an especially difficult problem, when we ask questions regarding their *existence.* For when we make our preliminary inquiries about the denotation of the name of these objects, we find that they purport to refer to things which are neither definite parts or aspects of the physical world, nor definite parts or aspects of any mental world. But rather, they refer to transcendental entities which are supposed to be just beyond the borders of the physical universe, or just beneath the springs of conscious mental life, or both.

Examples of such objects are the soul, immortality, and God. The name, "soul," denotes a "real" grounding for all our conscious activity. "Immortality" denotes a real duration, transcending temporal duration (which comes to a terminus at the physical death of the individual). "God" denotes a real entity which is supposed to exist *both* just beyond the borders of physical space and time, *and* just below the foundations of consciousness (along with our soul).

Such objects, in short, differ from physical or psychical objects, in that their name denotes something which is neither just physical nor just psychical but transcends the physical and/or the psychic realm altogether.

In regard to such transcendental objects, it seems obvious 1) that to say that they are non-existent physically or mentally would be *non ad rem,* since their *name* does not denote either of these types of existence: and 2) that a valid critique of such subjects will depend for its validity and significance on the prior establishment of the very *existence* of the subjects, in a manner appropriate to the sphere of reality being considered.

Here again, very different verification techniques would have to be used to establish or impugn transcendental existence. To establish the existence of a God transcending the physical universe, it would help not at all if our physical science could forge to the "edges" of the universe. For the name, "God," does not imply a physical or spatial boundary (and besides, the *totum* of space could not have *spatial* boundaries, i.e., boundaries which would themselves have to have a spatial context). To establish the existence of a soul transcending and grounding all our psychic life, it would not help if psychiatry plumbed the depths of consciousness, and disclosed its absolute "boundaries." For the name, "soul," does not imply anything that could be expressed in terms of a mental existence in the context of ideas; but rather a grounding for all mental life, which itself is not part of that life.

Rather, such "concepts" are independent of how much we know specifically of the physical world, or specifically of our psychic world. They seem to be relative to our experience of *experience* itself, *regardless* of the extent to which experience itself has expanded the frontiers of the knowable physical or psychic world. Thus we find the ideas of God, immortality, and the soul only in civilizations, advanced or primitive, that show some degree of rational consciousness. In order to verify their real existence, then, the most feasible approach would seem to be a scientific "observation" of experience—if such a thing be possible.

The most essential and fundamental aspect of our experience is that it is a unity-in-distinction of subjectivity and objectivity. *If* subjectivity is really distinct from objectivity (this seems to be the presupposition for all knowledge), as a really determinate pole; and *if* there is any way we might show *how* each pole is distinct (from *each other,* i.e., on the basis of some common criterion which is applicable both to thought and to being, and thus must not be merely a spatial or temporal distinction, or a logical distinction which applies only to thought and not to being);—then the clarification of *this* determinateness could conceivably put us in a position to pronounce definitively on the reality or non-reality of a transcendent context for experience as a whole. Or again: if subjectivity and objectivity are really united, and if we could examine this unity to determine how and (in a metaphorical sense) *where* it takes place, we might be in possession of an umbilical cord which could be traced back to some transcendent source (or, conversely, might prove to be merely immanent in the process as a whole).

   2. *The notion of the operations of synthesis vs. analysis:* a) *In general:* The differentiation of these two operations can perhaps be suitably illustrated by focusing for a moment on two very basic human operations: 1) The operation of building up a "collection." It makes no difference what the collection comprises—car parts, butterflies, trophies, books, friends, facts, arguments. Whatever is brought into the collection is systematized, compartmentalized, categorized. By this means "the world" is subordinated to human needs and brought into the focus of human cognition. This is a "synthetic" procedure—a procedure which draws discrete elements into a unity. 2) The operation of taking things apart—alarm clocks, automobiles, suspicious stories, arguments, etc. This involves an analytic procedure—separating a unified or organized entity into its diverse parts or aspects. Epistemologically, the process of "taking apart" *ideas* has come to imply a concomitant process of reflective withdrawal—taking ideas apart from their immediate empirical context, to examine meanings.

   But note that the "synthetic" operations indicated here not only are compatible with, but require, an apprehension of discrete elements, which could come only from analysis. And the "analytic" procedures likewise not only permit, but require, a pre-recognition of some unity which needs to be analyzed—a unity which could be recognized only through some sort of synthesis. And so, in general, we conclude that synthesis only connotes an emphasis of unification over differentiation, while analysis merely connotes a predominance of differentiation over unification. Neither of these reciprocals in any way connotes the *absence* of its complementary operation.[5]

   b) *As applied to judgements in the Kantian sense:* Analytic judgements, according to Kant, are simply instances of the non-inferential recognition of self-identity; and can be reduced to the form, $A = A$, or $P \to P$, in which there is no real inference. Thus they do not add anything to our knowledge, but are simply reaffirmations (often with a greater degree of clarity) of propositions already admitted to be true.[6] An example of such a judgement would be, "gold is a yellow metal." This amounts to the same thing as saying, "gold is gold"; because "yellow metal" is a definition of gold, inherent in its concept.

   Synthetic judgements, on the other hand, require a "middle-term." In the theoretical sphere, this middle-term must be supplied by "empirical" or "pure" intuition. I can say, "a straight line is the shortest distance between two points," only because by means of a "pure" intuition of the sensibility I go beyond the concepts of "straight" and "line," to discern certain spatial relationships accruing to these concepts.[7] I can make the judgement that "air is elastic" only on the basis of empirical intuitions of the sensibility, which are synthesized into an a priori format.[8] In the sphere of practical reason (morality), the middle-term is a positive concept of freedom.[9] I can make the synthetic judgement, "suicide is wrong" ("I ought to legislate preservation of life as the only maxim of my action which can be a universal law for the actions of all")—only because I perceive myself as a member of a suprasensible world, free from the laws of physical inclinations, and imposing my own laws, as a type of universal, necessary causality, on the activities of my phenomenal self. But in both the theoretical and the practical spheres, synthetic judgements expand an original notion, and add something to it.

Kant, adhering to the notion of synthesis and analysis as essentially *logical* processes, isolates them rigidly from each other, with good reason: since the *proposition,* P→P, or A = A, is only a pseudo-statement-about P, or A, and hence amounts to only a pseudo-expansion of our knowledge. But although we must isolate a horse's mane from its neck in our mind, in order to talk about it logically—we should not suppose that it is isolated in reality.

The fact that Kant does consider these two operations to be isolated in reality receives corroboration from his decision with regard to analytic judgements: All analytic judgements are a-priori. Why? Because they refer only to concepts *about* the phenomenal world, not to the phenomenal world itself. In other words, he seems to consider analytic judgement as a process taking place only in the understanding, independently of the understanding's unification of, or through, the schemata of the imagination; and having to do only with concepts as the a-priori determinants of reality, and not with the a-posteriori appearances which are determined.

This does not seem to be an exaggeration of the separation of the two processes in Kant's estimation—especially in view of the almost exclusive value which he placed on synthetic judgements for truly expanding (rather than just explicating or clarifying) our ideas about the world of appearances.

But if we accept the differentiation of analytic and synthetic judgements in such a strict "logical" sense, some problems arise: For instance, Kant says that analytic judgements help towards the clarification of concepts. But if they *really* amount to nothing more than A = A or P → P, how could they clarify anything? Wouldn't they be better left unsaid?

Other problems arise in regard to Kant's notion of "synthetic" judgements. For in the domain of mathematics and physics we supposedly have *a priori* synthetic judgements, which are based on a synthesis of pure or empirical intuitions, but go beyond these intuitions to take on necessary or universal a priori form. But does physics, for example, "go beyond" experience in formulating its "a priori synthetic" judgements? [10] If it does transcend experience, it would seem to be liable to the criticism that Kant levies against *metaphysics* for going beyond experience to formulate a priori synthetic judgements in an "autonomous" manner. . . . No. If Kant is to consistently maintain that there are valid a priori synthetic judgements, he must establish in some way that they never leave the domain of experience, although at the same time they are not simply immersed in the contingencies of experience. And this leads into problems concerning how judgements can be based on a posteriori experience, and still be classified as a priori. How is the necessity of universality of such judgements *any less* a "real use" of the understanding, forcing its modalities on experience—than we purportedly find in metaphysics? An example of Kant's confrontation with this very problem seems to be given in the note on p. 53 of his *Prolegomena,* where he comes to some rather equivocal conclusions about "experience":

"When I say that experience teaches me something," observes Kant, "I mean only the *perception* that *lies* in experience [Italics added] . . . That this heat necessarily follows the shining of the sun is contained indeed in the judgement of experience (by means of the concept of cause), yet is a fact not learned by experience."

1) This explanation seems to be called for by the fact that any judgement which contains necessity is by definition "a priori." "If wc havc a proposition which in being thought is thought as *necessary,* it is an *a priori* judgement."[11] Since Kant has just expounded (in the *Prolegomena*) on the fact that "the objective validity of the judgement of experience" in physics "signifies nothing else than its necessary universal validity"[12] —and since Kant has already[13] distinguished judgements of experience from *"a priori"* judgements—this explanation is certainly called for, since we apparently have a contradiction. If judgements of experience truly have necessity or universality, they are *ipso facto* a priori: therefore they *cannot* be "judgements of experience" in the aforementioned sense of "empirical judgements" which are absolutely distinguished from *a priori* judgements.

2) In spite of the ambiguity accruing to "experience" here, it is not at all unclear what Kant *means* by a judgement of experience, in view of the context. "The sun warms the stone" is a judgement of experience because it implies a necessary cause-effect relationship between the sun and the warming of the stone, a relationship which itself is not "learned" from the perceptual moment of experience.[14]

3) But whether we say that "experience" = the "perception in experience" or that "experience" = "that which is generated by the addition of the concept of the understanding"[15] —the problem remains: If the *a priori judgements* of experience are synthetic, they are not synthetic *via* the "middle term" of empirical intuitions. Neither are they synthetic *via* pure intuitions, which apply only in mathematics, not in physics.

If we say that the *schemata of the imagination* are the prime "middle terms" for such acts of syntheses, we seem to be following the example of Plato, who posited the "mathematica" as an intellectual bridge between the sensible world and the ideal world (a "bridge" which, instead of explicating a solution to the problem of the connection between the two "worlds," simply distracted one from that problem). Plato seemed to get himself into trouble by supposing a one-to-one relationship between the two worlds (cf. his own self-criticism in the *Parmenides*). The "mathematica" did not dissolve these troubles one whit. If he had supposed that there are autonomous connections, purely "spiritual" syntheses of the Forms among themselves, he might have had a more workable hypothesis.—So also, if Kant would allow that the concepts of the understanding admit of autonomous syntheses among themselves, on the basis of higher-order intuitions of *their content,* he would avoid making *each* category a *deus ex machina* which entered into the sensible world through the tabernacle of an appropriate "schema" of the imagination, to make the appropriate synthesis.—Otherwise, we are always left with the unanswered questions: a) Why is one schema more "appropriate" than another? b) why is one a priori synthesis more "appropriate" than another? and c) why do the Categories of the Understanding supply an absolute limit to the manifold of appearance?[16]

3. *The notion of the a-priori vs. the a-posteriori.* a) *In experience in general:* The a-priori in the widest possible sense[17] seems to be a stable context, which conditions the way in which our experience *must* be shaped. For instance, if I wear green glasses today, all my visual perceptions *must* be either green or a combination of some other color with green. If I am confined to prison for ten years, all of my sensuous experiences during those ten years must be presented in the background of prison life.

Now to widen the context a bit: *Culture* has an a-priori aspect. A child who is reared exclusively in a Chinese environment, if he has any experiences at all, must have them in certain general ways, dictated by that cultural context. And a child reared in an exclusively pastoral environment *cannot* experience sounds, sights, and social interaction in the way that a child in the city would. Our *language* also has a definite a-priori aspect in a similar sense. I *can't* think at all except according to the grammatical and logical rules of my language; and in all my thinking I must have as a *background* certain basic concepts that have been introduced into my language, or some language that I understand. (If I introduce new concepts myself, and name them, this would be an instance of the a-posteriori being introduced into, and becoming a part of, the a-priori.) And finally, our genetic make-up takes on the aspect of the a-priori. If I inherit certain physical features, or temperamental dispositions, or talents—this hereditary influence must, in a positive or negative way, color all the experiences of my life.

How do we come to separate the a-priori from the a-posteriori? Obviously, there is an aspect of relativity here. The a-priori is not fixed and stable of its very nature, but becomes a fixed or stable aspect in relationship to a definite context. For example, if I enter into a room that I have never seen before, observe it thoroughly, and then put on colored glasses to view it again, the superimposed color becomes a-posteriori to the background; but a-priori, if I put the glasses on before entering. And if I am a member of a committee of linguists producing a new international language, the language produced is a-posteriori with reference to the ideas held by the committee as to what the new international language *should* be like.

In the domain of philosophy, the presupposition, and sometimes also the express designation, of an "a-priori" as opposed to an "a-posteriori," seems to be based in large part on temperamental disposition.[18] For the rationalist, ideas, essential "forms," and pure subjective structures will characteristically take on the aspect of the a-priori, to be applied, with attitudes ranging all the way from tyranny through condescension to co-existence, to the world of facts. The empiricist, on the other hand, although he may sometimes pay lip-service to the distinctions of a-priori vs. a-posteriori introduced by some rationalist philosophy which supplies his intellectual milieu—will nevertheless, in all of his practical activities and judgements, consider the world of facts as having a stable, a-priori aspect, while the concepts according to which these facts are collected and unified are viewed as arbitrary epi-phenomena, especially when their applicability to facts is not readily apparent.

Is there any *essential* distinction between the a-priori and the a-posteriori, or is the distinction always arbitrary, i.e., relative to the situation or context being considered? Perhaps the examination of *consciousness* might provide the key to the solution of this problem. For consciousness—except when it is examining or observing *itself*—seems to take its immediate inception from its immediate distinction from some completely unassimilated otherness, from some "inorganic" sense manifold. All the activities and distinctions of consciousness would seem to be *dependent* on this initial distinction.

We will follow up on some of the consequences of this later in this chapter.

b) *As applied to judgements in the Kantian sense:* Kant, exemplifying the typical rationalist persuasion, emphasizes the fact that there are certain stable structures in our subjective awareness of the world, which determine the way that the world *has* to appear to us. That is, there are certain categories of ideas which supply a-priori conditions for our knowledge of the world. The fact that there *are* these categories, is attributable to our logic and the language in which it is expressed. We have to think in terms of subjects with predicates: therefore we see things as substances. We have to think of protasis and apodosis: therefore we see the world in terms of cause-effect relationships. We have to quantify subjects in terms of "All" of "Some," and therefore we see the world in terms of unities and pluralities. And so forth. The "world," in the Kantian context (which is concerned specifically with our knowledge of the world), is the manifold of sensuous appearances which supply the *content* of our experience, i.e., the determinable a-posteriori aspect which is formed into "objective reality" by synthesis with the a-priori categories. An a-posteriori judgement is simply a "judgement of perception" in which a sensuous content has not yet been fully determined according to the categories; but has been only incompletely synthesized with certain subsidiary predicates or ideas.

4. *The logic behind logic:* Since *logic* seems to play a major part 1) in Kant's designation of the a-priori as opposed to the a-posteriori; and 2) in his rigid dissociation of the operations of analysis and synthesis—it behooves us to first give some attention to the function of a "logical context," before applying the notion of a-priori synthetic judgments in the Kantian context, to Hegel's *Phenomenology*, which seems to diverge from the ordinary standards of logico-scientific thought:

a) A logic based on the law of identity and the law of contradiction [19] is a necessity of consciousness. For consciousness, which is always a consciousness *of* something, requires as its prerequisite an adequate distinction of the subjective sphere of the onlooker from the objective sphere of the world. By means of the traditional "logic of identity" we assure ourselves a) that there are stable facts in the objective world which we can use as a basis for logical inductions; and

b) that there are stable ideas, in the subjectivity, which can be applied in a univocal way, with continual reliability, in our processes of deduction. Thus the laws of induction require, not that the facts should remain stable, but that we focus only on predictably stable facts. And the laws of deduction require, not that our ideas should not undergo any evolution, but that we should deal with them only according to certain stable and publicly acknowledged significations. If we had not developed such a logic, the distinction of man from his environment (and all the ramifications of that distinction) would have been obstructed; and we would no doubt be in a state proximate to the "magic consciousness" still extant among primitive peoples—a consciousness characterized by an inability to adequately distinguish between symbol and reality, cause and effect, life and death, etc.

b) Distinction, in general, implies a unity. For we can ask, with regard to every distinction, "distinction in what respect?" Which implies that a thing must in some respects be congruent with something, in order for it to be distinguished from the latter in other respects. Otherwise, comparison would be impossible. In a converse manner unity, in general, guarantees some sort of distinctness. For we can ask about every unity, "a unity of what with what?" A unity which did not unify any disparity would be unintelligible.

c) The distinction of subject from object in consciousness implies their unity, and *vice versa*. But *this* unity-in-distinction is unlike all other unities-in-distinction, in that it does not just result from the convergence and divergence of certain finite aspects of objectivity, or certain finite aspects of subjectivity; but is a pivotal unity-in-distinction upon which all other distinctions *in* the objective world or *in* the subjectivity depend. The branches of a tree could never be distinguished from the roots, unless we first adequately distinguished *ourselves* from the *tree*. When the Pythagoreans based all the rational unity-in-distinction in the cosmos on the unitary *Henad*, they were recognizing implicitly that unity-in-distinction is a *process* that has to be traced back to one generative source.

d) Since logic in general is designed to further consciousness, and since the logic of identity tends to staticize facts and ideas to promote the distinctness of objectivity and subjectivity—another logic may be called for to promote and explicate their synthetic unity. This logic would not be concerned primarily with either objectivity or subjectivity, but rather with consciousness, which is the "middle term" which makes possible the unity of these two spheres. Hegel's "logic of non-identity"[20] seems to be oriented towards this goal, although it certainly has not been forged into as efficient and dependable an instrument as the traditional logic of Western philosophy.

e) A fundamental presupposition of a logic of *non*-identity is that consciousness has a content, or *is* a content. If this is true, and if consciousness is a unity of thought with being, and if *judgement* is the *process* of *synthesizing* thought with being and *vice versa*—then

(i) we discover that this content is essentially *judgement itself*, as a dynamic process, in all of its aspects, synthetic, a-priori, a-posteriori, and analytic.

(ii) we see that in *our examination* of this conscious experience of judgement, our "analytic" judgements are not simply explicitations of concepts to which phenomena must conform, since the "phenomenon" here *is* our repertoire of concepts (i.e., our "analytic" judgements are transparently "synthetic," drawing on a "phenomenal" manifold of concepts). And the Kantian distinction of a-priori vs. a-posteriori seems to be blotted out, since the categories seem to be part of the content being judged. (Even if the categories were judged *according to* the categories, there could not be "a-posteriori" preliminary judgements which would not yet have been brought into a synthetic thought-unity with the categories.)

We proceed now to the main problem of this chapter:

B. IS HEGEL'S "PHENOMENOLOGY" A METAPHYSICS?

In addressing ourselves to this question, we are using Kant as our criterion for checking on the speculative activities of Hegel. This is not to say that Hegel "ought" to stay within the limits set by Kant for philosophy. But we are simply considering the following as a philosophical question: was Hegel's *Phenomenology* the sort of philosophical work that Kant would have considered to be an "invalid" metaphysical enterprise? No value judgement is necessarily implied in regard to the *Phenomenology*, if it should succumb to the Kantian censure.

It should be noted, however, that in making comparisons of Kant with Hegel we will suffer some extreme restrictions as to the terminology we can use meaningfully. For instance, the "objective" in Hegel signifies otherness, while the "objective" in Kant signifies appearances which have been effectively subsumed under the proper subjective categories (i.e., our concepts make things formally "objective"). The "phenomenon" for Hegel is the content of consciousness, while for Kant it is an empirical content which receives form from consciousness. Kant's "noumenon" is a difficult concept which refers sometimes to illicit, sometimes to licit but unknowable transcendentals; while Hegel looks upon Kant's noumenon as illicit, and admits an absolute cognitive relationship to the transcendentals. And so on. The result of all this is that we cannot simply distinguish phenomenon from noumenon, subjective from objective, appearances from concepts, etc. in the scope of this *comparison*; but must try to use that terminology which has taken on as little as possible special technical significance in both the Kantian and the Hegelian "systems."

At the end of his *Prolegomena*, Kant issues the following challenge to an anonymous critic who sought to defend metaphysics against the unsympathetic sallies of Kant:

> I challenge my critic to demonstrate, as is only just, on *a priori* grounds, in his own way, any single really metaphysical proposition asserted by him. Being metaphysical, it must be synthetical and known *a priori* from concepts, but it may also be any one of the most indispensable propositions as, for instance, the principle of the persistence of substance or of the necessary determination of events in the world by their causes. . . .
>
> He finds . . . in my *Critique* eight propositions, of which one in each pair contradicts the other. . . . He has the liberty of selecting any one of these

eight propositions at his pleasure . . . and then of attacking my proof of the opposite proposition. . . . If . . . I cannot save my demonstration, then a synthetic proposition *a priori* from dogmatic principles is to be reckoned to the score of my opponent, and I shall deem my impeachment of ordinary metaphysics unjust. . . . [21]

The above passage is illuminating insofar as it gives us concrete examples of what Kant considered to be "metaphysics" in the pejorative sense. The examples are: 1) the notion of the persistence of substance; 2) the notion of a necessary "ground" for contingent events in the world; 3) the four "antinomies." Since no. 2 is included in the scope of the fourth antinomy, the number of examples mentioned here can be reduced, for our purposes, to five.

The first two antinomies in Kant's *Critique of Pure Reason* have to do with the mathematical conception of the world, and show that the phenomenal world can be considered—with equally good reasons—to be a) *either* finite or infinite in spatial and temporal extension; and b) *either* finitely or infinitely divisible into integral constituents. The second two antinomies have to do with the world as a physical dynamism, and conclude that the phenomenal world can be considered —again with equally good reasons—to have a) *either* a finite or an infinite series of causes,[22] and b) *either* a finite or an infinite series of contingencies.[23]

If we examine these examples, we note

a) that the antinomies are not concerned with the *physical* existence [24] of space and time, or of cause-effect relationships. For Kant had already demonstrated (in his "Transcendental Aesthetic" in the *Critique of Pure Reason*) that space and time were essentially forms of the mind, and nothing physical; and (in his "Transcendental Analytic" in the same *Critique*) that causality and contingency were essentially categorical concepts of the understanding, and nothing physical. If the antithetical statements in the antinomies were concerned with physical existence, Kant would simply have to *deny* both theses, instead of admitting them both. For no predicates can be admitted for admittedly non-real subjects.

b) that the antinomies are not concerned with the attribution of "finite" or "infinite" to space or time or the series of causes as *mental* realities, i.e., as ideas. For Kant had already demonstrated in the "Transcendental Aesthetic"[25] that space and time *qua* representations, i.e., *qua* mental realities, are infinite. And in the "Transcendental Analytic,"[26] he had already demonstrated that the category of causality is the unconditioned conditioning concept which gives determination to all successions of experience (i.e., that it is "infinite," in the sense that, while being unlimited and undetermined itself, it is an absolute determinant for phenomena). Therefore, since Kant had already decided that space and time and causality are "infinite" (in a special sense, i.e., as determinant a-priori conditions), it would make no sense to allow the possibility of their finitude in the antinomies, *if* the antinomies had to do with specifically mental realities.

c) that the antinomies seem to have to do with pseudo-transcendent realities, i.e., names which *seem* to denote realities which are within the domain neither of our physical nor of our psychic experience, but "exist" as the borders of our physical and/or psychic experience.

d) that the question of the "permanence of substance" also seems to relate to a pseudo-transcendent reality. For substance is either conceived as an external thing-in-itself which constitutes an absolute boundary-line for all our experiences of physical reality (in Aristotle and other "Classical Realists"); or it is conceived as an internal-thing-in-itself which constitutes an absolute grounding for mental reality (as for example, the idealism of Berkeley).

e) that the examination of problems relating to space and time and causality and substantiality, etc., does not necessarily have to result in an "invalid" metaphysics. For example, Kant himself in his "Transcendental Aesthetic" derives most of the attributes of space and time by "metaphysical" expositions. These are not invalid, because they do not consider space and time as "transcendent realities" (in the sense in which we have used that term in this chapter), but as mental realities which can be at least clarified by a process of reflection. A similar observation could be made in regard to Kant's *Metaphysic of Morals*, which treats of God, immortality, and freedom—and perhaps succeeds in avoiding the types of invalid statements made on these topics by "transcendent" metaphysics. But in the strict sense moral philosophy would not be properly called metaphysics.[27]

f) that *Kant* would seem to consider his valid metaphysical exposition of such concepts to be the result of a-priori analytic judgements, although he does not state this explicitly. For the main purpose of both the *Critique of Pure Reason* and the *Prolegomena* is to show that a-priori synthetic judgements are not possible in metaphysics.[28] But it is here especially that his consistency seems to break down. For it is extremely difficult to see how all the attributes applied to space and time in the "Transcendental Aesthetic," could be simply diverse ways of expressing the tautology that "space is space," or "time is time." In other words, in practice, if not in words, Kant seems to allow a-priori synthetic judgements about the purely mental world, leading to a metaphysics of some sort.[29]

g) that therefore (from the point of view of this criticism of Kant's critique) an invalid metaphysic obtains only when one (i) starts with certain mental realities; (ii) projects them invalidly into the status of transcendent realities;[30] and (iii) makes invalid judgements about them by means of a synthesis of the conceptual with the physical spheres.[31] (Note that there is a twofold "invalidity" here.)

Accepting this as the incontrovertible core of the Kantian notion of an invalid metaphysics, we come now to the question of whether Hegel's *Phenomenology*, subjected to Kant's criticism, shows itself to be an invalid metaphysics. We will concentrate on the three aspects of an invalid metaphysics which we have just mentioned:

(i) Hegel starts with certain mental realities; not, as with Kant, our concepts about the physical world, but our concepts about our experience of the physical world. He begins, in other words, with our concepts of consciousness, which he calls the "Forms of Consciousness."

(ii) Hegel seems to recognize throughout that the Forms of (Individual and Social) Consciousness are aspects *immanent* in the empirical ego. He keeps them fairly clearly distinguished from their transcendent backdrop—Absolute Being (Kant's thing-in-itself) and Absolute Self-Consciousness (Kant's transcendental ego). But though the immanent aspects of the empirical ego are not projected into either of these fundamental transcendent realities, they are considered to have both an a-posteriori side (the Forms of Individual Consciousness) and an a-priori side (the Forms of Social Consciousness, or "the World")—according to the *general* notions of a-priori vs. a-posteriori which we developed in the first half of this section, and in section I(a) of the Conclusion. These "two sides" are neither conformable to, nor refuted by, the restricted Kantian notion of "a-priori vs. a-posteriori."

(iii) Since the immanent aspects of the empirical ego are not projected into transcendent realities, it would be impossible for any question to arise as to whether they are invalid syntheses after the fashion of the Kantian *antinomies.*

Therefore, at least in regard to the formal stipulations which Kant proposed for testing invalidity, it would not seem that the *Phenomenology* is an invalid metaphysics.

But this doesn't mean it is a valid metaphysics.

That is, it could be the case that Hegel's *Phenomenology* is not an invalid metaphysics, because it is not *any* kind of metaphysic. It could be an invalid Critique; or a valid new poetic form.

Is the *Phenomenology* a metaphysics at all? And if so, is it valid?

Since we are using Kant as our criterion here, we will first make the following observations:

a) The closest thing we have in Kant's theoretical writings to a metaphysics would seem to be his "metaphysical expositions" of space and time, and his "metaphysical deduction" of the Categories. In the former we begin with the notions of space and time; in the latter, we begin with the notion of the various forms of judgement. But, as was mentioned above (B, paragraph f.), there is no evidence that the metaphysical exposition and the metaphysical deduction constitute a "valid" metaphysics, i.e. one which expands the frontiers of knowledge by means of a priori synthetic judgements. At least, *not in the Kantian sense.*

The point here is that one's logical vantage point dictates what he can and should see or admit. Kant's purpose was to serve the cause of a logic of identity by effectively, once and for all, distinguishing what comes from the mind from what is extrinsic to the mind. Since he was rationalistic in temperament, "what comes from the mind" takes on the aspect of form or actuality, while "what is extrinsic to the mind" takes on the aspect of matter or content. (If he had had an empiricist bias, and completely revolted against rationalistic standards in his cultural milieu, he might conceivably have served the cause of logic in the completely opposite direction, i.e., by presenting our ideas as content conditioned by external facts.) Thus in the Kantian context, by definition, the active operation of synthesis is something that must come "from the side of" the mind. The mind itself can never have, *in this restricted Kantian context,* a material or passive aspect which would admit of being actively synthesized. Even if, from our point of view, Kant seems to treat of the ideas of space, time, etc. as a content admitting of synthesis—in his own limited framework this can never be anything more than a logical analysis of the formal determinants of phenomena.[32]

Thus the metaphysical exposition and the metaphysical deduction are at most an example of the necessary restriction of metaphysics to *analytic* judgements (in the Kantian sense). But more properly, they are integral parts of the "Transcendental" or "Critical" philosophy of Kant, which does not aim to expand the frontiers of knowledge, but to draw up directives for its expansion.

b) But what if our ideas of space, time, causality, etc. were considered as mental "phenomena" which could be brought into higher unity by the understanding? Could we proceed then by means of a-priori synthetic judgements? At this point, and with the final, inevitable confrontation with this problem—we are finally in a position to understand the remarkable consistency, if not the wisdom, of Kant:

(i) *"The remarkable consistency . . ."* In the domain *purely* of a "logic of identity," analytic judgements can never become synthetic, a-posteriori judgements can never have a-priori stability. For the logic of identity requires that "synthesis" and "analysis" be used only in sharply differentiated, *univocal* senses. "Synthetic" judgement, in its universal logical meaning, signifies (according to Kant) only the uniting of the concepts of consciousness with that which appears as "other than" consciousness—the sense manifold; or coversely, bringing the manifold into the unity of some concept. "Analytic" judgement, in its univocal logical sense, signifies a temporary withdrawal from the sense manifold to reexamine and clarify the concepts of consciousness; and thus it cannot be "synthetic" in the aforementioned sense. We could conceivably define logical synthesis and analysis in some other way. But granted Kant's definition (which seems of its nature preeminently suited for preserving the logic of identity itself, in its purity), the "synthesis" of concepts with each other, or of different aspects of a single concept, could never be a synthesis; nor could an "analysis" of the undifferentiated sense manifold be conceivable. If we draw concepts or the aspects of concepts into higher unities, this might be "synthesis" in a wider sense, but not in *the* strict logical sense. If we tear a sense manifold apart to get at its meaning, this could be "analysis" in some wider sense, but again, not in *the* logical sense.

(ii) *". . . if not the wisdom, of Kant."* Granted that our analytic clarification of our concepts about the world cannot be synthetic in the strict Kantian sense—it is obviously synthetic in a wider sense. It does not increase our knowledge about the relationship of consciousness to the sense manifold. But it obviously does expand the frontiers of our knowledge about our mental world. Unless we are to presuppose arbitrarily that we *have* no mental world, but are acting like automatons impressing preordained forms on chaotic phenomena—we have to grant that we have a mental world, with existential content, just as we have a physical world. This, it would seem, is the world that "metaphysics," from time immemorial has been dealing with preeminently—the world of substances, essences, causes, privations, potentialities and actualities, purposes, truths, unities, etc.

True—metaphysics had often treated of these things as if they resided in pristine purity in the world of objectivity. And in this sense, metaphysics has been "invalid." But to deny metaphysics any validity would be to deny that we have any distinct mental world which we can call our own. Kant's implicit non-recognition of that world is perhaps the source of some of the difficulties he had with "freedom." For, as Kant himself avers, it is only insofar as we are members of a suprasensible world that we can be free. But how can we really be a "member" of a world without content, in which in Spinozistic fashion we seem to be caught in a monolithic hierarchical spiral convergence of pure forms into the unspeakable transcendent unity of apperception?

With these observations in mind, we can conclude as follows, in regard to Hegel's *Phenomenology*:

a) Metaphysics, as has been indicated above, should deal only with our mental constructs, or the world as reflected in and through our mental constructs. This is also the way in which Hegel defines metaphysics:

> Logic coincides with Metaphysics, the science of things set and held in thoughts—thoughts accredited able to express the essential reality of things.[33]

It is noteworthy that—at least in its wording—this definition bears some similarity to the definition of the philosophy of nature which Kant gives:

> The metaphysics of nature. . .contains all the principles of pure reason that are derived from mere concepts. . .and employed in the theoretical knowledge of all things.[34]

But we should note that for Kant a "metaphysics of nature" (if he had been able to accomplish this project) would involve the elaboration of empirical principles in the light of the pure categories; while for Hegel metaphysics (as identical with speculative Logic) involved the demonstration of the reciprocity (unity-in-distinction) between thought and being (or thinghood). The *Phenomenology* is not concerned specifically with our mental constructs, or the world as reflected in and through our mental constructs. (In a certain sense, we might say that the *Phenomenology* is concerned with our mental constructs. But more specifically it is concerned with elucidating the total range of our experience, including the formation of mental constructs.) Therefore, it would not be quite accurate to classify it as a metaphysics, in the way we have defined metaphysics above.[35]

b) The *Phenomenology* is concerned specifically with the consciousness of consciousness. In the consciousness of consciousness, insofar as it is a merger of the subjective and the objective, all the distinctions of the logic of identity converge and disappear. The distinctions into which the consciousness of consciousness can be "analyzed" are transparently "synthesized" among themselves. The a-posteriori content transparently furnishes its own a-priori form. The "phenomenon" here, in short, cannot be considered meaningfully and unambiguously according to a logic of identity, which is founded on *self-identical distinctions.*[36] Rather, as the phenomenon of the *union* of subjectivity and objectivity, it calls for a "logic of non-identity," based on *self-negating identities.*

Each logic, in other words, is naturally oriented to a distinct subject-matter. The logic of identity is oriented properly only to our examinations of the physical world. The logic of non-identity is oriented properly only to our examination of the consciousness of consciousness and of the mental constructs which we find in this examination.[37]

In the logic of non-identity, the various seemingly self-identical moments of empirical consciousness must be traced in their disappearance into other moments of consciousness as a whole. The various seemingly stable concepts that we formulate about our empirical consciousness must be traced in their disappearance into some absolute concept of consciousness about itself. And the "a-priori" in the *Phenomenology* is no longer consciousness in its logical distinction from the physical world but the social consciousness in its trans-logical distinctness from the individual consciousness. This a-priori social consciousness is the new self-identical distinctness which results in the wider context of a logic of non-identity, which includes the logic of identity by becoming non-identical with *itself.*

c) The *Phenomenology,* insofar as it is an "experience of experience," paradoxically seems to bring to fruition the Critical philosophy of Kant. For amidst the critical arrows of Kant, two "transcendental" realities survived unscathed— the thing-in-itself, and the transcendental ego. But they appear in Kant as rather tender and fragile presuppositions, insofar as we are sure neither of their existence nor of their attributes. And indeed, this is quite understandable; for, as we have observed above, the only approach germane to the consideration of transcendental realities would be in and through a reflection on experience. And such a reflection is what we find in Hegel's *Phenomenology.* Hegel, therefore, in the great attention that he gives to the thing-in-itself (Absolute Being[38]) and the transcendental ego (Absolute Self-Consciousness) seems in a very real way to be merely continuing the tradition of the Kantian Transcendental philosophy, addressing himself to problems that the Kantian philosophy had raised without solving. And one of the most important, but elusive, characteristics of the *Phenomenology* is that it seems to be calculated to *show* (in the only way in which it might possibly be "shown") the *existence* of something in what we designated at the beginning of this chapter as the "transcendent" sphere of discourse. This "something," of course, is *Absolute Spirit,* substance-becoming-subject-becoming-substance.

III. How is the Transition Made from the "Phenomenology" to the "Encyclopedia"?

What is portioned out to all mankind,
I shall enjoy deep in myself, contain

Within my spirit summit and abyss,
Pile on my breast their agony and bliss,
And thus let my own self grow into theirs, unfettered . . .
                                    —Goethe, *Faust: A Fragment* (1790)

Consciousness, having traced in Hegel's *Phenomenology* the avenues of its experience along all its winding paths, comes at last to the summit of Absolute Knowledge, at which all things become transparent to it—the world, itself, other selves, and society. All the trivial details disappear from sight, and it catches a total view of the main mechanisms in which it had previously been enmeshed in a blind and powerless immediate awareness. It sees Absolute Being partitioning itself out in space, and Absolute Self-Consciousness developing itself in time; and by means of post-Cartesian philosophical concepts, it stands at the point of their fusion—no longer the passive pawn of appearance and accident, but in possession of pivotal reality, and weaving the threads of its own Fate. There still remain, of course, opacities, problems, obstacles; but these no longer appear as alien to consciousness, since consciousness, in full possession of itself and its roots, has the key to deciphering the full meaning of all that appears to it.

Consciousness, as presented in the *Phenomenology*, is like an orphan who had been brought up among strange people, in an environment that it did not understand; and who one day, realizing his situation, fled to travel around the world, discover his origins, and find out his family name. So also, consciousness now, after many trials and mistrials, has discovered its homeland and its family name.[1]

But it merely has a home, and merely has a name. It has an immediate apprehension of identity with the Absolute Spirit transcending Being and Thought. But this is merely an immediate apprehension. It appears as something that has "happened" to it; as something which, though putting it beyond all accidents, has happened to it by accident. Just as the orphan tracking down his origins must assimilate these to himself, so also consciousness must now go through a process of "assimilation."

But this process can no longer be a "phenomenology" of consciousness, which has reached its absolute terminus. But having attained to the unity of Spirit in an empirical way, it must now proceed to deduce from this unity its own phenomenal consciousness of subject-object distinction (the mode according to which it must apprehend even the transcendent unity of Spirit); and all the differentiations which it finds in its new environment. It must start at its remote ancestry—the Absolute *Idea* of Spirit—and trace the genealogy of the world of Spirit whose presence it now apprehends.

This is the task which Hegel attempts in the *Encyclopedia*. The Concept is first, containing implicitly all being and subjectivity and spirit. He proceeds "from the side of Spirit" to deduce didactically the generations of the Spirit which appears to us. Thus he hopes to elaborate systematically the essential conditions according to which the experiences narrated in the *Phenomenology* must be understood.

CONCLUSION: I

1. *P.*, p. 564: *Das Ziel*, das absolute Wissen . . . hat zu seinem Wege die Erinnerung der Geister, wie sie an ihnen selbst sind und die Organisation ihres Reiches vollbringen. Ihre Aufbewahrung . . . nach der Seite ihrer begriffnen Organisation . . . die *Wissenschaft* der *erscheinenden Wissens* (ist).

2. *Op. cit.*, p. 42: Cette élévation de la conscience empirique au savoir absolu n'est possible que si on découvre en elle les étapes nécessaires de son ascension; ces étapes sont encore en elle, il faut seulement qu'elle descende dans l'interiorité du souvenir par une opération comparable à la réminiscence platonicienne.

3. Cf. *supra*, Intro., V.

4. I am using the term "a priori" here in the original Aristotelian sense, according to which A is prior to B in nature if and only if B is an effect which could not exist without its cause, A; and A is prior to B in knowledge, if and only if the knowledge of A is a pre-condition for knowing B.

5. Cf. Introduction, VI(c).

6. Cf. Introduction, VI(d).

7. "Progressively," not in a temporal or historic sense, but in an organic and dynamic sense.

8. Cf. the sections on morality and conscience.

9. Cf. Baillie, p. 440.

10. This refers to our mode of apprehension, not to that which is apprehended. Spirit is apprehended by *consciousness* to be in-itself a unity which *appears* as a distinction for-consciousness. It now remains for consciousness to trace these distinctions in their major outlines, until they produce transparent evidence of the intimation that they are "distinctions which are no distinctions."

11. This, again, refers to our mode of apprehension, not to that which is apprehended. What is apprehended is a plethora of distinctions in spirit—distinctions which merge into one another and disappear, and thus finally take on the appearance of unity; or, more precisely, of a unity (spirit), which has come to *appear* to consciousness as a unity, by means of a thorough mediation of all its distinctions.

CONCLUSION: II

1. There exists an object x, such that it does not have the property "G," but has the property "F."

2. It would not be within the scope of this study to show that these three spheres of discourse are an exhaustive set of possibilities, to which all other areas of discourse would be reducible. Rather, they should be considered as a provisional disjunction which, as we shall see, will prove useful when it comes to the problem of discussing Kant's critique of metaphysics, and the relevance of this to Hegel.

3. The conclusion of existence or non-existence in all the cases which we are considering in this section (A. 1. a, b, and c), would, of course, involve separate judgements of existence, judgements which are not derived by a process of deduction after the manner of predicative judgements, but are derived by an induction from some manifold of experience, which leaves a unitary impression, the impression of the existence or reality of that manifold, in terms of some determinate unified coherence.

4. For a discussion of the psychological basis for the notion of the two "realities," see the Introduction, V.

5. The merger of synthesis and analysis in the Speculative Method is also emphasized by Hegel in his *Logic*. See Murray Greene, *op. cit.*, p. 37.

6. *Prolegomena to any Future Metaphysics*, p. 14; on the subject of analytic

and synthetic judgements, cf. also *The Critique of Pure Reason* (A6 = B10)

7.*Prolegomena,* p. 16. This, at least, is Kant's reasoning. The theory of mathematics upon which he bases this reasoning has been challenged by some contemporary philosophers of science. See e.g. Reichenbach, *The Rise of Scientific Philosophy* (Berkeley, 1958), pp. 130ff.

8. *Ibid.,* p. 49.

9. *Fundamental Principles of the Metaphysics of Morals,* p. 64.

10. As Hegel notes in the *Enzyklopädie* (p. 46, para. 33) the Kantian notion of "experience" differs from the notion which we find in the British empiricists, insofar as it includes an "a priori" element. But since this a priori element is not itself derived *from* experience, it is difficult to see how the a priori synthetic judgement of physics can be produced without going *beyond* experience.

See George A. Schrader's discussion of empiricism in his article "Hegel's Contribution to Phenomenology" (*The Monist,* Vol. 48, No. 1, 1964, pp. 18-33), in which he shows how this general problem supplied an impetus to the development of phenomenology and dialectical method.

11. Cf. the *Critique of Pure Reason,* B 3.

12. *Prolegomena,* p. 46.

13. *Prolegomena,* p. 15; *Critique of Pure Reason,* B 12, A 8.

14. Cf. *Prolegomena,* p. 53, n. 6.

15. *Ibid.*

16. If the third category in each set of three categories is a synthesis of the first two (Cf. *Critique of Pure Reason,* B 110), in what sense does this synthesis differ from the synthesis of a manifold appearance? In other words, could not our *ideas* constitute valid first-level experiential data, capable of syntheses ad infinitum, even in metaphysics?

In regard to this third question (c), we cannot fail but notice a parallelism of problematics in Wittgenstein, who in his *Tractatus,* after stating that a proposition is an assertion of a fact, and a picture of that fact as an existent state of affairs, says that this propositional picture is also a fact (2. 141). But he doesn't make the next logical step (or what would seem offhand to be a logical step), to say that there can be verifiable and non-tautological pictures about *these* propositional pictures.

17. That is, in the sense which the notion of the "a-priori" has "prior" to being applied to synthetic or analytic judgements, or even to judgement itself as the specific cognitive operation of uniting subject with predicate. We are speaking, of course, in a non-Kantian framework here.

18. For a discussion of this, see Section V of the Introduction, *supra.*

19. For a discussion of the nature of a "logic of identity," see Section VI (d), *supra.* See also Hegel's *Enzyklopädie der philosophischen Wissenschaften,* 1st ed., section 12 (p. 33).

20. For a discussion of this type of logic, see Section VI (d), *supra.* See also Hegel's *Enzyklopädie der philosophischen Wissenschaften,* 1st ed., sections 15-17 (p. 35ff).

21. *Prolegomena,* p. 128.

22. If there is an infinite series of causes, then the world is a completely conditioned set of events, i.e., it is completely necessitated. If, however, there is only a finite series of natural causes, then there must be a sphere transcending the sphere of natural causality, i.e., there must be a sphere of freedom and "free" causality.

23. The assumption of contingency ad infinitum in the world leads us to the idea of a world as a self-contained whole; while the assumption of a Necessary Being limiting (as an unconditioned condition) this series, leads us to the threshold of the notion of a transcendent God.

24. We are using the term, "physical existence," here in the sense of the first "type of existence" discussed at the outset of this chapter (Part A, 1 (a)); that is, something which admits of sensuous verification through experimentation or observation. Translated into Kantian terms, the realm of "physical existence" would be equivalent to "Nature" considered *"materialiter,"* i.e., as the complex of all objects of experience—of all objects which are "given" to the understanding through empirical intuition (see the *Prolegomena*, p. 43). Space and time are pure subjective forms according to which Nature must be considered, but are not themselves a *part* of Nature considered *materialiter*.

25. Cf. *The Critique of Pure Reason*, A25=B40, A32=B47.

26. Cf. *Ibid.*, A189 = B234.

27. Cf. *Ibid.*, A842 = B870.

28. We might say, "in ordinary metaphysics." But this would be misleading. If Kant a) had been able to develop the "reformed" metaphysics of nature which is dimly adumbrated in the *Critique*; and b) had demonstrated that this reformed metaphysics utilized valid a priori synthetic judgements—then we would be able to distinguish meaningfully this valid metaphysics from the "ordinary," "traditional" metaphysics. But Kant was never able to accomplish this task (although he did start to write a metaphysics of nature). Even if he had finished his "metaphysics of nature," it is doubtful whether it would have been very different from the *Critique of Pure Reason* (as Walsh points out in "Kant's Criticism of Metaphysics," *Philosophy*, Vol. XIV, 1939, p. 314). And therefore we cannot say that "Kant distinguishes between two metaphysics—one being the traditional metaphysics which is invalid, and another being his own metaphysics which features valid a priori synthetic judgements." For when Kant criticizes metaphysics in the first *Critique* and the *Prolegomena* he is perhaps more effective than he wished to be: he leaves it in doubt whether *any* metaphysic, including his own projected metaphysics, could be based on valid a priori synthetic judgements.

29. It is perhaps because of this fact that Kant wavered in regard to whether or not his *Critique of Pure Reason* was a metaphysic. As W. H. Walsh observes on p. 313 of the above-mentioned article, Kant states in one of his letters that the *Critique* contains a "metaphysic of metaphysics"; but in the *Critique* itself he distinguishes what he is doing in the *Critique* from the system of reformed metaphysics that he hoped to elaborate at some later date (cf. *The Critique of Pure Reason*, B869 = A841).

It should be noted that if we take Kant at his word in characterizing the *Critique* as a "metaphysic of metaphysics," at least one problem looms large: Does this "metaphysic of metaphysics" utilize valid a priori synthetic judgements? If so, then what is the sense manifold that is being synthesized in accord with the categories? Also, would it be valid to utilize a priori synthetic metaphysical judgements to challenge the possibility of a priori synthetic judgements in metaphysics? (This challenge is made even stronger and more pointed in the *Prolegomena*, in which Kant tries to clear up misunderstandings which resulted from his *Critique*. See the *Prolegomena*, Appendix, where Kant responds to a critical review in the *Göttingische gelehrte Anzeigen*.)

30. In the first two antinomies, space and time are invalidly extrapolated into finite or infinite things-in-themselves, i.e., noumenal "containers" for the phenomenal universe as a whole. In the third and fourth antinomies, the totality of phenomenal contingencies or causes is either extrapolated into a self-contained, self-generating thing-in-itself, or is thought to be bounded by an absolute thing-in-itself which serves as a ground for the series *without* being outside the series itself. The "absolute" thing-in-itself in these latter two antinomies thus becomes a transcendent freedom which exerts *causality*; or a transcendent Necessary

Being which somehow becomes a prime *"mover,"* or a *source* of contingent being.

In the "Paralogisms" of Pure Speculative Reason, there is an invalid extrapolation of the category of substantiality into the trans-categorical transcendental ego.

In the "Ideal" of Pure Speculative Reason, finally, there is an invalid extrapolation of the sum-total of truth possibilities into an individualized transcendental substrate, an *omnitudo realitatis,* which is also thought of as having an intelligence corresponding to our own unity of apperception.

If we were to generalize from all these examples of the invalid "real" use of Pure Speculative Reason, we could say that the "invalidity" takes three essential forms: either a) it takes the form of a projection into massive metaphysical things-in-themselves; or b) it takes the form of a projection in the contrary direction, i.e., into a transcendental ego; or d) there is an admixture of both forms.

31. Hegel's criticism of pre-Kantian metaphysics is similar. He says that metaphysics, although concerned with problems at the heart of philosophy, nevertheless went astray insofar as it considered these problems after the manner of object-images (e.g. the soul, God, being, and space were wrongly considered as objects or persons over against some subject). Cf. *Enzyklopädie,* 1st ed., p. 38-40, paragraphs 19-20.

32. On the other hand, in the context of Hegel's logic of non-identity as applied in a phenomenology of pure consciousness, the ideas of the mind cannot be a content admitting of synthesis, precisely because in a consciousness of consciousness content is transparently form, and the condition of being synthesized is transparently the act of self-synthesis.

The only logical vantage point from which the ideas of the mind would be considered as "content" admitting of synthesis, would be a combination of the two "logics" from a rationalist point of view. For a discussion of the possibility of such a combination, cf. *infra,* comment 37.

33. Cf. *Logic,* Wallace tr., paragraph 24.

34. Cf. *The Critique of Pure Reason,* N. Smith tr. (B869 = A841).

35. The *Phenomenology,* however, insofar as it constitutes an introduction to the *Logic,* (see para. 24, *Enzyklopädie, ad fin.;* and also Ch. III of this book, in which the "introductory" nature of the *Phenomenology* is discussed), is an introduction to metaphysics.

36. Cf. *Enzyklopädie,* 1st ed., p. 34, paragraph 14.

37. What about the examination of our consciousness of the world (our concepts about the world)? What logic is oriented to this? The necessary distinctions of the logic of identity would begin to converge here, and thus lose their effectiveness. The transparent unity-in-distinction of the logic of non-identity would not be completely applicable here, where there still are some remnants of a phenomenon-noumenon dichotomy. In other words, we are one step beyond the physical world, but have not yet attained to the transcendent unity of consciousness with itself. In view of this, it would seem that the logic which would be most truly germane to the sphere of "our ideas about the world" would be a synthesis of the logics of identity and non-identity, which might be expressed in the following theorem of a logic of non-identity: $I \rightarrow [(I) \leftrightarrow - I]$.

If this is true, then it would seem to follow also, that the only subject upon which we could have a truly Hegelian type of "phenomenology" (using only the logic of non-identity) would be the subject which Hegel actually *did* treat of—the consciousness of consciousness. If one were to do a "phenomenology" of anything *other* than the consciousness of consciousness, he could not meaningfully restrict himself to the logic of non-identity, but would have to apply a synthesis of the two procedures.

Hegel's *Encyclopedia,* insofar as it involves a systematic reconstruction of phenomenological consciousness of consciousness, also, of course, presents apt "subject-matter" for an exclusively "dialectical" methodology, although, to repeat an analogy utilized several times in this book, the dialectic of the *Phenomenology* is "inductive" while that of the *Encyclopedia* is "deductive". However, it must be admitted that the rationale and the appropriateness of the dialectic seems much more obvious both in the early sections of the *Phenomenology* (on Consciousness and Self-Consciousness) and in the first section of the *Encyclopedia* (the Logic), where (in both cases) the subject matter is more patently and explicitly "introspective". Hegel himself seemed to realize this fact, especially with regard to the Philosophy of Nature, which he characterized in several places as frustrating, opaque, and hard to systematize dialectically.

38. For Hegel's own summary of the various appearances of Absolute Being in the *Phenomenology,* see the beginning of Ch. VII.

CONCLUSION: III

1. Although in a certain sense he has always been in his "homeland" while making the phenomenological "voyage of experience." See Greene, *op. cit.,* p. 22.

Select Bibliography

The following listing is only partial. It does not include many books and articles which are referred to only obliquely or peripherally in the course of this book, or which exerted an indirect influence on the author.

Bogen, James, "Remarks on the Kierkegaard-Hegel Controversy," *Synthesis* (1961)

Collins, James, *History of Modern and Renaissance Philosophy* (Milwaukee: Bruce Publ. Co., 1954)

Dove, Kenley, "Hegel's Phenomenological Method," *Review of Metaphysics* XXIII, 4, 1970

Fichte, Johann Gottlieb, *Science of Knowledge (Wissenschaftslehre)*, edited and translated by P. Heath and J. Lachs (N.Y.: Appleton-Century Crofts, 1970)

Findlay, J. N., *Hegel: a Re-examination* (N.Y.: Collier, 1962)

Glockner, Hermann, *Hegel-Lexikon* (Stuttgart, 1957)

Gray, J. Glen, *Hegel and Greek Thought* (N.Y.: Harper Torchbooks, 1968)

Greene, Murray, *Hegel on the Soul* (The Hague: Martinus Nijhoff, 1972)

Harris, Errol E., "Dialectic and Scientific Method," *Idealistic Studies* III, 1, Jan. 1973

Harris, H. S., *Hegel's Development: Towards the Sunlight (1770-1801)* (Oxford: Clarendon, 1972)

Hegel, G.W.F., *The Logic of Hegel,* Wallace tr. (London: Oxford, 1931)

—— *On Christianity,* Knox tr. (N.Y.: Harper-Cloister, 1961)

—— *Phänomenologie des Geistes* (Hamburg: F. Meiner Verlag, 1952)

—— *Phenomenology of Mind,* Baillie tr. (London: Allen & Unwin, 1961)

—— *Philosophische Propädeutik,* "Sämtliche Werke" (Stuttgart: Fr. Frommann Verlag, 1961, Dritter Band)

—— *Lectures on the History of Philosophy,* Haldane tr. (London: Routledge & Kegan Paul, 1968), Vol. III

—— *Geschichte der Philosophie* (Stuttgart: Frommans, 1959)

——*Philosophy of Mind,* Wallace-Miller tr. (Oxford: Clarendon, 1971)

—— *Enzyklopädie der Philosophischen Wissenschaften,* Lasson ed. (Leipzig: Felix Meiner, 1905)

—— *Phenomenologie de l'Esprit,* Jean Hyppolite tr. (Paris: Aubier, 1939)
—— *Wissenschaft der Logik,* (Stuttgart: Frommanns Verlag, 1958), (Sämtliche Werke, Vierter Band)
Heidegger, M. *Holzwege* (Frankfurt: Vittorio Klostermann, 1952)
—— *Hegel's Concept of Experience* (N.Y.: Harper, 1970)
Husserl, Edmund, *Ideas,* Gibson tr. (N.Y.: Collier, 1962)
Hyppolite, Jean, *Genèse et Structure de la Phénoménologie de l'Esprit de Hegel,* Tome I & II (Paris: Aubier, Editions Montaigne, 1946)
—— *Marx and Hegel* (N.Y.: Basic Books, 1969)
Jung, C. G., *Archetypes of the Unconscious, The Collected Works of C.G. Jung,* Vol. 9, Part I, Hull tr., Bollingen series XX (N.Y.: Pantheon, 1959)
—— *Psychological Types,* H. Baynes tr. (London: Routledge & Kegan Paul, 1964)
—— *Two Essays on Analytical Psychology,* Hull tr., *Collected Works of C.G. Jung,* Bollingen series (N.Y.: Pantheon, 1953)
Kainz, H.P., "Hegel's Theory of Aesthetics in the *Phenomenology,*" *Idealistic Studies* II, 1, Jan. 1972
—— "A non-Marxian Application of Hegel's Master-Slave Dialectic to Some Current Socio-Political Problems," *Idealistic Studies* III, 3, Oct. 1973
Kant, Immanuel, *Critique of Judgement,* Bernard tr. (N.Y.: Hafner, 1951)
—— *Critique of Practical Reason,* Beck tr. (Indianapolis: Liberal Arts Press, 1956)
—— *The Critique of Pure Reason,* Kemp tr. (N.Y.: St. Martin's Press, 1956)
—— *Fundamental Principles of the Metaphysics of Morals,* Abbot tr. (N.Y.: Library of Liberal Arts, 1949)
—— *Prolegomena to any Future Metaphysics,* Beck ed. (Indianapolis: Liberal Arts Press, 1950)
Kaufmann, Walter, *Hegel: Reinterpretation, Texts, and Commentary* (London: Weidenfeld and Nicholson, 1966)
Kierkegaard, Søren, *The Concept of Dread,* Lowrie tr. (New Jersey: Princeton U. Press, 1957)
—— *Either/Or,* Vols. I & II, Swenson tr. (N.Y.: Anchor-Doubleday, 1959)
—— *Fear and Trembling and Sickness unto Death,* Lowrie tr. (N.Y.: Anchor-Doubleday, 1954)
Kline, George, "Recent Interpretations of Hegel," *The Monist* XLVIII, 1, 1964.
Kosok, Michael, "The Formalization of Hegel's Dialectical Logic," *International Philosophical Quarterly* VI, 4, 1966
Kroner, Richard, "Kierkegaard's Hegelverständnis," *Kant-Studien* XLVI (1954)
Loewenberg, Jacob, *Hegel's Phenomenology: Dialogues on the Life of Mind* (Illinois: Open Court, 1965)
Löwith, Karl, *From Hegel to Nietzsche* (New York, 1967)
Marcuse, H., *Reason and Revolution* (Boston: Beacon, 1960)
Marx, Karl, *Economic and Philosophic Manuscripts of 1844* (N.Y.: International, 1964)
—— *Frühschriften* (Stuttgart, 1953)
Merleau-Ponty, *Sens et non-sens* (Paris: Les Éditions Nagel, 1948)
—— *Sense and Nonsense* (Illinois: Northwestern University Press, 1964)
Mure, G.R.G., *The Philosophy of Hegel* (London: Oxford U. Press, 1965)

O'Malley, Algozin, *et al, The Legacy of Hegel* (Proceedings of the Marquette Hegel Symposium 1970–The Hague: Martinus Nijhoff, 1973)

Pöggeler, Otto, "Zur Deutung des Phänomenologie des Geistes," *Hegel-Studien* I, 1961

Richardson, *Heidegger* (The Hague: Nijhoff, 1963)

Schelling, F.W.J., *System des transzendentalen Idealismus* in *Werke,* II (Munich, 1927)

Schrader, George, "The Thing-in-Itself in Kantian Philosophy," *The Review of Metaphysics* II, 7, 1949

Solomon, R.C., "Hegel's Concept of 'Geist,' " *Review of Metaphysics* XXIII, 3, 1970

Travis, J. *A Hegel Symposium* (University of Texas, 1962)

Walsh, W.H., "Kant's Criticism of Metaphysics," *Philosophy,* XIV, 1939

Weiss, F., and Kainz, H.P., "Recent Work on Hegel," *American Philosophical Quarterly* VIII, 3, July 1971. Revised version published in *Teorema* (Valencia) V, 1972

Glossary

A GLOSSARY OF TERMS COMMONLY USED IN THE "PHENOMENOL-
OGY"

*EXISTENCE-IN-SELF (*Ansichsein*): a state of potentiality; any status quo in
which the positive content shows promise of unfolding many properties or
aspects which are as yet only implicit in that content.
*EXISTENCE-FOR-SELF (*Fürsichsein*): the movement of an in-itself towards
actualization; a simultaneous alienation from explicit content and extension
towards projected implicit content.
*EXISTENCE-IN-AND-FOR-SELF *(An-und-für-sichsein):* the state in which there
is a synthesis of old explicit content (existence in-self) and new implicit content (existence for-self) into a new unity.
SUBSTANCE (*die Substanz*): that which is both in-itself and "other," i.e., other
to individual self-consciousness—and thus appears in the guise of an "object"
or as thinghood.
SUBJECT (*das Subjekt*): that whose existence in-itself consists precisely in becoming for-itself.
NEGATIVITY *(die Negativität):* the spiritual "space" in which alone all positive
determinations can take on meaning: the bordering context which relates constituent elements precisely by keeping them apart from one another.
THE UNIVERSAL (*das Allgemeine*): a negative medium which draws together
manifold isolated unities into a higher unity.
THE PARTICULAR (*das Besondere*): an isolated unity superseded by the higher
unity of a universal, and thus set in the context of some manifold.

*The translation of-*sein* is a problem. "Being" has a substantive denotation in English,
unsuitable for expressing activity in some contexts. "Existence" is used in the *Logic* for a
translation of the technical term, *Existenz.* To complicate matters, Baillie often translates
Dasein as "existence." It seems best to me to use "existence" in its ordinary English sense.
An awkward alternative would be the use of the hyphenated "be-ing."

THE ABSTRACT (*das Abstrakte*): particularity** insofar as it innately resists being drawn into the higher unity of the universal.

THE CONCRETE (*das Konkrete*): particularity completely synthesized with its congruent universals under the agency of thought.

AN INDIVIDUAL *(das Einzelne):* a particular being which actively and intrinsically manifests its relationship to the universal. Note: the technical distinction of *Einzelne* from *Besondere* is only incipient in the *Phenomenology*. It becomes more apparent in Hegel's later works.

IMMEDIACY (*die Unmittelbarkeit*): the state of the relatively passive "givenness" of an in-itself which is potential to further elaboration.

MEDIATION (*die Vermittlung*): the elaboration or development of any "immediate" object or aspect or state into the stages of existence-for-self and existence-in-and-for-self.

SCIENCE (*das Wissenschaft*): the systematic exposition of all truths—including the truth of self-consciousness—in their dialectic interrelationship.

SUBJECTIVITY (*die Subjectivität*): the ego in all of its relationships to "otherness" (the non-ego).

OBJECTIVITY: Baillie uses this term to translate *"Dingheit," "Seinde,"* etc. In general, it implies "otherness," including the ego's otherness to itself.

ABSOLUTE BEING (*das Absolute Wesen*): objectivity considered as an infinite thing-in-itself; often referred to simply as "the Absolute."

ABSOLUTE SELF-CONSCIOUSNESS (*das Absolute Selbstbewusstsein*): the transcendental ego attaining to infinite self-consciousness by a negative realization of absolute Being.

THE CONCEPT (*der Begriff*): a determinate synthesis of subjectivity and objectivity which simultaneously manifests truth (various aspects of the object in-itself) and certitude (various ways in which the subject in-itself can be also for-itself).

SPIRIT (OR MIND) *(der Absoluter Geist):* a complete synthesis of subjectivity and objectivity, such that self-consciousness had made itself into an "object," and/or substance has come to manifest subjectivity.

UNDERSTANDING (*Verstand*): the power of forming abstract general concepts and making laws.

REASON *(Vernunft):* the unification of dialectical opposites.

ESSENCE (*Das Wesen*): a unified determinate being in its aspect of existing in-itself, and as containing implicitly the multiple determinations of *form.*

EXISTENCE (*Dasein*): In the Preface to the *Phenomenology*, Hegel defines existence as "quality, determinateness identical with itself or determinate sim-

---

**"Particularity" in the Hegelian sense could include an *abstract concept* which is isolated from its context. This can result in terminological confusion, since in a non-Hegelian sense we very often refer to such abstract concepts as "universal" ideas. A "universal" idea—e.g. the idea of man (in general)—can be (in Hegel's usage) either universal or particular: universal, insofar as it applies to all individual men and draws them into a unity; particular, insofar as it can be viewed as an isolated unity, set in the context of other ideas, and set in the context of objective physical referents, sense impressions, etc.

plicity, determinate thought." Existence is best contrasted with *Being-in-general,* the indeterminate, abstract notion of that which supplies a background for all determinate beings or existents, but is not equated with any of these determinate expressions.

EGO (*das Ich*): The meaning of this term depends on the context. For example, if the "I" is contrasted with the body, it takes on the aspect of the subjective pole as opposed to the objective pole; if it is contrasted with the "we," it takes on the aspect of the individual ego as compared with the ethical substance or social consciousness.

MIND (see SPIRIT)

CATEGORY (*die Kategorie*): Preeminently, this refers to the dialectical unity-in-distinction of being and thought. In a subsidiary sense, it refers to all the subordinate and corollary dialectical "syntheses" that manifest or are deduced from this primal category.

Table of Hegelian Opposites

This table should not be understood as indicating clearly-defined oppositions in the *Phenomenology*. In actual practice, the "opposites" mentioned here often are converted into each other in the processes of dialectical experience. However, it may be of some utility to the beginning student to acquire, prior to reading the *Phenomenology,* some familiarity with some of the kinds of "opposites" he will encounter there.

From the side of the "I"	*From the side of the "it"*
thought	being
universal	particular
self	other (or otherness)
ego	non-ego
subjectivity	objectivity
self-consciousness	consciousness
abstract idea	abstract sense datum
selfhood	thinghood
the for-itself (which becomes for-another)	the in-itself (which becomes for-consciousness)
freedom	necessity
essence	existence
subject	substance
soul	body
individual consciousness	ethical substance
pure ego	empirical ego
unity	multiplicity
mind	world
the present	the "beyond"

TERMS USED TO DESCRIBE THE SYNTHESIS
(RECONCILIATION) OF OPPOSITES

The Concept of concepts
The Idea of infinity (or the infinite Idea)
Absolute Spirit as the transcendent synthesis or unity or reconciliation of
 opposites
The Category (in Hegel's sense) of Reason (in Hegel's sense)
The negation of negations (the ultimate Positive)
Unity-in-distinction
The *Sache Selbst*
The in-and-for-itself

Correlation of Indices

Index

The following abbreviations are used:

H	for Hegel
Knowl.	for Knowledge
Conss.	for Consciousness
Ency.	for *Encyclopedia*
Phen.	for *Phenomenology*
S/O I	for Subjective/Objective Individuality
Kier.	for Kierkegaard
T-A	for Thesis-Antithesis
T-A-S	for Thesis-Antithesis-Synthesis

SUBJECT INDEX

unity-in-distinction of being with 57
Time
  and force of understanding 36
  in picture of "movements" 24f.
  is time, and Kant 179
  life as object parceling out in space and 83
  negative dynamism of 57
  non-temporal progression 10
  problems relating to space and 179
  temporal as historical 10
  thought and 10
  universe as temporal reality and traditional formal logic 32
Transcendence (Transcendent) (Transcendental)
  aspects of, Absolute Being and Absolute Self 26f.
  necessity of 36
      in *Phen.* 37
  pseudo-transcendent reality 179
  transcendent realities and invalid metaphysics 179
  transcendent unity, endowed by unifying ego, and Kant, Hegel, and Heidegger 39
  transcendental existence, sphere of 169
Transcendental ego
  as Absolute
      for-itself, and H 21f.
      self 26
          and potentiality of conss 42
      subject for itself 40
  as primary analogate 149
  as transcendental reality surviving Kant 183
  as unifying force in conss 42ff.
  Husserl & 47
  Kant's, as absolute self in H 145
  Kant's, as absolute self-conss 180
  of Kant and Fichte, H & 148
  unifying ego as, by Kant 39
Transcendentals
  as difficulties regarding their existence 169
  of Kant, continued in H 183
Truth
  absolute 130
  and certainty, barest minimum of in sensory contact of world 63
  and representatives of self-conss 60
  apparent, and apparent certitude 129
  approximation to 1
  as extent of being property of conss 56
  categories of 'true" & "false" 19
  citadel of, and science 56
  concepts reveal, in moments not explicitly themselves 69
  epistemological criterion of 59
  falsity of principle in philosophy 55
  in strict sense in *Phen.* 140
  no probability is tantamount to 103
  objective, and subjective certainty 125
  of free self-conss, and Slave 90
  self-conss as harbinger of, to conss 82
  true knowl. and negations of mediation 55
  true world, form of, and inner being of world 55
Unconditioned Absolute Universality *See* Universality
Understanding
  attitude of 69
  culminating in self-conss 167
  force of and natural necessity in *Phen.* 36
  from, to self-conss, and transition of adolescent 17
  in glossary 194
  in *Phen.*, empirical reflections on transcendental conss and 44
  is electricity and Schelling 137
  limits of, and Kant 138
  progression of conss in stage of 116
  progression through sensory awareness to 24
  proper gives way to self-conss proper 144
  schemata of 42
Understanding, schemata of 42
Unhappy consciousness
  and Kierkegaard's "The Unhappiest Man" 148

AUTHOR INDEX